THE MARINES

THE MARINES

Edwin Howard Simmons, Editor-in-Chief
J. Robert Moskin, Editor

MARINE CORPS HERITAGE FOUNDATION
BEAUX ARTS EDITIONS

Marine Corps Heritage Foundation

The Marine Corps Heritage Foundation, originally the Marine Corps Historical Foundation, was established in 1979 as a private, nonprofit organization dedicated to the preservation and promotion of Marine Corps history and traditions. The Foundation directly supports the historical program of the Marine Corps in ways that might not be possible through government funding. Such support largely takes the form of grants, fellowships, awards, and special projects.

The logo of the Foundation is the oldest military insignia in continuous use in the United States. It first appeared on the Marine Corps buttons adopted in 1804. With the stars changed to five points, this device has continued on Marine Corps buttons to this day.

Marine Corps Heritage Foundation
3800 Fettler Park Drive
Suite 104
Dumfries, Virginia 22025
www.marineheritage.org
e-mail: info@marineheritage.org
(703) 640-7965; fax: (703) 640-9546

Beaux Arts Editions
Published by Universe Publishing
A Division of Rizzoli International Publications, Inc.
300 Park Avenue South
New York, NY 10010
www.rizzoliusa.com

2010 2011 2012 / 10 9 8 7 6 5 4 3

Design: Lori S. Malkin
Project Editor: James O. Muschett

ISBN-13: 978-0-88363-663-3

Printed in China

Contents

A Word
to the Reader

This aims to be the most beautiful and comprehensive word-and-picture book ever produced about the United States Marine Corps. It was conceived in Virginia, published in Connecticut, printed in Hong Kong, and distributed from California. More than a year of many people's time has gone into researching and writing these essays and locating the historical pictures and producing the new ones.

Among the participants who have brought this book to life are two commandants of the Marine Corps, Marines who have fought in World War II and every war since then, and civilians who care deeply about the Corps. The result, we hope, is a book that will be read with great interest, browsed through again and again, and treasured for years and generations to come.

The U.S. Marine Corps has defended and fought for our people ever since the Corps was born on 10 November 1775, even before the Continental Congress approved Thomas Jefferson's Declaration of Independence.

Today, if you are abroad and walk into an American embassy, the first person you are likely to face is a Marine. If you watch on TV as the president of the United States lands on the White House lawn, the pilot of that helicopter is a Marine. And when war threatens, the armed service that lives the motto "First to Fight!" is the United States Marine Corps.

The Corps is a relatively small service but it really has fought from the shores of Tripoli to the halls of the Montezumas. And in other places with strange names—Belleau Wood, Guadalcanal, Tarawa, Iwo Jima, Chosin, Da Nang—made meaningful because Americans in Marine uniform have died there.

As we write these words, our country is at peace. But you need only think of the surprise attack on Pearl Harbor in 1941; the North Korean attack against the South in 1950; the Cuban missile crisis of 1962; or the Iraqi invasion of Kuwait in 1990. To protect us from such surprises, all of our armed services are standing by. And one of the best—one that yields to no other—is the Marine Corps.

The Marines' greeting is "Semper Fi." They use it all the time. It means Always Faithful, and that is what the Corps is. If this book is faithful to the best of the Marine Corps, it will meet the challenge we set for ourselves.

Edwin Howard Simmons
Editor-in Chief

J. Robert Moskin
Editor

11 July 1998

Chronology of the U.S. Marine Corps

J. Robert Moskin

"We have fought in every clime and place . . ."

Whenever trouble brews, the U.S. Marine Corps steps forward and faces the world for the nation. This chronology touches on the highlights of the Corps' story in synch with that of the United States year by year since the beginning.

1775	19 Apr	*American Revolution begins when British troops fire on Minutemen on Lexington (Mass.) Common.*
	10 Nov	Continental Congress authorizes two battalions of American Marines; the birthday of the Corps.
	28 Nov	Samuel Nicholas commissioned as Captain of Marines.
1776	3 Mar	Capt Nicholas and his Marines land at New Providence, Bahamas, seize military stores. And in January fight for Gen Washington at Princeton.
	4 Jul	*Congress approves the Declaration of Independence.*
1778	27 Jan	Capt John Trevett leads twenty-six Marines in capture of Fort Nassau, Bahamas.
	22 Apr	John Paul Jones and Lt Samuel Wallingford spike cannon at Whitehaven, England. Later, Wallingford is killed when *Ranger* defeats *Drake*.
1779	28 Jul	Capt John Welsh and thirteen Marines killed in assault on Fort George at Penobscot Bay, Maine.
	23 Sep	John Paul Jones's French-Irish Marines in epic battle between *Bonhomme Richard* and *Serapis*.
1781	19 Oct	*Lord Cornwallis surrenders at Yorktown, Virginia.*
1798	11 Jul	President John Adams signs Act establishing the U.S. Marine Corps.
1805	27 Apr	Lt Presley O'Bannon and seven Marines lead attack against Derna, Tripoli.
1812	18 Jun	*United States declares war on Great Britain.* The following March on board *Essex*, 1stLt John Marshall Gamble commands first Marines in the Pacific.
1813	10 Sep	Marine Lt John Brooks killed when Oliver Perry defeats British fleet on Lake Erie.
1814	24 Aug	In Battle of Bladensburg 114 Marines help defend Washington, D.C.
	24 Dec	*Britain and U.S. sign treaty ending war.*
1815	8 Jan	Andrew Jackson, including Marines under Maj Daniel Carmick, defeats British at New Orleans.
	20 Feb	Capt Archibald Henderson leads Marines in *Constitution*'s victory over *Cyane* and *Levant*.
1820	8 Oct	LtColComdt Anthony Gale cashiered.
	17 Oct	Archibald Henderson appointed commandant, holds position for thirty-eight years until his death.
1824	12 Mar	Brevet Maj Robert D. Wainwright and Marines from Boston quell riot in state prison. Story in McGuffey's Reader spreads Marines' fame.
1832	8 Feb	Brevet Capt Alvin Edson leads attack at Quallah Battoo, Sumatra.
1836	23 Jun	ColComdt Henderson and 462 Marines report for duty in the Second Seminole War.
1837	27 Jan	Col Henderson wins Battle of Hatchee-Lustee River against Seminoles in Florida.
1845	30 Oct	President James Polk sends 1stLt Archibald Gillespie to California with secret orders.
1846	13 May	*U.S. Congress declares war on Mexico.*
	30 Jul	lstLt Jacob Zeilin leads Marine detachment ashore at Santa Barbara, California. Two weeks later Commodore Robert Stockton, with 360 Marines and sailors, enters Los Angeles.
1847	9 Mar	Capt Alvin Edson leads Marine battalion ashore with Army forces at Veracruz, Mexico.
	13 Sep	In Mexico City, Marines help seize fortress of Chapultepec and next day occupy the National Palace on site of the Halls of Montezuma.
1853	14 Jul	Marines under Maj Jacob Zeilin land as Commodore Matthew Perry opens Japan.
1856	20 Nov	Marines in landing party that captures four barrier forts guarding way to Canton, China.
1859	18 Oct	86 Marines under 1stLt Israel Green, USMC, and LtCol Robert E. Lee, USA, capture abolitionist John Brown at Harpers Ferry, Virginia.
1861	12 Apr	*Confederate shore batteries fire on Fort Sumter in Charleston harbor. The Civil War begins.*
	21 Jul	Battalion of 365 Marines led by Brevet Maj John G. Reynolds fights in Battle of Bull Run.
1862	15 May	Cpl John F. Mackie on board ironclad *Galena* is first Marine to receive the Medal of Honor.
1863	1 Jan	*Lincoln issues Emancipation Proclamation.*
	26 Apr	250 Marines under Capt John L. Broome seize New Orleans custom house and city hall.
	3 Jul	*Battle of Gettysburg, highpoint of the Confederacy.*
1865	15 Jan	365 Marines in naval landing force attack Fort Fisher at Wilmington, North Carolina.
	9 Apr	*Gen Lee surrenders at Appomattox Courthouse.*
1871	10 Jun	Capt McLane Tilton leads 109 Marines in naval attack on Han River forts in Korea.
1880	1 Oct	John Philip Sousa appointed 17th leader of the Marine Band.
1885	18 Jun	Marines land in Panama to protect trans-isthmus railroad.

1898	15 Feb	28 Marines among 250 Americans killed when cruiser *Maine* is blown up in Havana harbor.
	1 May	***Admiral George Dewey destroys Spanish fleet in Manila Bay.*** Marines occupy Cavite Naval Station.
	10 Jun	1st Marine Battalion led by LtCol Robert W. Huntington lands at Guantanamo Bay, Cuba. Sgt John Quick signals under Spanish fire to save Marine unit, receives Medal of Honor.
	10 Dec	***U.S. and Spain sign Treaty of Paris.***
1899	8 Oct	Marines attack Filipino insurgents at Novaleta.
1900	31 May	Marines reach Chinese capital to defend Legation Quarter from Boxer rebellion.
	4 Aug	Marines in International Relief Force that marches out of Tientsin to lift siege of Peking. Pvt Dan Daly wins first of two Medals of Honor.
1901	28 Sep	Maj "Tony" Waller takes out 314 Marines to destroy Filipino insurgents who slaughtered U.S. Army company on Samar.
1903	5 Nov	Maj John Lejeune lands battalion to ensure Panama's independence from Colombia.
1906	28 Sep	Provisional Marine Brigade of 2,800 men lands at Havana; Marines stay until 1909.
1908	12 Nov	President Theodore Roosevelt removes Marines from warships, but six months later President Taft restores them.
1912	22 May	1stLt Alfred Cunningham is first Marine aviator.
	14 Aug	Maj Smedley D. Butler leads Marines ashore, beginning intervention in Nicaragua.
	4 Oct	Marines fight at Coyotepe, Nicaragua.
1914	21 Apr	Marine regiments land at Veracruz, Mexico, to keep German guns from Mexican dictator.
	2 Aug	***World War I begins. Shortly thereafter the Panama Canal opens for traffic.***
1915	28 Jul	Marines land in Haiti beginning their longest Caribbean intervention.
	18 Nov	Maj Butler leads Marines in attack on Fort Riviere in Haiti, awarded his second Medal of Honor.
1916	15 May	Marine battalion begins occupation of Dominican Republic.
1917	**6 Apr**	***United States declares war on Germany.***
	6 Jun	5th Marine Regiment sails for France.
1918	6 Jun	Marines advance into Belleau Wood against German machine guns.
	29 Jun	Marines from USS *Brooklyn* go ashore at Vladivostok, Siberia.
	18 Jul	Marines in vast Allied counter-offensive meet Germans south of Soissons.
	3 Sep	In Haiti, native leader Charlemagne Peralte starts revolt of "Cacos" against Marine rule.
	12 Sep	In France, 2d Division including Marine Brigade begins offensive in Saint Mihiel salient.
	3 Oct	4th Marine Brigade assaults Blanc Mont in fierce fighting. Next day is Marines' bloodiest.
	14 Oct	Marine fliers 2dLt Ralph Talbot and GySgt Robert G. Robinson win Medals of Honor.
	1 Nov	Marine Brigade enters Meuse-Argonne.
	10 Nov	5th Marines make night crossing of the Meuse River against German resistance.
	11 Nov	***Armistice between Germany and Allies.***
1919	31 Oct	Marine Sgt Herman Hanneken and Cpl William Button sneak into "Cacos" camp and kill Peralte.
	19 Nov	***U.S. Senate rejects Versailles Treaty.***
1924	12 Jul	Marine Brigade leaves Dominican Republic.
1927	6 Jan	Marines begin second Nicaraguan intervention, fight Augusto Sandino in the mountains.
	16 Mar	4th Marines land at Shanghai to stay fourteen years.
	27 Dec	***Josef Stalin takes control of USSR.***
1928	6 Jan	1stLt Christian Schilt begins ten flights to aid besieged Marine patrol at Quilali, Nicaragua.
	8 Mar	Capt Merritt A. Edson sets out on epic Coco River patrol to hunt for Sandino.
1930	25 Jul	Lt Lewis Puller wins first of five Navy Crosses chasing Sandino guerrillas in Nicaragua.
1931	**18 Sep**	***Japanese Army occupies Manchuria.***
1933	2 Jan	5th Marine Regiment departs Nicaragua.
	30 Jan	***Adolf Hitler named chancellor of Germany.***
	4 Mar	***Franklin D. Roosevelt inaugurated as president.***
	14 Nov	Marines at Quantico, Virginia, begin work on *"Tentative Landing Operations Manual."*
	7 Dec	Navy Department creates Fleet Marine Force.
1934	15 Aug	Marines end intervention in Haiti.
1937	**7 Jul**	***Japanese and Chinese clash at Marco Polo Bridge outside Peking.***
	7 Dec	Marine Capt Evans Carlson goes to Yenan to observe Communist Chinese armies in action.
1939	**1 Sep**	***Germany invades Poland; Great Britain and France declare war on Germany.***
1940	**17 Jun**	***France surrenders to Germany.***
1941	**22 Jun**	***Germany attacks USSR on 2,000-mile front.***
	7 Jul	1st Provisional Marine Brigade lands at Iceland.
	27 Nov	4th Marines leave Shanghai marking end of era.
	7 Dec	Marines try to fight back when Japanese attack U.S. Pacific fleet at Pearl Harbor. Marines at Tientsin and Peking are forced to surrender.
	10 Dec	Japanese defeat American garrison on Guam.
	23 Dec	Japanese overwhelm garrison on Wake Island.
	28 Dec	Most of 4th Marines move from Bataan to Corregidor Island in Manila Bay. Fortress island falls 6 May 1942.
1942	9 Apr	105 Marines among Americans on Bataan Death March.
	1 Jun	First black Marines enlist in Corps; 19,168 will join Corps during World War II.
	7 Aug	1st Marine Division lands on Guadalcanal.
	17 Aug	2d Raider Battalion raids Makin Atoll.
	13 Sep	On Guadalcanal, Marines turn back Japanese attack in Battle of Edson's Ridge.
	9 Dec	MajGen Alexander Vandegrift turns over command of Guadalcanal to Army.
1943	**18 Jan**	***Soviets crack German siege of Leningrad, followed two weeks later by German surrender after siege of Stalingrad.***
	13 Feb	Woman's Reserve program is announced; birthday of women Marines.
	21 Jun	4th Raider Battalion lands on New Georgia.
	13 Jul	***Russians win war's largest tank battle at Kursk.***
	3 Sep	***American Army invades Italy.***
	16 Sep	Maj Gregory "Pappy" Boyington shoots down five planes; he would claim 28, the most of any Marine.
	1 Nov	3d Marine Division lands on Bougainville.
	20 Nov	2d Marine Division assaults Betio Island of Tarawa Atoll in Central Pacific.
	26 Dec	1st Marine Division lands on Cape Gloucester, New Britain.
1944	1 Feb	4th Division's 23d and 24th Marines land on Roi and Namur of Kwajalein Atoll in Marshalls.

	17 Feb	22d Marines help Army seize Eniwetok Atoll.
	6 Jun	***D-Day—Americans land in Normandy.***
	15 Jun	2d and 4th Marine divisions assault Saipan.
	21 Jul	3d Marine Division opens battle for Guam.
	24 Jul	2d and 4th Marine divisions land on Tinian, clear airfield from which "Enola Gay" will take off for Hiroshima a year later.
	15 Sep	1st Marine Division assaults Peleliu.
	21 Oct	***Gen MacArthur returns to the Philippines.***
1945	19 Feb	4th and 5th Marine divisions assault Iwo Jima, raise flag on Mount Suribachi four days later.
	26 Mar	Iwo Jima secured. Marines suffer 25,851 casualties.
	1 Apr	On Easter Sunday, U.S. Tenth Army, including 1st and 6th Marine divisions, lands on Okinawa.
	12 Apr	***Franklin D. Roosevelt dies; Harry S. Truman is president.***
	7 May	***Germany surrenders unconditionally.***
	18 Jun	LtGen Simon Buckner, USA, killed; Marine MajGen Roy Geiger takes command of Tenth Army.
	21 Jun	***Americans victorious on Okinawa.***
	16 Jul	***Trinity test of atomic device at Alamogordo, NM.***
	26 Jul	***President Truman issues Potsdam Declaration calling on Japan to surrender unconditionally.***
	6 Aug	***B-29s drop atomic bomb on Hiroshima; three days later atom-bomb Nagasaki.***
	8 Aug	***Soviet Union joins war against Japan.***
	14 Aug	***Japanese surrender.***
	30 Aug	4th Marines land at Yokosuka on Tokyo Bay.
	2 Sep	***Japanese sign surrender on USS Missouri.***
	30 Sep	Marines of III Amphibious Corps start landing in North China, disarm 630,000 Japanese.
	6 Oct	On Tientsin–Peiping road, Marines have first fire fight with Chinese Communists.
1946	6 May	Commandant Archibald Vandegrift tells Senate Naval Affairs Committee "the bended knee is not a tradition of our Corps."
	23 Nov	***French Indochinese war begins.***
1947	**26 Jul**	***President Truman signs National Security Act organizing armed forces under single Secretary of Defense and establishing separate Air Force.***
1948	23 May	First Marines brought ashore by helicopter for amphibious exercise at New River, North Carolina.
	18 Jul	Twelve Marines at consulate in Jerusalem begin modern Marine Security Guard program.
	10 Nov	First eight enlisted women are sworn in as Regular Marines. The following summer, first black women Marines enlist.
1949	18 Nov	Corps orders all male Marines, regardless of race, be assigned to vacancies in any unit.
1950	**25 Jun**	***North Korean forces invade South Korea.***
	2 Aug	1st Marine Provisional Brigade lands at Pusan, South Korea.
	15 Sep	1st Marine Division makes assault landing at Inchon on west coast of Korea, retakes Seoul.
	2 Nov	Marines engage Chinese Communists in North Korea near the Chosin Reservoir.
	23 Nov	Thanksgiving Day, 7th Marines take Yudam-ni.
	28 Nov	After repulsing eight Chinese divisions, Marines begin epic "breakout" on 1 December.
1951	**9 Apr**	***President Truman relieves Gen MacArthur.***
	20 Jun	1st Marine Division reaches "the Punchbowl" in Korea.
1952	28 Jun	Congress sets Marine Corps' strength and gives commandant equal status on Joint Chiefs of Staff in matters of concern to the Corps.

1953	27 Jul	*Armistice signed at Panmunjon, Korea.*
1954	**8 May**	***French strong point of Dien Bien Phu falls in Indochina.***
	10 Nov	Marine Corps War Memorial dedicated next to Arlington National Cemetery.
1956	7 Jan	Marine Security Guard fights off mob at consulate in East Jerusalem.
	8 Apr	Six recruits drowned in Ribbon Creek at Parris Island, South Carolina.
	26 Jul	***Egypt's President Gamal Nasser nationalizes Suez Canal precipitating international crisis.*** Marine battalion from Sixth Fleet evacuates civilians from Alexandria.
1958	15 Jul	2d Marines land near Beirut and seize airport at Lebanese government's request.
1959	**16 Jan**	***Fidel Castro overthrows Cuban dictator Fulgencio Batista.***
1961	**17 Apr**	***Anti-Castro Cubans land at Bay of Pigs.***
1962	20 Feb	Marine LtCol John H. Glenn, Jr, orbits earth in first manned American space capsule.
	15 Apr	Marine helicopter squadron (HMM-362) arrives in the Mekong Delta of South Viet Nam.
	20 Oct	***Cuban Missile Crisis brings U.S. and Soviet Union to brink of nuclear war.***
1963	**2 Nov**	***Coup topples President Ngo Dinh Diem of South Viet Nam.***
	22 Nov	***President John F. Kennedy assassinated in Dallas.***
1965	8 Mar	9th Marine Expeditionary Brigade lands at Da Nang, South Viet Nam.
	28 Apr	6th Marines land in Dominican Republic.
	27 Oct	Viet Cong raids wreck Marine aircraft at Marble Mountain and Chu Lai.
1967	28 Feb	PFC James Anderson, Jr, is first black Marine to win the Medal of Honor.
1968	20 Jan	North Vietnamese open battle against 26th Marines for Khe Sanh.
	31 Jan	***Vietnamese Communists launch Tet offensive.***
	5 Jul	Americans give up Khe Sanh base.
1969	**8 Jun**	***President Nixon announces first sizable withdrawal of U.S. troops from Viet Nam.***
1970	19 Feb	Combat patrol of 7th Marines charged with deaths of eleven civilians at Son Thang, Viet Nam.
	30 Apr	***President Nixon orders troops into Cambodia.***
1971	25 Jun	Last Marine ground troops leave Viet Nam.
1972	**30 Mar**	***North Vietnamese sweep south in Easter offensive.***
1973	**28 Jan**	***Cease-fire begins in Viet Nam. Last U.S soldiers leave by end of March.***
1974	**8 Aug**	***President Nixon resigns; President Ford pardons him.***
	19 Aug	Marines defend embassy in Nicosia, Cyprus, after mob kills U.S. ambassador.
1975	**25 Mar**	***Hue falls to the Vietnamese Communists.***
	12 Apr	Marines evacuate foreigners before Khmer Rouge seize Phnom Penh, Cambodia.
	30 Apr	4th Marines under Col Alfred M. Gray complete evacuation by helicopters from Saigon embassy and Tan Son Nhut airfield.
	14 May	Marines board American container ship *Mayaguez,* which Cambodians had seized

	2 Jul	***North and South Viet Nam united as Socialist Republic of Viet Nam with capital at Hanoi.***
	10 Nov	Marine Corps celebrates its 200th birthday.
1979	**30 Jan**	***Ayatollah Khomeini replaces Shah of Iran.***
	30 Oct	Embassy Marines drive off crowd with tear gas in San Salvador, El Salvador.
	4 Nov	Mob overruns embassy in Teheran, Iran; thirteen Marines are among sixty-five Americans taken hostage; fifty-two are held captive for 444 days.
	21 Nov	In Islamabad, Pakistan, mob burns embassy as seven Marines defend building.
1980	24 Apr	Three Marines killed in desert accident during effort to rescue Teheran hostages.
	12 May	Embassy Marines in San Salvador use tear gas to rescue U.S. ambassador from mob.
	6 Jun	***Israel invades Lebanon.***
	23 Jun	Marines land in Lebanon to evacuate civilians.
1983	18 Apr	One Marine among sixty-three killed when terrorists blow up U.S. Embassy in Beirut, Lebanon.
	23 Oct	Terrorist truck-bomb blows up headquarters of 1st Battalion, 8th Marines at Beirut airport, killing 241 Americans, of whom 220 are Marines.
	25 Oct	Marines and Army intervene in Grenada, West Indies.
1984	31 Jul	All Marines except embassy guard leave Lebanon after 533-day intervention.
1989	**9 Nov**	***Berlin Wall is torn down.***
	20 Dec	Marines are part of force that tries to capture Panama's dictator, Manuel Antonio Noriega.
1990	**2 Aug**	***Saddam Hussein's Iraqi Army invades Kuwait.***
	5 Aug	Marines land in Monrovia, Liberia, and evacuate civilians threatened by civil war.
	25 Aug	7th Marine Expeditionary Brigade begins Persian Gulf buildup (Operation Desert Shield).
1991	4 Jan	Marine helicopters evacuate 281 people from U.S. Embassy at Mogadishu, Somalia.
	16 Jan	Operation Desert Storm begins as Marines fly in first waves of allied planes.
	24 Feb	Marine 1st and 2d divisions, commanded by LtGen Walter Boomer, breach Iraqi line.
	28 Feb	***President George Bush calls off Persian Gulf War after exactly 100 hours.***
	14 Apr	Marines ordered to Iraq–Turkey border to help multinational relief force protect Kurds.
	30 Apr	Marines assist millions of homeless after cyclone kills 125,000 in Bangladesh.
	21 Dec	***Soviet Union disbanded and replaced by Commonwealth of Independent States.***
1992	9 Dec	Marines land in Somalia to rescue foreigners.
1993	20 Jun	Marine unit returns to Mogadishu, Somalia, to maintain peace.
1994	12 Apr	Marines evacuate foreigners from Rwanda.
	20 Sep	Army and 1,900 Marines land in Haiti.
1995	3 Mar	Marines complete their support of the withdrawal of UN force from clan war in Somalia.
	8 Jun	Team of forty Marines rescues Air Force pilot shot down over Bosnia-Herzegovina on 2 June.
1997	30 May	Marines are diverted from Kinshasa, Zaire, to help evacuate 2,500 from Freetown, Sierra Leone.
1999	24 Mar– 25 Jul	AV-8B Harriers from the 24th and 26th Marine Expeditionary Units (Special Operations Capable) take part in Operations Allied Force and Joint Guardian against Serbian forces in Kosovo.
	14 May	The first production MV-22 Osprey is delivered to Patuxent Naval Air Station, Maryland.
	1 Jul	Gen James L. Jones becomes the thirty-second Commandant of the U.S. Marine Corps.

	1 Jul	Sergeant Alfred L. McMichael becomes the fourteenth Sergeant Major of the Marine Corps.
	2 Jul	Marine Corps bases at El Toro and Tustin close.
	30 Sep	31st Marine Expeditionary (Special Operations Capable) helicopters deploy to East Timor in support of peacekeeping operations.
	26 Oct	The 11th Marine Expeditionary Unit (Special Operations Capable) deploys to East Timor to support peacekeeping operations, remaining there until December 7.
2000	8 Apr	A MV-22 Osprey crashes near Marana, Arizona, killing all 19 Marines on board. Osprey flight operations are briefly suspended following the accident.
	12 Oct	Following a terrorist attack on the USS *Cole* in Aden, Yemen, Marines of the 2d Fleet Antiterrorism Security Team Company deployed to secure the ship.
	11 Dec	A MV-22 Osprey operating from Marine Corps New River Air Station, North Carolina, crashes near the base, killing all four Marine crew members. As a result of this latest mishap, the Osprey is grounded for 18 months.
2001	11 Sep	Terrorists from the al Qaeda terrorist network hijack four airliners and crash two into the World Trade Center in New York City and a third into the Pentagon. A fourth crashes in rural Pennsylvania. Marines take part in rescue operations at the Pentagon.
	1 Oct	Gen Peter Pace becomes the first Marine to serve as Vice Chairman of the Joint Chiefs of Staff.
	7 Oct	Operation Enduring Freedom begins against Taliban and al Qaeda forces in Afghanistan. VMFA-251 and VMFA-314 based on carriers in the Indian Ocean take part, along with AV-8 Harriers from the 15th Marine Expeditionary Unit.
	29 Oct	The 4th Marine Expeditionary Brigade (Anti-Terrorism) is reactivated in response to the September 11 terrorist attacks.
	25 Nov	Elements of 15th Marine Expeditionary Unit begin landing in Afghanistan and establish a fortified base, Forward Operating Base Rhino.
	7 Dec	Marines kill and wound dozens of enemy fighters and destroy several vehicles in one of their largest firefights to date of Operation Enduring Freedom.
	10 Dec	Marines of 26th Marine Expeditionary Unit secure the long-abandoned U.S. Embassy in Kabul, Afghanistan.
	13 Dec	Elements of the 26th and 15th Marine Expeditionary Unit take control of Kandahar Airfield in Afghanistan.
2002	15 Jan	The first enemy detainees from Afghanistan arrive at Camp X-Ray, Guantanamo Bay, Cuba. Marines from II Marine Expeditionary Force help provide security.
	18 Oct	The I Marine Expeditionary Force, commanded by Lieutenant General James Conway, is ordered to move its headquarters from Camp Pendleton, California, to Kuwait for possible action against Iraq.
	12 Dec	Marines from the 2d Marine Division, II Marine Expeditionary Force, arrive in Djibouti as part of Combined Joint Task Force-Horn of Africa.
2003	4 Jan	Units and equipment of the I Marine Expeditionary Force (1st Marine Division, Task Force Tarawa, and 3d Marine Aircraft Wing) are ordered to Kuwait.
	14 Jan	General Michael W. Hagee becomes the thirty-third Commandant of the U.S. Marine Corps.
	19–20 Mar	***Operation Iraqi Freedom begins with a massive aerial bombardment called "Shock and Awe."***
	20–21 Mar	Led by the 5th Marine Regimental Combat Team, 1st Marine Division, the I Marine Expeditionary Force crosses into Iraq and secures Iraq's southern oil fields.

	20 Mar	15th Marine Expeditionary Unit leads the British 1st Armoured Division into Iraq from Kuwait.
	23 Mar	Task Force Tarawa (2d Marine Expeditionary Brigade) and 1st Marine Division began the bloody battle for An Nasiriyah. The town will not be completely secured until early April.
	2 Apr	The 1st Marine Regimental Combat Team destroys much of the Republican Guard Baghdad Division at Al Kut and crosses the Tigris River.
	2–3 Apr	The 5th Marine Regimental Combat Team reaches An Numaniyah and captures bridges over the Tigris River, opening the path to Baghdad.
	4 Apr	AV-8 Harriers and F/A-18 Hornets from the 3d Marine Aircraft Wing attack masses of Iraqi armor and artillery deploying out of Baghdad under the cover of darkness, inflicting heavy losses.
	9 Apr	Baghdad falls as Marines link up with the Army's 3d Infantry Division and drive into the capital's center, where they are greeted by cheering crowds.
	11 Apr	Elements of the 26th Marine Expeditionary Unit are deployed to northern Iraq to support Special Operations forces already there.
	13 Apr	Marines locate seven American soldiers held prisoner by the Iraqis near Samarra.
	13 Apr	Marines from Task Force Tripoli enter the city of Tikrit, Saddam Hussein's hometown.
	14 Apr	***CENTCOM commander Gen Tommy Franks announces that all major Iraqi cities are under coalition control and organized resistance has all but ceased.***
	16 Apr	Marines attempting to secure Baa'th Party head-quarters in Mosul return fire from a hostile crowd, killing seven Iraqis.
	18 Apr	Marines secure the office of Iraqi Dr. Riyadh Taha, better know as "Dr. Germ" and leader of Iraq's biological weapons program.
	1 May	***President George W. Bush announces an end to major combat operations in Iraq.***
	26 Jun	SgtMaj John L. Estrada becomes the fifteenth Sergeant Major of the U.S. Marine Corps.
	14 Aug	More than 200 Marines from the 26th Marine Expeditionary Unit (Special Operations Capable) deploy to Monrovia, Liberia, in support of peace keeping efforts.
	10 Sep	The Navy announces it will base two squadrons of the new F/A-18 Super Hornet strike fighter at Marine Corps Air Station Cherry Point, North Carolina.
	3 Nov	The I Marine Expeditionary Force is awarded the Navy Presidential Unit Citation for its service in the initial combat operations of Operation Iraqi Freedom. It is the first unit to earn the citation since the Viet Nam War.
2004	23 Feb	A team of 50 Marines arrives in Port-au-Prince, Haiti, to protect the U.S. embassy as Haiti is wracked by political unrest; hundreds of additional Marines soon follow to serve as part of a multi-national peacekeeping force.
	8 Mar	The 2d Battalion, 1st Marines, takes over for elements of the Army's 82d Airborne Division in Fallujah, Iraq.
	25 Apr– 10 May	The 22d Marine Expeditionary Unit (Special Operations Capable) conducts Operation El Dorado, its first major operation since arriving in Afghanistan.
	4 May	The 11th and 24th Marine Expeditionary Units are ordered to Iraq to replace Army units.
	5 Jun	***Former President Ronald Reagan dies. Hundreds of Marines take part in ceremonies honoring the former president in the following days.***
	8 Jun	The first elements of the 24th Marine Expeditionary Unit arrive in Iraq.
	27 Jun– 10 Jul	Marines from the 22d Marine Expeditionary Unit (Special Operations Capable) conduct Operation Thunder Road in the Afghan province of Oruzgan.
	7 Jul	The Department of Defense announces new troop rotations to Iraq and Afghanistan. Among the units to deploy are the II Marine Expeditionary Force, which will be stationed in central western Iraq, and the 3d Battalion, 6th Marines (with a Marine Aviation Combat Element), which will deploy to Afghanistan.
	Oct–Nov	Marines of I Marine Expeditionary Force take part in heavy fighting during operations against Iraqi insurgents in and around Fallujah.
	26 Dec	After a tsunami devastates South Asia, Marines from the 15th and 26th Marine Expeditionary Units are among thousands of U.S. servicemen deployed in support of relief operations.
2005	30 Jan	Marines help to provide security during Iraq's first democratic elections.
	10 Mar	The 5th Provisional Civil Affairs Group, the Marines first provisional civil affairs unit, begins operations in Al Anbar, Iraq.
	7–14 May	Marines from Regimental Combat Team-2, 2d Marine Division, conduct Operation Matador near the Iraqi-Syrian border, killing more than 125 insurgents. Nine Marines are killed and 40 wounded.
	8 May	Marines from 3d Battalion, 3d Marines, engage in a five-hour battle in Laghman province in Afghanistan. Fifteen insurgents and two Marines are killed in the fighting.
	5 Jun	Marines of Regimental Combat Team-8, 2d Marine Division, uncover a massive underground insurgent bunker complex west of Baghdad near Karmah.
	17–22 Jun	Approximately 1,000 Marines from Marine Regimental Combat Team-2, 2d Marine Division, conduct Operation Spear in northwestern Anbar province against Iraqi insurgents and foreign fighters.
	28 Jul	Marines from the 3d Battalion, 25th Marines, supported by air strikes from the 2d Marine Aircraft Wing and Iraqi Security Forces, attack insurgent positions in Cykla, killing nine terrorists.
	1–4 Aug	In a particularly violent four-day period in Iraq, 22 Marines are killed in action, including six members of a sniper team killed in an ambush and another 14 killed when their AAVP7A1 Amphibious Assault Vehicle is destroyed by a mine. Most of the Marines killed are from Lima Company, 3d Battalion, 25th Marines, a reserve unit from Ohio.
	3–10 Aug	Marines from Regimental Combat Team-2 and Iraqi soldiers conduct Operation Quick Strike against insurgents in western Iraq, capturing weapons and suspected terrorists.
	10–20 Aug	Marines from 2d Battalion, 3d Marines, conduct security operations in the Korengal Valley region of Afghanistan in support of September elections.
	30 Aug	Marine Reservists from 3d Platoon, Alpha Company, 4th Assault Amphibian Battalion, based in Gulfport, Mississippi, rescue dozens of people in Mississippi devastated by Hurricane Katrina. Hundreds of additional Marines are deployed to the region to assist with disaster relief.
	10 Sep– 3 Oct	The 13th Marine Expeditionary Unit takes part in the Bright Star 2005 joint military exercise in Egypt.
	24 Sep	Hurricane Rita strikes Louisiana and Texas. Hundreds of Marines are deployed to the region to assist with relief operations.
	28 Sep	The Department of Defense approves full production of MV-22 Osprey.
	30 Sep	Gen Peter Pace is sworn in as Chairman, Joint Chiefs of Staff, the first Marine to hold that position.
	1 Oct	Marines from Regimental Combat Team-2, 2d Marine Division, launch Operation Iron Fist against Iraqi insurgents in Anbar province.

11

THE Marine Corps Experience

THE
Marine Corps
Experience

General Carl E. Mundy, Jr., USMC (Ret)
Thirtieth Commandant of the Marine Corps

Warriors "coming from the mystique of the sea . . ." Marines of a modern-day expeditionary force practice their trade in a landing exercise at Camp Pendleton, California. The amphibious assault—projecting power from the sea onto the shore—has been a specialty of Marines since 1775. (Photo: USMC)

The world over, the word Marine defines something more than a soldier. It arouses the image of a warrior on the boundlessness of the oceans, coming from the mystique of the sea onto the land—an amphibian, a soldier of the sea. The aura is of one who is different and of whom more is expected.

To be a United States Marine requires more than mastery of the skills and techniques of soldiering or seamanship—the practical abilities that come through training and experience. Being a Marine is a state of mind that comes from an imbedded belief that he or she is, in fact, unique, a cut above. A Marine is, most of all, part of an organization that demands a difference—and delivers excellence beyond others in all it is and does. This is The Corps, the strongest brotherhood in the world.

Among those not in the profession of arms, the notion exists that military service is simply another job alternative; that soldiers go to work with only pay and benefits in mind. Being a Marine has never been just a job, just a paycheck, an occupational specialty, or an insignia of rank. Being a Marine comes from the Eagle, Globe, and Anchor that is tattooed indelibly on the innermost being of those privileged to earn the title. It is a searing mark, one that does not fade over time. "There's no such damned thing as an ex-Marine! Once a Marine, always a Marine!" To dispute this is to invite a brawl.

Few who have borne the title fail to identify with it throughout their entire lives. Former Secretary of State James Baker, long after his active service, was known, on light-hearted occasions, to identify himself as "Secretary of State, and Captain, United States Marine Corps." Pride and cockiness are marks of a Marine: a belief in self, a confidence in

Above: On the last night of World War I, 10 November 1918, the 4th Brigade of Marines crossed the Marne River, broke through the German defenses, and were still fighting when word of the Armistice reached them. ("The Last Night of the War," F. C. Yohn, Marine Corps Art Collection)

Below: Their drill instructor congratulates these recruits on becoming Marines. They have successfully completed their recruit training—the toughest in the world. (Photo: USMC)

Previous spread: Marine recruits at San Diego present their rifles to their drill instructor for inspection. "Every Marine a rifleman" is the creed ingrained in every Marine. (Photo: Rick Mullen)

15

Top: *In Viet Nam in May 1969, Marines pay final tribute to men of their unit killed in a recent action. Each dead Marine is represented by a helmet on a rifle bayoneted into the ground, a tradition begun in France during World War I when rifles and helmets were used to mark temporary graves. (Photo: USMC)*

Above: *Marines salute, whether it is to honor a fallen comrade or to acknowledge receipt of an award at a stateside ceremony. (Photo: USMC)*

fellow Marines, and an almost emotional belief in the institution. The Corps is holy to Marines. Their unabashed pride in the organization breeds a selflessness unique in the American culture. As a leathery gunnery sergeant put it to a recruit many decades ago, "Lad, if you must, it's okay to die for the Corps, but it's not okay to soil its battle flag on the way down!" This dedication to institution, and to those who comprise it, harkens to the days of loyalty to kings, the loyalty of Napoleon's Old Guard at Waterloo, and to Henry V's band of brothers at Agincourt. Indeed, "band of brothers" describes those who are the Corps—men and women alike—as it describes no other organization anywhere.

Pride runs deep in Marines. The story is told of an American lady visiting a French field hospital in World War I who noticed among the fiercely whiskered Gallic faces one unlike the others. "Oh," she said, "surely you are an American!" "No, ma'am," the casualty answered, "I'm a Marine."

Being a Marine has been likened by some to a calling—an almost religious commitment to the Corps. Among the proud marching songs of the five American armed services, only one is titled "hymn"—"The Marines' Hymn." Years before it became fashionable among the other services to stand when one's service song is played, Marines stood to attention for their hymn on every occasion. Today, as proud members of other services applaud and cheer their song, Marines still stand, almost reverently, at attention for their hymn. Newly commissioned Marine lieutenants, experi-

encing the tradition of the formal officers' mess dinner, stand solemnly at its conclusion to sing, from memory and in unison, the verses of the hymn. The pride, commitment, and dedication to the Corps in their eyes and in the strength of their young voices is palpable and moving.

Marines enjoy a reputation for prowess in combat, a reputation earned in battles "in every clime and place" throughout our nation's history. Yet, it

has been said that the most important contribution the Marine Corps has made to our nation is not that it has fought and won battles. Rather, its most enduring contribution is that it makes Marines, imbues them with extraordinary mettle, and returns the great majority to civilian life with exceptional qualities of confidence, determination, leadership, and a winning spirit that gives strength to our national character. These "once a Marine, always a Marine" citizens, whatever their successes, never abandon the pride instilled in them for, or their identification with, the Corps.

The process of making a Marine is thought by many to begin with recruit training. Indeed, and unique to the Corps, it begins well before that, as part of the recruiting process. On high school career days, when

In response to their drill instructor's challenge, "I can't hear you!" recruits sound off loud and clear: "Yes, sir!" (Photo: Rick Mullen)

Left: *Newly arrived recruits, on their first day of processing, stand back-to-breast, heads shaven, awaiting their uniform issue. The civilian world is being left behind. (Photo: Rick Mullen)*

Facing page: *Recruit training is a non-stop physical challenge including rolling over logs ("Keep your head down!"), working for that last chin-up, calisthenics in place, marching under full pack, and rappelling down a rope from a dizzying height. (Photos: Rick Mullen)*

U.S. MARINE CORPS
RECRUITING SERVICE.

Wanted, for the United States Marine Corps,

Able-bodied MEN, between the ages of 18 and 40 years, not less than 5 feet 5 inches high, and of good character.

SOLDIERS serving in this Corps perform duty at Navy Yards and on board United States Ships of War on Foreign Stations. which affords a splendid opportunity to travel and see the world.

The term of service is FOUR YEARS: and if a soldier re-enlists at the expiration of that time. his pay will be increased **two dollars** per month for the first re-enlistment. with a further addition of **one dollar** per month for all subsequent re-enlistments.

By good conduct and attention to duty. a soldier will certainly rise to the position of a non-commissioned officer.

SERGEANTS in the Marine Corps frequently have independent command of guards on Sloops-of-War, and always on Gunboats. The following is the rate of pay as now established:

GRADE.	PAY OF UNITED STATES MARINE CORPS.		
	Pay per Month.	Pay per Annum.	Pay for Four Years.
To the First or Orderly Sergeant of a Company or Guard,	$24 00	$288 00	$1.152 00
All other Sergeants, each.	20 00	240 00	960 00
Corporals,	18 00	216 00	864 00
Musicians,	16 00	192 00	768 00
Privates,	16 00	192 00	768 00
At Sea, the extra pay is	1 50	18 00	72 00

In addition to the pay as above stated, one ration per day and an abundant supply of the best clothing is allowed to every soldier. A soldier who is careful of his clothing can save during his enlistment from 50 to 80 dollars. Quarters, fuel, and medical attendance are always provided by the Government, without deduction from the soldier's pay. If a soldier should become disabled in the line of his duties, the law provides for him a Pension.

All other information which may be desired, will be given at the Rendezvous.

LIEUT. H. C. COCHRANE,
Recruiting Officer.

RECRUITING RENDEZVOUS,
PARDEE'S BUILDING, CHICAGO.

May, 1866.

recruiters appear from each of the armed services to give a presentation of benefits, education opportunities, job selections and pay incentives, Marine recruiters want to speak last. Following the sales pitches, the Marine sergeant stands, looks at the audience, and with almost arrogant disdain, announces: "There may be one or two of you good enough to be Marines. If you think you are, I'll talk to you!"

Marine recruiting posters do not promise material benefits, but,

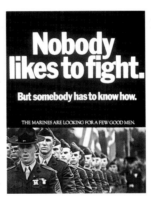

Marine Corps recruiting posters have historically offered a clear challenge of service and commitment and a promise of adventure—but no "rose garden."

rather, "Maybe you can be one of us." "We never promised you a rose garden"; "Nobody likes to fight, but somebody has to know how"; "We're looking for a few good men and women." A challenge—not a guarantee—is laid down, and the gauntlet is picked up by young Americans of ordinary fiber seeking to attain the extraordinary aura of the Corps.

Arched over the gate at one of the Corps' oldest and most legendary bases—Parris Island, South Carolina—is a sign: "Where the Difference

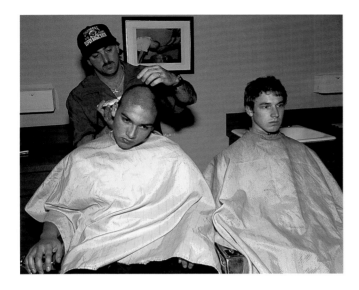

Begins." Through this gate, and others like it in San Diego, California, and Quantico, Virginia, thousands of young Americans pass to accept the challenge to become a Marine. Here, in the intense and impassioned weeks that follow, they will undergo trials of stress and physical endurance beyond those they believed themselves capable. Here, self-discipline and personal responsibility are ingrained. "Yes, sir! No, sir! No excuse, sir!" reflect the Corps' intolerance of excuse for failure. "I'm sorry, sir" gets thunderous disapproval from the drill instructor: "You're never sorry for anything you do in the Corps!"

During the weeks in this forge, young bodies harden, maturity emerges, minds focus, confidence grows, brotherhood takes form, and pride begins to tingle. At their conclusion, "recruit" or "candidate" becomes "Marine" in the euphoria of accomplishment. The new Marine knows that he or she has passed through a trial that others have not dared, and has gained acceptance in a storied band of brothers: "The few . . . the proud . . . the Marines."

Top left: *The skin-tight "boot haircut" takes the barber less than thirty seconds. It is a great leveler. (Photo: Rick Mullen)*

Top right: *Teamwork is taught by such simple joint efforts as scrubbing the "deck" of the barracks, a step in a "field day" that will make the barracks immaculate—or else. (Photo: Rick Mullen)*

Facing page: *A Marine puts on his "war face" with a camouflage stick. It is designed to do more than camouflage: the Marine confronts his enemy as a fierce, depersonalized warrior. (Photo: USMC)*

Below: *A drill instructor drives home his point "up close and personal" to the erring recruit who must stand frozen at attention or invite further wrath. (Photo: Rick Mullen)*

Previous spread: *Hand over hand, a Marine recruit climbs a cargo net, good physical training and a reminder that this was how Marines in times past went over the side of troop transports and down cargo nets into landing craft—and it still sometimes happens. (Photo: Rick Mullen)*

Marines respect tradition. Their uniforms change little over time. Their buttons are emblazoned with the oldest American military insignia worn in any service. The collar of their ageless blue uniform harkens to the leather stock worn around the necks of their American Revolution–era predecessors. Their officers wear the replica of a sword presented by an Arab bey after a Marine victory on "the shores of Tripoli" two centuries ago. They fervently believe the scarlet stripe on their trouser leg is the "blood stripe" earned in "the halls of Montezuma." Their hats are marked by a quatrefoil, symbolic, they have been told, of a white cross used in the

Marines in their "blues" can be seen at their smartest during ceremonies held at Marine Barracks, Washington, during the summer parade season. (Photo: USMC)

Below: *These Marines defended the Legation Quarter in Peking, China, during the Boxer Rebellion of 1900. They wore as their fighting uniform "blues" that were not much different from today's "dress blues." (Photo: USMC)*

26

Women Marines stand by, ready to graduate from recruit training—separate from, but just as tough as that given the men—at Parris Island, South Carolina. Their drill instructor, a sergeant, wears three rows of ribbons, a rifle expert's badge, and an NCO sword unchanged since 1859. (Photo: Greg E. Mathieson)

This Marine's infantry training continues at Camp Lejeune, North Carolina, after his graduation from Parris Island. (Photo: Greg E. Mathieson)

days of sail to identify their officers to Marines perched high in the ship's rigging and clearing the enemy's deck with musketry.

With these visible manifestations of tradition, Marines cling also to standards that have sustained the Corps over its history and been passed down to them from generations before. The most defining among these is the Marine Corps creed: "Every Marine a rifleman." In a world of fantastic technology, this statement seems antiquated. Yet, generations of Marines learn to know the rifle first, and with it, the fundamentals of infantry—the backbone of combat. Sophisticated specialties come later. Whatever their assignments, all Marines spend time each year polishing their marksmanship with the rifle. Officers, for their first half year as lieutenants, carry and learn to fight with rifles. Only then are they armed with pistols.

Unique to the Corps, would-be pilots learn first the tactics and techniques of infantry; only afterward are they trained in the intricacies of piloting sophisticated aircraft. As testament to the bedrock of this creed, it is not insignificant that the first Marine officer to receive the Medal of Honor in World War II, Captain Henry T. Elrod, was a pilot, his aircraft no longer flyable, who died leading Marines as infantry on Wake Island. "Every Marine a rifleman."

Flowing from spirit, tradition, pride, comradeship, and dedication are the fundamental hallmarks of Marines. Courage is foremost among these. As the fledgling Corps began to take form in the early years of our nation, Marines wore their motto, "Fortitudine"—"Courage"—on their cap badge. Courage under fire, tenacity, determination to stand when others would turn are the historic badge of Marines.

Young Lieutenant Clifton B. Cates, destined to become the Corps' 19th commandant, reported during a World War I battle: "I have only two men left out of my company, and twenty out of other companies . . . I have

Marines slog through the "green hell" of an island in the Pacific during World War II. For much of its history the Corps has fought in tropical jungles. Now its battlefields are more apt to be urban. ("Ghost Trail," Kerr Eby, Navy Art Collection)

To a Marine going down a cargo net in World War II, the distance from the deck of the transport down to the landing craft bobbing in the water below seems infinite. (Cpl Richard E. Gibney, USMC, Marine Corps Art Collection)

no one on my left, and only a few on my right. I will hold." Twenty-five years later, during the desperate fight for a toehold on a Pacific atoll called Tarawa, Colonel David M. Shoup, who would be the 22d commandant, reported similarly: "Casualties many; percent dead not known; we are winning." And in the frozen snows of the Korean winter, Major General Oliver P. Smith, commanding the 1st Marine Division and surrounded by outnumbering communist Chinese divisions, responded to a reporter's query: "Retreat, hell! We're just attacking in a different direction!"

"First to fight for right and freedom, and to keep our honor clean, we are proud to claim the title of United States Marine." So proclaims the first verse of "The Marines' Hymn." Courage, honor and faithfulness are held high by Marines. Integrity, ethical behavior, a respect for fellow human beings (even an enemy), devotion to a cause, commitment to an organization, and an unyielding bond of faith with those beside you are principles to be inculcated into and believed by those in whom the nation places its ultimate trust for survival, and its authority to inflict violence on others in its behalf. They are keystone values in the character of those who are Marines. "It's not okay to soil the battle flag on the way down" says it. "No Marine leaves another Marine on the battlefield" says it. But "Semper Fidelis" . . . "Always Faithful," the motto of the Corps since 1883, says it best.

This faithfulness to country and Corps has, over time, brought Marines to an extraordinary relationship with America's leaders, and its commander-in-chief in particular. Our third president, Thomas Jefferson, designated the Marine Band "The President's Own," and it has played for the inauguration of every American president since. "Hail to the Chief," the president's march, came from the Marine Band. By tradition, the Marine Band can leave Washington to play elsewhere only with the permission of the president. Presidential ambassadors in embassies throughout the world are guarded by Marines. A Marine opens the door to the east wing of the White House—the president's office. Marines guard the presidential retreat at Camp David, Maryland. Marine helicopters lift the president from the lawn of the White House and, wherever he travels—worldwide—are there to meet and transport him. Indeed, the relationship

between Marines and the American presidency is special and enduring.

"Send in the Marines" has been the American response to countless crises distant from our shores over the history of our nation. "Expeditionary" is the word that embodies this historic role of Marines—who are created and shaped not for home service, but for overseas expeditions. In 1775, the first American soldiers sent forth from the fledgling nation's shores were a detachment of Marines dispatched to New Providence, Bahamas. That amphibious raid—the first in what remains today a Marine specialty—aimed to seize guns and gunpowder from a British fort. Three decades later, Marines again sortied with the fleet to Derna, Tripoli, to put down Barbary Coast pirates taking a toll of American merchant ships in the Mediterranean. And in the same century, as America engaged in conflict with its neighbor to the south, Marines were first to reach the site of the palace of the Aztec chieftain, Montezuma. By such deeds over their entire existence, Marines lay claim to distinction as America's premier expeditionary force.

Unlike the emblematic shields of their sister services, signifying defense, the Marine emblem—eagle, globe, and anchor—symbolizes distant service under the American eagle, by land and sea, to represent their nation's interests "in every clime and place."

Below: *The Marine Corps' "eagle, globe, and anchor," adopted in 1868, is perhaps the most recognized military insignia in the world.*

Bottom left: *A Marine reconnaissance team moves by inflatable rubber boat to a raid site during an exercise at Camp Lejeune. (USMC)*

Bottom right: *The broad deck of USS* Essex *provides plenty of room for Marines to do push-ups when flight operations are not in progress. (Photo: Rick Mullen)*

Marines march in a long double column of files through the rugged hills of Camp Pendleton. (Photo: Rick Mullen)

Some have likened Marines to the legionnaires of history. Historian T. E. Fehrenbach, accounting the Korean War of the mid-twentieth century, articulated this expeditionary image of Marines:

> *The man who will go where his colors go, without asking, who will fight a phantom foe in jungle and mountain range, without counting, and who will suffer and die in the midst of incredible hardship, without complaint, is still what he has always been, from Imperial Rome to sceptered Britain to democratic America. He is the stuff of which legions are made. . . . He has been called United States Marine.*

These same remarkable qualities were poignantly characterized by Lieutenant General Victor H. Krulak, one of the Corps' great leaders, when he wrote:

Flares light up the night, silhouetting Marines, during a night exercise. (Photo: Rick Mullen)

The face of a modern-day legionnaire—a United States Marine. (Photo: USMC)

The Marine Corps War Memorial in Arlington, Virginia, is visited by millions each year and is the scene of hundreds of ceremonies. (Photo: USMC)

Although the Corps contains its share of visible heroes, its triumphs, in an aberration of history, are triumphs of the institution itself and not the attainments of individual Marines. We remember that Marlborough defeated the French, that Togo defeated the Russians, that Scipio defeated Carthage. But we know only that it was the Marines who won at Belleau Wood, the Marines who won at Guadalcanal, the Marines who led the way at Inchon. And that is exactly the way the Corps' heroes—big and small—would have it, for the Corps is less of the flesh than of the spirit.

The memorial on Wake Island in the Pacific, dedicated to the Marines who during the first weeks of World War II defended that island in what has been called the "Marine Corps' Alamo," is now a lonely place, almost never visited—but a U.S. flag still flies over the island. (Photo: Rick Mullen)

Indeed, the Marine experience, for all those who have lived it, and for those who will live it, is special and to a higher standard in countless forms of measure. If there is a single distinction that stands out, among the many, marking the experience in the lives of the men and women who are Marines, it is their extraordinary and selfless dedication to and identification with The Corps.

This is the Marine Corps experience.

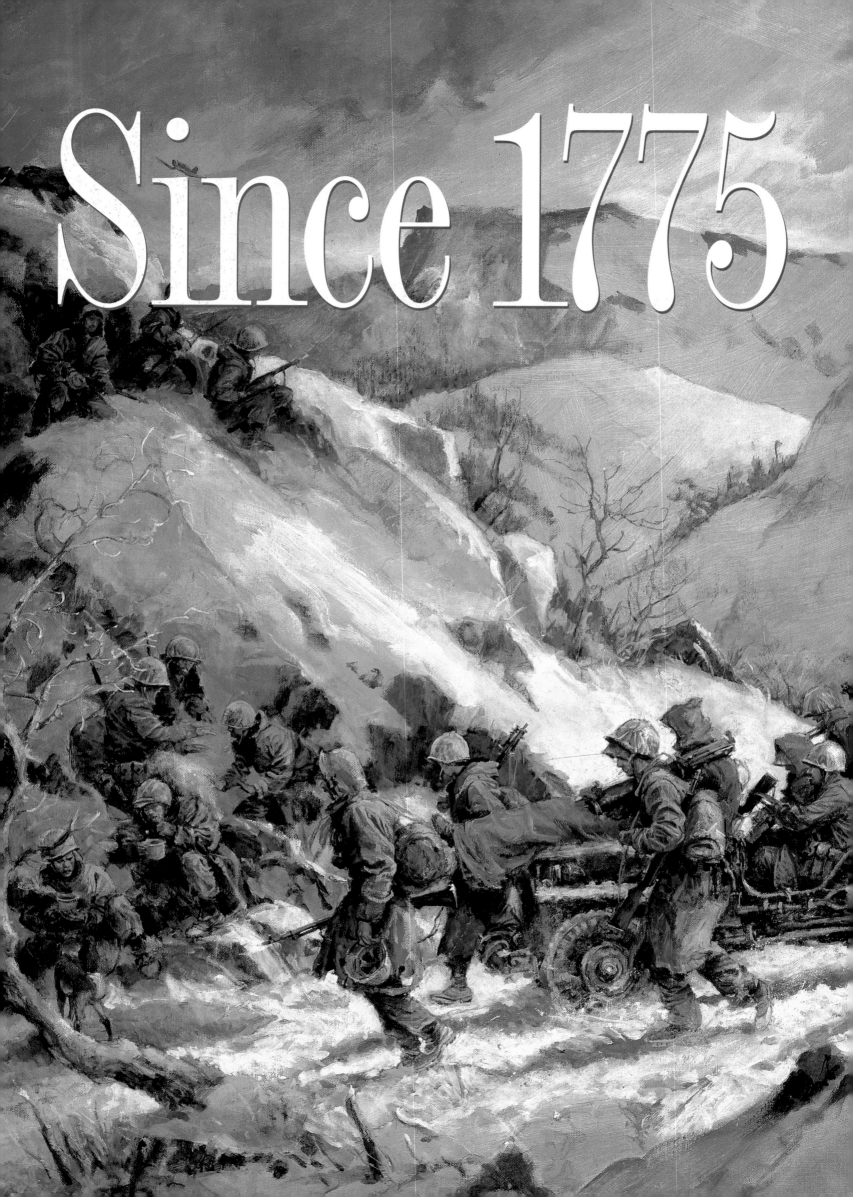

Since 1775

Since 1775

Brigadier General Edwin H. Simmons, USMC(Ret)

Three small companies of Continental Marines get a taste of General Washington's temper when they momentarily falter during the battle of Princeton on 3 January 1777. ("Marines with Washington at Princeton," Col Charles Waterhouse, USMCR (Ret), Marine Corps Art Collection)

The Continental Marines

On 10 November 1775—which the Marines take as their birthday and celebrate around the globe—the Continental Congress passed a resolution to raise two battalions of American Marines. They were to be part of a naval expedition to help the inhabitants of Nova Scotia secure "the preservation of their rights and liberties." But George Washington, as commander of the Continental Army, was cool on the idea of the expedition, and it didn't happen.

The Continental Congress still went ahead with raising the Marines. Captain Samuel Nicholas, the ink not yet dry on his commission, was authorized to recruit Marines for service with Commodore Ezek Hopkins's squadron, the Continental Navy's first, then forming at Philadelphia.

About three hundred Marines were in the eight ships that sortied in mid-February 1776, destination New Providence in the Bahamas. Nicholas took a landing party—his Marines and some seamen—ashore on 3 March and, despite a few random shots, captured two small stone forts and a significant amount of military stores. The first landing by American Marines on a foreign shore was a success.

Nicholas, on his return to Philadelphia, was promoted to major and told to recruit four companies for service in the four frigates then being built in the Delaware River. One company went to sea in the fall of 1776 in the *Randolph* (and would go down with the ship in 1778). In December 1776 Nicholas crossed the Delaware with his remaining three companies, hoping to join Washington at Trenton; and they did arrive in time for the battle at Princeton. After that, Nicholas's Marines shriveled to a minor garrison in Philadelphia. Elsewhere, Marine officers, their recruiting broadsides sometimes trumpeting they were looking "for a few good men," raised their ship's detachments locally for service afloat.

John Paul Jones used his Marines in the *Ranger* especially well when he harried the British ports on the Irish Sea. Later, he recruited his Marines for the *Bonhomme Richard,* 137 of them, from the expatriate Irish Brigade of the French Army. The French-Irish Marines gave a good account of themselves; but in the 42-gun *Bonhomme Richard's* epic victory over the 50-gun *Serapis* off Yorkshire's coast in September 1779, it was a seaman, not a Marine as legend would have it, who dropped the decisive grenade through the open hatch of the *Serapis*, exploding her magazine.

In the summer of 1779 an expedition mounted out from Boston intending to dislodge the two battalions of Scots who had ensconced themselves in hastily built Fort George at Penobscot Bay in what is now Maine. The landing force numbered about a thousand, mostly militia but a quarter of them Continental and states' Marines. In the amphibious assault that began at dawn on 28 July, Captain John Welsh, who had come from Ireland to fight the British, was killed leading the Marines. So were thirteen more Marines, and an additional twenty were wounded. The militia came ashore and then the attack stalled. The landing force commander would not assault the main works until the ships brought their guns to bear, and the naval commander would not risk his ships "in that damned hole."

On the evening of 13 August, a British squadron appeared in the bay, and the next morning an out-gunned Continental naval commander flew the signal: "All ships fend for yourself." Nineteen American ships were lost, but most of the militia, seamen, and Marines made their way overland to Boston. The largest amphibious effort of the war ended in failure. The United States would not try another major amphibious landing for nearly seventy-five years.

Service Under Sail

On 11 July 1798, President John Adams signed a bill creating the United States Marine Corps as such and authorizing a strength of five hundred privates, plus necessary officers, non-commissioned officers,

John Adams reviews John Paul Jones's Marines at Brest, France, in May 1779. He was shocked to find them wearing what he thought were English red coats. The Marines, however, were soldiers drawn from France's Irish Brigade, bitter enemies of Britain. ("John Adams Reviews Jones' Marines, 13 May 1779," Col Charles Waterhouse, USMCR (Ret), Marine Corps Art Collection)

and musicians. Marines of the new Corps would share in the glory of the romantic victories of the frigates in the Quasi-War with France (1798–1801), the Barbary Wars (1801–1815), and the more important Second War of Independence (1812–1815). Legends began to cluster around the exploits of young officers, often rash, sometimes disagreeable, and always completely self-assured.

One such was Lieutenant Presley O'Bannon. In 1805 he and seven Marines marched across six hundred miles of North Africa's Libyan desert with a polyglot "army" that successfully stormed the fortified Tripolitan city of Derna. Marines today sing about the victory in the second line of their "Hymn," ". . . to the shores of Tripoli." The Marine Corps' officers sword, adopted in 1826, is modeled, they say, after the Mameluke scimitar given O'Bannon for his exploits.

Britain, by its impressment of seamen from American merchant ships, pushed the United States into declaring a new war on 18 June 1812. Muster rolls show that at the war's beginning the Marine Corps consisted of ten officers and 483 men. Half the Corps was at sea in ships' detachments; the rest were in navy yards or at Washington and New Orleans. There would be adventures enough for all of them. Marines served in sea battles—including those on the Great Lakes—and fought ashore, notably in the defense of Washington in August 1814 and at New Orleans at the end of that year.

One of those early young heroes, Lieutenant John Marshall Gamble, commanded the Marine detachment in the bantam frigate *Essex* when in 1813 its captain, David Porter, ventured into the southern Pacific to destroy the British whaling fleet. Porter took so many prizes that he used

When the American frigate Constitution *engaged the British frigate* Guerriere *off Newfoundland on 19 August 1812, eager Marine Lt William S. Bush went to the rail and called to Navy Capt Isaac Hull, "Shall I board her, sir?" A Royal Marine shot him dead, but Bush's Marines cleared the* Guerriere's *decks with musket fire, while "Old Ironsides" pounded the enemy's hull with zero-range broadsides. The American victory jolted the proud British Royal Navy. ("USS* Constitution *and HMS* Guerriere," *Michael F. Corne, U.S. Naval Academy Museum)*

Maj John Marshall Gamble, who took the first U.S. Marines into the Pacific in the Essex *and was left crippled from a musket ball in his heel, mounts an Arabian horse given to him by his brother. (Marine Corps Art Collection)*

up all his Navy officers as prize captains and gave command of one ship, the 10-gun *Greenwich*, to Gamble. With it, Gamble captured the biggest prize of all, the 14-gun *Seringpatam*. Porter and his squadron sailed on to the Marquesas Islands, where he took possession of the island of Nukuhiva. There, Porter departed and left Gamble behind as island commander with three ships and twenty-two men. His garrison, mostly captured British seamen, mutinied, and, with Gamble, as a prisoner, a musket ball in his heel, sailed off in the *Seringpatam* flying the Union Jack. The mutineers put Gamble and a few loyal hands into an open boat. Gamble made his way back to Nukuhiva where he and seven others manned the prize ship *Sir Andrew Hammond* and sailed it to the Hawaiian Islands.

In the summer of 1814, Rear Admiral George Cockburn, Royal Navy (who had already burned Havre de Grace and ravaged much of Norfolk), reinforced by Major General Robert Ross with four thousand veteran troops, approached Washington. Defending the American capital were mostly militia whose numbers did not make up for their lack of training. Captain Samuel Miller marched 103 Marines from Marine Barracks, Washington, out to Bladensburg, Maryland, to join them. On 24 August the British crossed the Potomac's Eastern Branch (now the Anacostia River). The militia melted away, but Commodore Joshua Barney, with five guns and about four hundred seamen, and Capt Miller and his Marines made a stand, futile though it was. The Marines lost eight killed, fourteen wounded, Miller among the latter. The British burned a good part of Washington but failed to take Baltimore.

In December, Major Daniel Carmick and about three hundred Marines at New Orleans took their place in the line that Major General Andrew Jackson formed behind the Rodriguez Canal. Major General Sir

Edward Pakenham, the Duke of Wellington's brother-in-law, first attacked on 28 December 1814. Carmick was wounded and would die within a year. Pakenham, rebuffed that time, attacked again on 8 January 1815 with sixty-five hundred men. The Americans had possibly forty-five hundred, but they stood behind cotton-bale barricades. The British advanced in close formation across an open field, and about seven hundred of them died, among them Pakenham whose body went home to Ireland in a cask of rum.

From then until the War with Mexico (1846–1847), the Marine Corps, which seldom numbered as many as a thousand men, served largely at sea, fighting "pirates" in the Mediterranean, the Caribbean, and the Far East, and slave runners in the South Atlantic.

In 1835, the U.S. government decided to relocate the Seminole Indians from Georgia and Florida to what is now Arkansas. The Seminoles objected and so did their allies, the Creeks. A Marine regiment was pulled together to help the U.S. Army, which had more on its hands than it could handle. It was an ugly, unfortunate six-year war with not much glory and a lot of tropical fever. Sixty-one Marines died.

Lieutenant Archibald H. Gillespie, an impetuous firebrand, arrived in California in the spring of 1846 with secret orders, or so it was commonly accepted, from President James Polk to begin one of the most bizarre events in Marine Corps history. He rendezvoused with Army Captain John C. Fremont and his exploration party (including the intrepid scout Kit Carson). Gillespie acted as Fremont's adjutant, a battalion of mounted riflemen was quickly recruited, and soon the Bear Flag was run up at Sonoma, and California was declared a republic. On learning that the United States

For six long years (1836–1842) Marines serving with the U.S. Army chased Seminole Indians in Florida. Other Marines served in the Navy's "Mosquito Fleet" that patrolled the coast and pushed on into the Everglades. Marines would renew their acquaintance with "riverine warfare" during the Civil War and again in Viet Nam. ("Seminole Wars," SSgt John Clymer, USMCR, Marine Corps Art Collection)

Top: *Commodore Matthew Perry's East India Squadron, which "opened up" Japan in 1853–1854, included two hundred Marines under Capt Jacob Zeilin. The Marines' brilliant uniforms, bayoneted muskets, and precision drill made a lasting impression on the Japanese. (Marine Corps Art Collection)*

Above left: *A Japanese artist, recording the scene for Prince Hosokawa, one of the six Japanese lords who received Perry, saw the Marines, in his version, marching in column behind a red-striped American flag lacking its star-spangled blue union. (Marine Corps Art Collection)*

Above right: *The Japanese artist, who chronicled Perry's visit in a long scroll, portrayed Zeilin's Marines in not an entirely complimentary way. (Marine Corps Art Collection)*

was at war with Mexico, Fremont took his battalion to Monterey and placed it under Commodore Robert F. Stockton, commander of the Pacific Squadron. Fremont's battalion and ships' landing parties seized the villages of San Diego and Los Angeles for the United States.

Gillespie was sent out to meet Army Brigadier General Stephen W. Kearny who was nearing San Diego with his grandly named Army of the West, consisting of about a hundred dragoons mounted on worn-out horses. Mexican lancers beat them at San Pascual on 6 December 1846. With a third of his force dead or wounded (Gillespie among the latter), Kearny took up a position on Mule Hill and held until a relief party, including the Marine guard from the frigate *Congress*, could be led in by Kit Carson. Stockton and Kearny then joined forces and completed the conquest of California.

In the Gulf of Mexico, a provisional battalion of Marines under Captain Alvin Edson raided a string of Mexican ports and then joined Army Major General Winfield Scott off Veracruz. Scott's bold landing on 9 March 1847 opened the way to Mexico City. Edson's battalion went back on board its ships and a battalion under Lieutenant Colonel Samuel E. Watson took its place with Scott. The Marine battalion was brigaded with Brigadier General John A. Quitman's division, Watson moved up to brigade command, and command of the Marine battalion went to Major Levi Twiggs.

Marines from the East India or Asiatic Squadron helped the British win a lopsided victory in 1856 over the four "Barriers Forts" protecting the treaty port of Canton. At the time, China was almost helpless against such Western incursions. (Marine Corps Art Collection)

Twiggs was killed in the assault of Chapultepec Castle on 13 September. Marine Captain George C. Terrett and his company stormed the San Cosme Gate and entered Mexico City itself. Next morning a Marine party ran up the Stars and Stripes over the Palacio Nacional (which was built on the foundations of the Halls of Montezuma). When the Marine battalion got back to Washington a grateful citizenry presented it with a set of colors emblazoned with "From Tripoli to the Halls of the Montezumas."

Commodore Matthew Perry's East India Squadron, which went to Japan in 1853 (after stopovers in the Bonins and Okinawa) and again in 1854, had a special Marine complement of six officers and two hundred men under Captain Jacob Zeilin. The East India Squadron also pecked away at the China coast, cooperating with British landings at Shanghai and near Hong Kong. The biggest action came in 1856 with the reduction of the four "Barrier Forts," which barred the way to the treaty port of Canton, and the capture of 170 cannon.

During these same antebellum years, Marines made repeated landings in Panama to protect the railroad that crossed the isthmus and shortened the route to the California goldfields. The sovereignty of lesser nations was not taken seriously; the Marines made landings in Nicaragua, Uruguay, Paraguay, and even the Fiji Islands.

The Blue and the Gray

On Sunday night, 16 October 1859, Lieutenant Colonel Robert E. Lee, USA, was informed by the secretary of war that the abolitionist John Brown had seized the U.S. arsenal at Harpers Ferry, Virginia, and was stirring up a slave insurrection. Lee left Washington for Harpers Ferry on the five o'clock train, taking Army Lieutenant J.E.B. Stuart with him as his aide. On arriving they found Lieutenant Israel Green already there with eighty-six Marines from the Washington Marine Barracks. With a

wave of his plumed hat Stuart signaled the assault on the arsenal's brick firehouse in which Brown and his men had fortified themselves. Green and his Marines stormed the firehouse and captured Brown.

On 1 January 1861, the eve of the Civil War, the strength of the Marine Corps was 1,892 officers and men. Half of the officers and two-thirds of the lieutenants, among them Israel Green, resigned to take commissions in the Confederacy. The Federal army that marched south from Washington, headed for Bull Run, had in it a battalion of Marines—thirteen officers and 336 men—under Major John Reynolds. The Marine battalion did a good job for a time defending Griffin's West Point battery at Henry House Hill, then the whole Union line began to break. Reynolds marched his Marines back to the barracks, less the forty-four who were casualties.

Marines landed repeatedly on the Confederacy's Atlantic coastline and in the Gulf, and performed admirably at New Orleans and Mobile Bay. By the end of 1864, Wilmington, North Carolina, defended by Fort Fisher, was the last Atlantic port still accessible to Confederate blockade runners. The Union tried an assault on Fort Fisher on Christmas Day; it failed. In a more determined effort on 15 January 1865, Rear Admiral David Dixon Porter, son of Commodore David Porter of *Essex* fame, pounded the fort with the six hundred guns of his assembled fleet. Some four hundred Marines were to land on the beach in front of the seaward face of the fort and hold a beachhead, while sixteen hundred sailors passed through them to "board" the fort with cutlass and pistol. At the same time, eighty-five hundred Army troops would land farther up the beach and attack the long breastworks that made up the fort's land face.

The Navy landing party bogged down, but the Army troops got through a mine field and took the fort.

The war ended three months later. Marine casualties were 148 killed, and 312 dead from other causes. During the war, the Corps had tripled to a peak of 4,167 officers and men.

The Empire Years

The Marine Corps' part in the Civil War had been small and not altogether impressive. In the years immediately after the war, the Corps examined itself and its mission. There were those in both the Army and the Navy that did not regard Marines as useful. If the Corps was to survive, it would have to prove its worth.

The United States, having conquered much of North America, was expanding overseas. Marines made small-scale landings in response to real or perceived affronts to U.S. diplomatic or economic interests. Before the end of the century, landings "to protect American lives and property" were made, some of them repeated three or more times, in China, Formosa, Japan, Korea, Samoa, Hawaii, Panama, Nicaragua, Uruguay, Mexico, Argentina, Chile, Colombia, Haiti, and Egypt. Of these, the most significant were the 1871 landing in Korea, where a brigade of bluejackets followed a battalion of Marines in assaulting and capturing the Han River forts guarding the approaches to Seoul, and the 1885 landing in Panama, which grew to brigade size to protect, once again, the trans-isthmus railroad.

Earlier the Corps' motto had been "Fortitudine" ("with courage"). About 1883 it became "Semper Fidelis" ("always faithful"). The Marines would come to take their new motto very seriously.

America's outward thrust climaxed in war with Spain in support of Cuban independence. Ten days after war was declared on 22 April 1898, a Marine battalion formed at the Brooklyn Navy Yard and was on its way to Key West in the ex-banana boat USS *Panther*. On 10 June the battalion landed inside Guantanamo Bay forty miles from Santiago, Cuba, and did some modest fighting to secure a coaling station for the Navy.

The "splendid little war" with Spain ended on 12 August with the occupation of Manila by American troops; the next day, the Philippine Insurrection began. A battalion of Marines went out to the Philippines in May 1899 and another followed in September. On 8 October a two-battalion Marine regiment attacked the fortified town of Novaleta and drove out the insurgents. A third battalion arrived in December, and the pacification of the Philippines continued.

The Marines' next scene of trouble was on the mainland of Asia. In China, the "Righteous Fists of Harmony"—or "Boxers" as Westerners called them—objected with force to the arrogant presence of the "foreign devils." The legations in Peking cabled their respective governments for protection. Captain John Twiggs "Handsome Jack" Myers landed at Taku on 24 May 1900 from the USS *Oregon* with twenty-eight Marines and five sailors. Captain Newt H. Hall joined him five days later with twenty-six more Marines from the USS *Newark*. They commandeered a tug boat that carried them forty miles upstream to Tientsin where they joined a milling mass of French, Russian, German, Austrian, Italian, and Japanese

soldiers, sailors, and marines—all eager to get to Peking and aid the legations. They loaded into two trains on 31 May and reached the imperial capital of China that night.

By mid-June, a 2,500-man Anglo-American relief column was formed in Tientsin to relieve the Legation Quarter in Peking, by now quite cut-off. The Boxers stopped the column twenty-five miles from Peking. Larger international forces converged on China. On 19 June a Marine battalion, under pugnacious Major Littleton W. T. "Tony" Waller and with nineteen-year-old Lieutenant Smedley Darlington Butler, from a politically prominent Pennsylvania Quaker family, as one of his company commanders, arrived at Taku and set off for Tientsin along with a battalion of Russian infantry.

Meanwhile, the Legation Quarter in Peking was still under siege. The allies riposted with an attack against a Boxer lodgment on the city's Tartar Wall. A Chinese spear tore open Capt Myers's leg; Capt Hall moved up to command of the U.S. Marines. One of them, Private Daniel Daly, would receive the Medal of Honor for his steadfast action on the wall.

When a second battalion joined Waller at Tientsin, the two battalions formed the 1st Marine Regiment. The international force, now numbering six thousand, attacked Tientsin's native quarter on 13 July. Smedley Butler took a bullet in the thigh. Next day the Japanese blew up the south gate and the native city was taken—and subjected to much burning and looting.

By the beginning of August the international force at Tientsin had grown to 18,600, of whom some 3,000 were Americans under overall command of Major General Adna R. Chaffee, USA. Another battalion of Marines arrived under Major William P. Biddle; being senior to Waller, he assumed command of the regiment.

The international column marched on Peking. On 14 August the Russians precipitated the assault. Waller's 1st Battalion, with the help of a battery of the U.S. 5th Artillery, breached the Chien Men Gate. Butler received a second wound; this one in the chest. The Legation Quarter was reached by late afternoon. Its defenders had numbered fewer than

The color guard of the Marine garrison at Guantanamo presents the colors during a visit by inspecting officer Maj Albert S. McLemore in early 1914. (Photo: USMC)

five hundred. Of these, 65 had been killed and 135 wounded; 17 of the 56 U.S. Marines and sailors were casualties.

The 1st Marine Regiment returned to the Philippines and in October 1901 Tony Waller was sent with his battalion to the island of Samar to avenge the massacre of a company of the U.S. Army's 9th Infantry. Waller moved against some three thousand Moros, "burning and killing" in accordance with orders he had received from Army Brigadier General Jacob M. "Hell-Roaring Jake" Smith. In mid-November, Waller successfully assaulted the Moros' stronghold above the Sojoton River.

His Army boss now ordered him to lay out a telegraph route on the east coast of Samar. Waller started off with a company-sized party a few days after Christmas, got lost in the jungle, and emerged at Basey on 6 January. Some Marines had been left behind. In all, ten Marines were lost. Waller, sick with fever and convinced that the debacle had been caused by the treachery of his Filipino guides, held a drumhead court-martial and had eleven of them shot. An Army court-martial tried Waller on charges of murder, but he squeaked out an acquittal on a technicality.

Marine landings in Samoa and the Hawaiian Islands in the last decade of the nineteenth century helped the United States solidify its claims to these insular possessions. In 1905 Marines took over the Legation Guard in Peking from their old comrades, the 9th Infantry, beginning the long run of "China duty" that would not end until 1941. And that same year Marines were assigned to guard the embassy in St. Petersburg.

But the main events were taking place in the Caribbean. A French company had tried to dig a canal across the Isthmus of Panama and failed. The U.S. bought up the French rights. When the Colombian government proved uncooperative, President Theodore Roosevelt switched his support to a group of revolutionaries bent on breaking off Panama from Colombia. A landing party from the gunboat *Nashville* went ashore on 3 November 1903 at Colon on the Atlantic side. A Marine battalion under Major John A. Lejeune landed two days later. Other battalions arrived in quick succession until a provisional brigade of two regiments was in place. When most of the brigade went home in February, one battalion stayed on. That May digging the canal began.

Bottom left: In about 1902, Marines, in blue flannel shirts, khaki trousers, and field hats, skylark for the cameraman in camp near Olongapo, Luzon. Their weapon, in addition to the toy machine gun, is the Krag-Jorgenson rifle, and the slogan of the times, referring to the Filipino guerrillas, was "Civilize 'em with a Krag." (Photo: USMC)

Bottom right: A Marine sentry stands silhouetted against the sky in Peking in 1915. The Marines assumed the Legation Guard from the Army in 1905 and would stay until December 1941 when they were taken prisoner by the Japanese. (Photo: USMC)

The "Platt Amendment" to the new Cuban constitution gave the United States the right to intervene in Cuban affairs and was invoked eight times between 1906 and 1917. Although little fighting took place, Marine units up to brigade strength were involved. The Marines did a great deal of guard duty and patrolling, riding trains and protecting U.S.-owned sugar plantations.

In Nicaragua an endemic civil war between the Liberals and Conservatives waxed and waned. Marines, reflecting U.S. support of the

Officers of the 2d Regiment muster at Bas Ospispo in Panama in January 1904 to have their picture taken. Seated in center of the first row with a white scarf around his neck is the commanding officer, the redoubtable Col Littleton W. T. "Tony" Waller. The tall figure behind Waller is Capt Charles H. Lyman. Standing in the rear row, fourth from the left, is Capt Robert H. Dunlap. Next to the last man on the right is Capt Smedley D. Butler, and the last man in the rear row is Capt Logan Feland. All were future major generals with large roles to play in the Caribbean and World War I. (Photo: USMC)

Marines and sailors from the gunboat Nashville *landed at Colon, Panama, in November 1903 to protect American interests. The intervention grew in size to a Marine brigade and gained Panamanian agreement to United States' aspirations to build the Panama Canal. (Photo: USN)*

47

A Marine patrol moves to an outpost at Veracruz. A few years later German machine gunners would teach them not to move at shoulder arms or at such close interval. (Photo: USMC)

SgtMaj John Quick aids another Marine and a sailor in raising the flag over Veracruz, Mexico, on 21 April 1914. The Mexicans, in the grip of a revolution, offered little resistance. (Photo: USMC)

Conservatives, landed again and again, in battalion or regimental strength, sometimes on the west coast at Corinto and sometimes on the east coast at Bluefields. Major Smedley Butler, now commanding a battalion in Panama, was a perennial visitor. By early 1913, and after some fairly serious fighting, most of the Marines had gone home, leaving just a legation guard at Managua. To give more finesse to these kinds of expeditions, a Marine Advance Base Force—a brigade of two small regiments—was formed at Philadelphia at the end of 1913.

Mexico was in the throes of a violent revolution, and U.S. President Woodrow Wilson decided on a landing at Veracruz to preempt the unloading of arms from a German merchant ship. The 2d Marine Regiment under Lieutenant Colonel Wendell C. "Buck" Neville, led off on the morning of 21 April 1914 and found a fire fight in the railroad yards. They were followed ashore by a provisional 3d Marine Regiment made up of fleet Marines and several battalions of sailors in coffee-dyed whites. By evening, Maj Butler and his Panama battalion had arrived. For a day or so there was brisk house-to-house fighting. Lejeune, now a colonel, brought in the rest of the Marine brigade, most notably the 1st Marine Regiment, and by 24 April Veracruz was pacified. An Army brigade arrived a few days later and took over.

An ebullient Teddy Roosevelt had warned the European imperial powers to stay out of Latin America and, in return, promised to indemnify legitimate debts stemming from loans and bond offerings (a provision that also pleased certain U.S. bankers). Both Haiti and the Dominican Republic went into a kind of financial receivership, and the United States took over their customhouses since import duties were considered the most reliable form of government revenue. Haiti demurred and in December 1914 the Marine detachment from the gunboat *Machias* went ashore and seized the last half-million dollars in the Haitian treasury.

At the end of July 1915, after a Port-au-Prince mob pulled apart the Haitian president pro tem Vilbrun Guillaume Sam and ate his heart, the disapproving United States began a serious intervention. It quickly built to Marine brigade strength under Col Tony Waller. The ever-present Maj Butler, as his agent extraordinary, chased down the "Cacos," as the rebels—half patriots, half bandits—were called. Butler captured one

mountain stronghold after another. While on patrol with Butler, Dan Daly, now a gunnery sergeant, earned his second Medal of Honor. He pulled the patrol's only machine gun out of the bottom of a mountain stream while under fire. Butler, who had received a Medal of Honor for Veracruz, also received a second one.

The Marines formed a Gendarmerie d'Haiti, and Butler at its head was given the local rank of major general. The Haitian gendarmes, officered by Marine Corps officers and NCOs, soon showed an astonishing proficiency at drill and in marksmanship with their cast-off Krag rifles. The young assistant secretary of the Navy, Franklin D. Roosevelt, visited Haiti early in 1917 and, much impressed, rode horseback the north-south length of the country with the Marines.

Top left: *Marine 3-inch field pieces were useful in the Dominican Republic in sizeable fights such as Las Trencheras on 27 June 1916, but mounted or foot patrols handled most action in the eight-year intervention (1916–1924). (Photo: USMC)*

Top right: *Patrolling in tropical Dominican Republic bore a marked resemblance to such patrols in the Philippines, Haiti, Nicaragua, and as recently as Viet Nam. (Photo: USMC)*

Bottom right: *To augment and eventually replace the 2d Marine Brigade, the Marines formed a Policia Nacional Dominicana—as they had also formed a Gendarmerie d'Haiti—of native troops officered by U.S. Marines. (Photo: National Archives)*

In the other two-thirds of the island of Hispaniola that was the Dominican Republic, a civil war caused Marines to be landed in May 1916 at Santo Domingo, the capital, on the south coast. In further landings on the north shore, the 4th Marine Regiment under Colonel Joseph "Uncle Joe" Pendleton arrived at Monte Cristi in mid-June. Marine units scattered about the republic were combined under his command into a 2d Marine Brigade (the 1st Brigade was in Haiti).

Pendleton and the 4th Marines started across rough country toward Santiago de los Cabelleros, some sixty-five miles away. They fought a battle at Las Trencheras where the Dominicans had beaten the Spanish in 1864. Joining up with a battalion under Major H. I. "Hiking Hiram" Bearss, which had landed at Puerto Plata, they marched together into Santiago. A Navy captain was made military governor and the 2d Marine Brigade settled in for what became an eight-year stay. The Marines organized a Guardia Nacional Dominicana, modeled on the Haitian Gendarmerie, early in 1917. One of the best of its native officers was a sugar plantation police-man named Rafael Leonidas Trujillo, who in due time would become the long-lasting dictator of the Dominican Republic.

Over There

The United States declared war against Germany on 6 April 1917. Spurred by the slogan "First to Fight," volunteers flocked to Marine Corps recruiting stations. By 14 June three oversized battalions of Marines, designated the 5th Regiment of Marines and commanded by Colonel Charles A. Doyen, were ready to join the first American troop convoy to sail for France. General John J. Pershing, commanding the American Expeditionary Forces, parceled them out for guard duty in French ports and as military police.

A second regiment, the 6th Regiment of Marines, and the 6th Machine Gun Battalion were formed at the new training camp at Quantico, Virginia, and sailed during the fall of 1917. At the beginning of 1918, the 6th Marines joined the 5th Marines, pried loose from line-of-communications duty, as the 4th Brigade of Marines, commanded by Doyen, now a brigadier general. The Marine brigade was one of two infantry brigades in the new U.S. 2d Division, the other being the 3d Brigade of Infantry.

In mid-March 1918, the 2d Division was fed into the salient near Verdun, now a quiet bit of the front. Quiet sector or not, the Marines learned the ugly realities of the Western Front: mud, shelling, barbed wire, rats, corpses in various states of disintegration, an almost invisible enemy, trench raids, gas attacks (the Marines' 74th Company in a reserve position was virtually wiped out), body lice called "cooties," and overhead an aerial ballet danced by French and German aircraft and balloons. The Marines came out of the line early in May feeling quite pleased with themselves. Pershing was weeding out his generals and he sent Charles Doyen home. He turned over the Marine brigade to Army

Top left: Marine recruits arrived in enthusiastic droves at Paris (later changed to "Parris") Island, South Carolina, after the United States declared war in April 1917. In "boot camp" they learned the rudiments of soldiering and a good deal about discipline before moving on to Quantico, Virginia, and then to France. (Photo: USMC)

Top right: The 5th Regiment of Marines was in the first convoy to sail for France in June 1917 and was followed by the 6th Regiment of Marines in the fall and winter of that year. Together with the 6th Machine Gun Battalion, they made up the 4th Brigade of Marines. More Marines would follow at the rate of one or two battalions a month until the war's end in November 1918. (Photo: USMC)

Below: Marines got their first taste of action in a quiet sector near Verdun from March through May 1918. They were paired off with French units until considered capable of holding a position on their own. (Photo: USMC)

Marines, rifles slung and wearing "tin hats," relax en route on the march at the beginning of June 1918 that would take them to Belleau Wood. A French poilu (right) appraises them thoughtfully. (Photo: USMC)

Brigadier General James G. Harbord, who had been the American Expeditionary Forces' chief of staff.

In late May the tired French divisions gave way to a massive German offensive. The Germans reached the Marne at Chateau-Thierry, and the road leading to Paris seemed open. On 1 June the 2d Division formed a line across the road, the Marine brigade in the center, and the Army brigade's regiments—the 9th (old friends from China) and the 23d Infantry—on the flanks.

The Germans attacked the next day and learned a lesson in rifle fire that began to kill at eight hundred yards. For three more days the Germans attacked. Then on 6 June the 2d Division counterattacked. In

Magazine illustrators, such as Frank Schoonover, used their imaginations in painting what the fighting was like in Belleau Wood. The Marines won, but not this easily. (Marine Corps Art Collection)

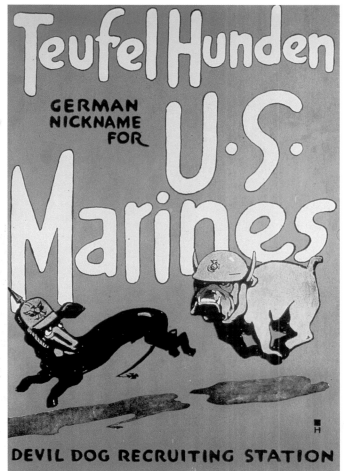

Left: *S. J. Woolf did this thoughtful portrait of an unidentified Marine in France in late summer 1918. The Marine is quietly confident, but war is no longer a game. (Marine Corps Art Collection)*

Right: *After Belleau Wood, the Marines told each other that the Germans were calling them "Teufel Hunden" or "Devil Dogs," which would come to rival "Leathernecks" as a favorite nickname. (Marine Corps Art Collection)*

front of the Marines stretched a hunting preserve, Belleau Wood, roughly peanut-shaped, about a square mile altogether, filled with underbrush and tumbled boulders. In the first attacks Marines in well-dressed lines crossed open wheatfields. Nineteenth-century tactics and raw courage barely carried the attack forward. Machine guns in the competent hands of veteran German gunners exacted a terrible cost. Once into the woods, the fragments of the Marine lines instinctively reformed into small combat groups, a hard lesson expensively learned. In the first day alone more than a thousand Marines were killed or wounded, more than had been lost in all the Corps' previous battles. But after a week's fighting, the Marines held most of the wood. The Marine brigade, having taken more than 50 percent casualties, pulled out on 16 June for a week's rest, and then went back and finished the job.

Harbord, promoted to major general, moved up to command of the 2d Division on Bastille Day, 14 July. And "Buck" Neville, who had been commanding the 5th Marines, took over the Marine brigade. The Germans tried one more offensive on 15 July, and the French riposted with an already planned counterattack. On the morning of 18 July, the 2d Division, loaned to the French, went in southeast of Soissons, and by nightfall the 5th Marines had taken the village of Vierzy. The following morning the 6th Marines continued the attack, crossing an open field behind a thin line of French tanks. The two days' fighting cost the Marines two thousand dead and wounded, but they had punctured the enemy line. The Germans would never attack again.

Harbord was detached to direct the AEF's troubled Service of Supply, and the Marine Corps' own John A. Lejeune, now a major general, took command of the 2d Division. For nearly two months the division rebuilt

from the losses at Soissons. Then on 12 September it went back into the attack at St. Mihiel as part of the newly formed U.S. First Army. By nightfall on the 15th, the Marine brigade held its objectives.

The 5th Marine Brigade arrived in France in September and was held at Brest for port duties. Smedley Butler, promoted to brigadier general, commanded the brigade, but there would be no fighting in this war for the "Fighting Quaker."

After St. Mihiel the 2d Division moved over to the French Fourth Army for the Meuse Argonne offensive. The French wanted to parcel out the big, strong American regiments to their infantry-short divisions. Lejeune argued to keep his division together and promised to take Blanc Mont, the "White Mountain," key to cracking the German line. The 6th Marines led off on 3 October followed by the 5th Marines. In three days of perhaps the brigade's heaviest fighting in the war they seized Blanc Mont.

The 2d Division then moved back to join the American First Army's V Corps for the final drive of the war. On 1 November the division attacked on a narrow two-kilometer front and in hard fighting pierced what the Allies called the "Hindenburg Line." The Marines' war ended with a costly flourish, a night crossing of the Meuse on 10 November, just hours before the Armistice. After that came the long march on foot into Germany and occupation duty in the American sector around the Rhine bridgehead at Koblenz. The 4th Marine Brigade finally came home in the summer of 1919 and marched proudly past the White House before disbanding at Quantico.

The Corps' strength had risen from 15,000 to almost 76,000 during the war. Of the approximately 32,000 Marines who served in France, 11,351 became casualties and 2,457 of these were dead or forever missing in action. In the years that followed the war the Corps shrank back to about 20,000 and then to 15,000.

Above: *The objective of this poster by Howard Chandler Christy was to attract male, not female, recruits. (Marine Corps Art Collection)*

Facing page: *Two good-looking women Marines are decked out for picture-taking with Sam Browne belts, worn by officers in France but never by women. In August 1918, three months before the end of the war, "Reservists (Female)" were authorized and by the war's end just over three hundred had signed up for clerical duties, mostly in Washington. (Photo: USMC)*

Below: *After serving in the Army of Occupation in Germany, the 4th Brigade of Marines on 12 August 1919 passes by the White House and President Woodrow Wilson in a last review before proceeding to Quantico and demobilization. (Photo: USMC)*

"Travel? Adventure? Answer: Join the Marines" promises this recruiting poster of the 1920s. Adventures in the Caribbean did not stop for World War I. The Corps had almost as many men deployed in Haiti, the Dominican Republic, Nicaragua, on the Mexican border, and in China as went to France. (Marine Corps Art Collection)

The 2d Marine Brigade had a hundred fire fights in the Dominican Republic in 1918, two hundred in 1919. Not until 1924 were the Marines withdrawn. (Photo: USMC)

Banana Wars

More than half of the Marine Corps did not go to France. The battleships and cruisers of the fleet continued to land their Marine detachments in such unlikely places as Vladivostok. The Legation Guard was maintained in Peking. The 1st Brigade was still in Haiti and the 2d Brigade in the Dominican Republic. A 3d Brigade went to Cuba and then moved to the Texas border where there were fears of a German-fomented incursion from Mexico. A 6th Brigade filled in behind in Cuba. At Philadelphia, the headquarters of the Marine Advance Base Force, under the command of now grizzled MajGen Tony Waller, continued to plan and train for the defense of advanced naval bases with such esoterica as searchlights and underwater minefields.

In Haiti in 1919, Herman H. Hanneken, captain in the Gendarmerie, sergeant in the Marine Corps, blackened his face so as to pass as a Haitian and with two companions worked his way into the camp of a new Caco leader, Charlemagne Massena Peralte, and shot him. In those uncomplicated days this won Sgt Hanneken a Medal of Honor. He went on to command a battalion and regiment in World War II and retired as a brigadier general.

Another Caco leader, Benoit Batraville, who had the nasty habit of roasting and eating the hearts and livers of dead Marines, took over from Charlemagne. The Gendarmerie and the 1st Brigade, under Colonel John H. Russell, hunted him down. In May 1920 a Marine patrol found Batraville and killed him. Russell, promoted to brigadier general, became Haiti's high commissioner.

Across the border in Santo Domingo, Brigadier General Ben Fuller relieved "Uncle Joe" Pendleton as commander of the 2d Brigade in October 1918. The brigade fought Dominican "bandits" in a hundred fire fights that year and two hundred more in 1919. Marine Brigadier General Harry Lee became military governor in 1923. And by October 1924 a constitutional government was installed, the Policia Nacional Dominicana

took over policing the countryside, and all the Marines departed.

The Legation Guard left Nicaragua in 1925, but unrest in the country brought the Marines back the next year. The 2d Marine Brigade, reactivated under Brigadier General Logan Feland, created a Guardia Nacional on the Haitian and Dominican model and stayed on to supervise free elections.

Augusto Cesar Sandino, the most fiery of the Nicaraguan leaders, did not agree with these arrangements. He took his men up into the mountains next to the Honduran border. For the next six years the Marines and the Guardia fought him, sometimes in good-sized battles. But mostly they were patrol actions in which junior officers who would play big roles in World War II made their reputations. One was a hatchet-faced captain, Evans Carlson, who would develop his own ideas on guerrilla warfare. Another was Captain Merritt A. "Red Mike" Edson, who led sensational patrols in native boats up the wild Coco River along Nicaragua's border with Honduras. Best known of all was Lewis B. "Chesty" Puller, who as a captain in the Guardia applied lessons learned in Haiti. All three received Navy Crosses.

Nicaragua proved to be a tougher nut to crack than either Haiti or the Dominican Republic. but the formula was the same: collecting weapons, extensive patrolling, and forming a Guardia Nacional (whose director general, Anastasio "Tacho" Somoza, following his friend Trujillo's example, made himself president and dictator after the Marines' departure in 1933). (Photo: USMC)

After one of the stiffest actions in Nicaragua, the defenders of Ocotal form up in ranks for a victory picture. Thirty-eight Marines and 48 Guardias, with the help of close-in bombing by Marine DH-4 DeHavillands, held off a siege by Augusto Sandino in July 1927. (Photo: USMC)

Top left: *Pvt Gerald C. Merchant, Jr., in his tailor-made khaki uniform, stands by his carefully groomed pony in Peking in 1935; both are members of the legendary "Horse Marines" of the Legation Guard. (Photo: USMC)*

Top right: *The 4th Marines join with a battalion of the Scots Guards (on the left) in a ceremony in Shanghai about 1929. Marine regimental commander Col Charles H. Lyman stands at the flag pole. British pomp and circumstance left its mark on U.S. Marine Corps parades and ceremonies and on customs such as mess nights. (Photo: USMC)*

Above: *The color guard of the 4th Marines passes in review in a parade at the Shanghai Race Course in 1933. In the first half of the 20th century, "China duty" had a lasting effect on two generations of Marine officers and NCOs—and on the Corps. (Photo: USMC)*

China was the scene of a more enjoyable intervention. The Legation Guard was ensconced in Peking and living was easy. Civil war was endemic and at first more a titillation than a bother. But things grew serious in 1927. A Marine battalion from Guam landed at Shanghai in February to help protect the International Settlement, followed two weeks later by the 4th Marines from San Diego. The reactivated 6th Marines arrived in May. The two regiments formed the 3d Brigade under command of the old war horse, Smedley Butler. Butler left the 4th Marines in Shanghai—where it would stay until the eve of the American entry into World War II—and took the rest of his brigade north to Tientsin. There was a good deal of parading but no real fighting, and the brigade returned to the States in January 1929. Eight years later, in September 1937, with China's war with Japan heating up, the 6th Marines came back briefly to Shanghai.

President Franklin D. Roosevelt brought the Marines out of Nicaragua at the beginning of 1933 and out of Haiti in August 1934. They had not caught Sandino. A year after they left, Sandino was killed by the director of the Guardia Nacional and future president, Colonel Anastasio "Tacho" Somoza.

The 1st Marine Brigade was home-based at Quantico and the 2d Brigade at San Diego. The East Coast and West Coast Expeditionary Forces were redesignated as the Fleet Marine Forces of their respective Atlantic and Pacific Fleets. The Marines were studying a possible war with Japan. By 1934, at Quantico, the lessons being learned in amphibious warfare were put down on paper as the crucially important *The Tentative Manual for Landing Operations*.

When war began in Europe in September 1939, America, gradually and reluctantly, rearmed. Marine Corps enlisted strength increased to twenty-five thousand, and in the fall of 1940 the call-up of the Organized Reserve added another five thousand. The 1st Marine Brigade left Quantico that fall for training in the Caribbean with the Atlantic Fleet. On 1 February 1941, while at sea, the brigade became the 1st Marine Division under Major General Holland M. (not yet "Howlin' Mad") Smith. On the West

Coast the 2d Brigade metamorphosed into the 2d Marine Division. Defense battalions were formed and dispatched to Oahu and Samoa and eventually Midway, Johnston, Palmyra, and Wake.

A great swampy tract of land was taken over at New River, North Carolina, and in due course became Camp Lejeune. The huge Rancho Santa Margarita north of San Diego, with twenty miles of Pacific beach, was converted into Camp Pendleton.

World War II and the Pacific War

Among those caught off-guard that slumbering Sunday morning, 7 December 1941, were the Marine air and ground forces on Oahu. The Japanese attack knocked out all of Marine Aircraft Group 21's planes on the ground. The 3d and 4th Defense Battalions, unable to get their ancient 3-inch anti-aircraft guns into action, angrily but ineffectually pecked away at the low-flying Japanese aircraft with pistols, rifles, and an occasional machine gun.

The Fleet Marine Force, still no more than a half-fleshed-out, half-trained skeleton, was stretched thin by worldwide deployments. A 1st Provisional Marine Brigade, which had been pulled from the 2d Division and sent to Iceland in July, was on its way home to California. In North China, contemptuous Japanese soldiers marched the Peking Legation Guard off to prison. The spit-and-polish 4th Marines, in garrison at Shanghai, had embarked just days earlier for the Philippines and escaped temporarily. Guam, with its company-size Marine garrison, fell after a day or so of desperate fighting. On other mid-Pacific islands the outpost line of defense battalions waited for the onslaught. Most of the 1st Defense Battalion and Marine Fighting Squadron 211 had just arrived at Wake Island. Major James P. S. Devereux was credited with saying, "Send us more Japs." He didn't, but his little force held out

Prime Minister Winston Churchill takes the review of the provisional 1st Marine Brigade, which in the summer of 1941 freed British troops garrisoning Iceland to fight elsewhere. Churchill later wrote that The Marines' Hymn *"bit so deeply into my memory that I could not get it out of my head." (Photo: USMC)*

Young Americans, eager to be the "first to fight," filled Marine Corps recruiting offices throughout the country the day after Pearl Harbor, 7 December 1941. (Photo: Library of Congress)

against Japanese air and naval assault until 23 December when the Japanese rammed two destroyer-transports onto the beach and put ashore a Special Naval Landing Force, their version of marines.

A 2d Marine Brigade, pulled out of the 2d Marine Division, sailed for American Samoa the first week in January 1942; a 3d Brigade, taken from the 1st Marine Division, went to British Western Samoa in March. The 4th Marines was given the beach defenses on Corregidor, the besieged "Rock" in Manila Bay, and met the final Japanese assault there on the night of 5 May 1942. Next day the regiment and its surviving Marines were surrendered. Some slipped away to join the Philippine guerrillas. At dawn on 4 June the 6th Defense Battalion on Midway received the first preliminary blows from what would become the pivotal Battle of Midway. Two Marine squadrons—VMF-221 and VMSB-241—sacrificed their mostly obsolescent aircraft and gained a bit more time for the Navy to reassemble its carrier strength.

In June the 1st Marine Division, under Major General Alexander A. Vandegrift, arrived in New Zealand expecting to have months to train. Instead, the division staff was sent scrambling for maps of the Solomon Islands. The Japanese had seized Tulagi, the Solomons' colonial capital, and its good harbor. Across Sealark Channel on the much larger island of Guadalcanal they had begun building an airstrip from which medium bombers would be able to reach Australia.

With a herculean effort, the Marines landed early in the morning of 7 August 1942—exactly eight months after Pearl Harbor. On the smaller islands there was serious fighting. The 1st Raider Battalion, under Colonel Merritt "Red Mike" Edson of Coco River patrol reputation, led the way at Tulagi. The 1st Parachute Battalion came in, by surface craft not parachute, onto the fly-speck islets Gavutu and Tanambogo. Elements of the 2d Marines came ashore on neighboring Florida Island. The 5th Marines, followed by the 1st Marines, made the main effort, landing on Guadalcanal itself almost without a shot being fired.

By early afternoon Japanese bombers came down from the north and pounded the Marines unloading supplies across Guadalcanal's beaches. After two days of aerial attack, the Navy withdrew its thin-skinned transports and supply ships and would fight a series of savage surface actions, mostly cruisers and destroyers against better Japanese cruisers and destroyers. The Marines were left alone and on short rations.

Marine engineers and Navy Seabees quickly finished the airstrip,

Captured rice and dried fish supplemented the Marines' meager rations during the first weeks ashore at Guadalcanal. They landed on 7 August 1942 and battled for possession of the island until 8 February 1943. (Photo: USMC)

Leaders of a patrol get last-minute instructions at the command post of the 5th Marines on Guadalcanal. Painting is by then-Capt Donald L. Dickson, a Marine Corps reservist, already a well-known artist and cartoonist in civilian life. ("Final Instructions, Guadalcanal," Marine Corps Art Collection)

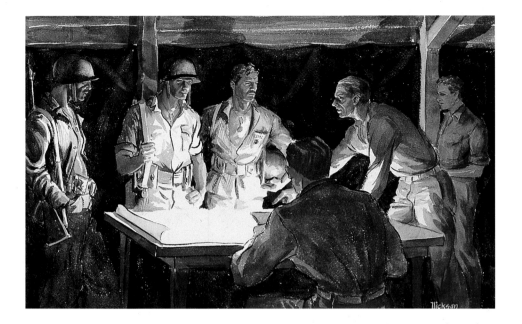

and the first Marine squadrons came winging in on 20 August. The Japanese Seventeenth Army was converging on the island and attacked in increments of ever-increasing size: the Ichiki Detachment, the Kawaguchi Brigade, the 2d (Sendai) Division, and the 38th Division. The Marines, riddled with malaria, grimly held on.

The worst night at Guadalcanal must have been 12–13 September when Kawaguchi's brigade nearly broke through Edson's thin line of raiders and parachutists holding a grassy knoll overlooking Henderson Field. Five days later the 7th Marines came in from Samoa, its 1st and 2d Battalions commanded respectively by Lewis "Chesty" Puller and Herman "Haiti" Hanneken. The American buildup continued, and on 13 October the Army's 164th Infantry arrived. That night the battleships *Kongo* and *Haruna* pulverized the airfield with their 14-inch guns.

Additional Army and Marine regiments reached Guadalcanal in November. Repeated actions were fought along the Matanikau River. On 9 December, after four months of battle and with the Americal Division now in place, command of the island passed to the Army. The Marine regiments' losses were more than a thousand dead and something under three thousand wounded, about the same as the Marines had had at

Left: *Men of the 2d Marine Division pause after overrunning a Japanese communication center on Guadalcanal in the last days of the campaign. (Photo: Sgt J. F. Fitzgerald, USMC)*

Right: *A Marine ashore at Tarawa pauses in the blistering heat for a sip of water from his canteen. He wears canvas leggings and his rifle sports the long bayonet of World War I. (Photo: USMC)*

Belleau Wood. And this time, at least ten thousand had malaria.

First step up the Solomons was New Georgia in June 1943, a complicated and predominantly Army operation involving seven landings. The Marines had part in four, mostly by raider and defense battalions. By mid-August New Georgia could be said to be secure.

The new 3d Marine Division and the Army's 37th Division landed in the lee of Cape Torokina on Bougainville on 1 November. The fighting was hard but the issue was never in doubt. On 15 December the Army's XXIV Corps took over from the I Marine Amphibious Corps, and the Marines' large-scale ground fighting in the Solomons was over.

On the day after Christmas 1943, the 1st Marine Division, having rebuilt for nearly a year in Australia and now under the theater command of General Douglas MacArthur, landed at Cape Gloucester at the northwest corner of the long, skinny island of New Britain. In that "green hell" the fighting was hard and in many ways shapeless, but the division kept moving eastward until relieved by the Army at the end of April 1944. Then, instead of returning to fondly remembered Australia, the 1st Division was sent to a miserable "rest camp" at Pavuvu in the mid-Solomons.

The long-envisioned drive across the Central Pacific began with the landing of the 2d Marine Division at Tarawa Atoll in the Gilbert Islands on 20 November 1943. Optimism that a high tide would carry landing craft over the reef proved misplaced. Most of the reef-crossing had to be done in new untested amphibian tractors or simply by wading. Losses were horrendous. In seventy-six hours, which was the official length of the battle, a thousand Marines died and another two thousand were wounded. Of the more than five thousand Japanese, only a handful still lived.

The next island group was the Marshalls. The new 4th Marine Division made a series of preliminary landings on 31 January 1944 and

Finding the guts to move over the coconut-log seawall that edged the narrow beach at Tarawa in the face of deadly Japanese fire is exactly what their tough, disciplined Marine Corps training was all about. (Photo: USMC)

Fighting on Tarawa, a 76-hour battle beginning on 20 November 1943, was of unprecedented savagery for the Marines. Photographs of American dead stunned the U.S. public. (Photo: USMC)

The 1st Marine Division wades ashore at Cape Gloucester on New Britain the day after Christmas 1943, beginning a campaign in a "green hell" that lasted until April 1944. (Photo: Sgt Howard, USMC)

followed a day later with its main landings on the twin islands of Roi and Namur. In mid-February a brigade-size force—half-Marine, half-Army—landed on Eniwetok atoll on the northwest edge of the Marshalls nearest Japan.

The Marianas, a giant step to the west, offered more land area than the coral atolls of the mid-Pacific, but the violence of the fighting

Left: Weary Marines of the 4th Marine Division, worn down by two days and two nights of violent fighting in February 1944 to take Eniwetok Atoll, drink welcome cups of coffee on a Coast Guard landing ship. (Photo: USCG)

Facing page, bottom: On a ship off Saipan, a Navy chaplain reads the funeral service as Marines in the burial party get ready to consign their dead comrades to the deep. Traditionally, a large caliber Navy shell weighs the canvas shroud. (Photo: USMC)

was much the same. First came Saipan; the 2d and 4th Marine Divisions assaulted on 15 June, with the Army's 27th Division following in reserve. Some thirty thousand Japanese defenders were waiting for them. The landing was tough; the swinging drive to the north was tougher. The 27th Division was fed into the center of the line and it sagged behind the charging Marines. Lieutenant General Holland M. Smith (and now he was being called "Howlin' Mad"), commander of V Amphibious Corps,

Top left: *Men of the 3d Marine Division get their first hot meal on Guam three days after hitting the beach on 21 July 1944. Freeing Guam, American territory lost to the Japanese in December 1941, was of particular satisfaction to the Marines. (Photo: Sgt Simpson, USMC)*

Top right: *Combat artist Sgt John McDermott caught the mood of both the liberating Marines and the liberated Guamanian children, the little boy clutching a hand-made American flag in one hand and his sister's hand in the other. The Japanese imposed frightful conditions on the Chamorros, the native people of Guam. They still celebrate "Liberation Day," 21 July, each year as the most notable secular holiday on their calendar. (Marine Corps Art Collection)*

relieved Major General Ralph C. Smith, commander of the lagging 27th Division, and caused an Army-Marine Corps controversy that would have repercussions for years to come. The last of the Japanese defenders went over the cliffs at Saipan's northern tip, urging into similar suicide a good part of the frantic civilian population.

Guam followed Saipan and was played to the same scenario. The III Amphibious Corps under Marine Major General Roy S. Geiger—3d Marine Division and 1st Provisional Marine Brigade in assault, followed by the Army's 77th Division in reserve—landed on two widely separated beaches on 21 July, converged, and swung to the north. Most of the close to twenty thousand Japanese defenders died. Some—not many—surrendered, and some slipped away into the jungle where a few would survive for years and even decades.

SSgt Federico Claveria, his carbine slung over his shoulder, pauses on Tinian in July 1944 to pass some candy to a Chamorro child held for his own safety in a barbed-wire enclosure. (Photo: PFC Mattson, USMC)

The 2d and 4th Marine Divisions made a textbook landing on Tinian, immediately south of Saipan on 24 July and crushed the nearly seven thousand defenders by 1 August. Tinian's flat plateau, planted in sugar cane, was soon surfaced for B-29 bombers. Air strips were also pounded into the coral of Saipan and Guam. The Japanese home islands were now just within bombing range of the big Superforts.

The capture of Peleliu in the Palaus was supposed to clear the flank of MacArthur's reentry into the Philippines; but by the time the landing came off on 15 September 1944, the American command knew it was unnecessary. The Japanese could not seriously interfere with MacArthur's approach. The Palaus were another assault for the III Amphibious Corps, still commanded by Geiger. The heavily reinforced 1st Marine Division landed against Peleliu itself. It was a terrible, grinding battle, and eventually the Army's 81st Division had to relieve the exhausted Marines.

Halfway from the B-29 bases in the Marianas to the Japanese home islands were the Bonins. One of these, Iwo Jima, demanded immediate attention to prevent the Japanese from using it for interceptors to meet the B-29s. Even more importantly, it was needed as a recovery site for disabled American bombers. Command of V Amphibious Corps was now in the hands of Marine Major General Harry Schmidt; "Howlin' Mad" Smith went along as a kind of overseer. Schmidt used the 4th and the new 5th Marine Division in the assault and held the 3d Division in floating reserve. Seven assault battalions landed on 19 February 1945 over the eastern beaches. Their left flank almost touched the beginning of the slope of Mount Suribachi, the 556-foot-high extinct volcano that

Reserve troops land at Peleliu while shore party Marines float in oil drums across the reef. In retrospect, the bitterly fought assault of Peleliu in the Palau Islands in September and October 1944 was unnecessary: the war had already passed it by. (Photo: Sgt Fitzgerald)

The Iwo Jima landing beaches were starkly exposed to the Japanese on Mount Suribachi. The dead volcano was captured on the fourth day but the fighting went on for a month. (Photo: SSgt Lou Lowery, USMC)

Below: *A Marine scout dog stands as a vigilant sentry while his exhausted handler, covered by a poncho, sleeps in a hole scooped into Iwo Jima's volcanic sand. Marines used war dogs—Dobermans and some German shepherds—as both scout and guard dogs. Scout dogs were trained to remain silent; guard dogs were taught to bark. (Photo: Sgt Kauffman, USMC)*

Right: *Navy doctors and hospital corpsmen work at an Iwo Jima first aid station, nothing more than a crowded spot on the beach. Here they attempt to stabilize the wounded until they can be evacuated to a ship for definitive treatment. (Photo: USMC)*

dominated the island. One of the new regiments, the 28th Marines, reached the summit the morning of 23 February. The flag went up and the world-famous picture was taken.

The main effort, though, was to the north where the island widened. The Japanese had dug and cemented themselves in so incredibly well that scarcely a defender was seen above ground. In what was the Corps' bloodiest battle, the Marines took the three airfields one by one. The island was declared secured on 26 March. More than seventy-one thousand Marines had gone ashore, nearly six thousand Marines died, and more than seventeen thousand were wounded. All but a handful of the twenty-three thousand Japanese defenders were killed.

A Tenth Army, consisting of the Army's XXIV Corps and the Marines'

III Amphibious Corps (still under Geiger), was formed to invade Okinawa. Marines thought that Holland M. Smith should have command. It went instead to Lieutenant General Simon Bolivar Buckner, Jr., a fine soldier, but one with very little combat experience and none at all in amphibious warfare. The Tenth Army landed across the Hagushi beaches on the west side of Okinawa's narrow waist on Sunday, 1 April 1945, which everyone was quick to point out was both Easter and April Fool's Day.

The Army landed on the right—on the left, the new 6th Marine Division (actually an expansion of the brigade used at Guam) and the 1st Marine Division. Hardly a shot was fired. The 2d Marine Division, faking a landing across a southeast beach, took heavier casualties than the assault divisions. The 1st Marine Division charged ahead to the opposite coast. The 6th Division, on the very left flank, curled to the north and did some fairly stiff fighting on Motobu Peninsula above Nago Bay. But it was the Army's XXIV Corps, which had pivoted to the right and was driving south, that ran into the enemy's main defenses.

Top: *Marines found the landing at Okinawa on 1 April 1945 strangely unopposed. They would learn that the Japanese commanding general was saving his troops for a battle-winning counterattack. (Photo: USCG)*

Above: *Army LtGen Simon B. Buckner (left), commanding the Tenth Army, and Marine MajGen Roy S. Geiger, commanding the III Amphibious Corps, walk along a deceptively quiet Okinawa road in April 1945. Two months later, Gen Buckner was killed by a Japanese shell while observing an attack by the 8th Marines, and Gen Geiger became the first Marine to command a field army in combat. (Photo: Sgt Torrie, USMC)*

Marines lunge forward on Tarawa in what became a three-month battle. To defend Okinawa, the Japanese used kamikaze *or suicide tactics on land, sea, and air. (Photo: USMC)*

69

The Japanese had prepared a series of fortified lines crossing the southern, most populated part of the island and now fought a defensive land battle, while kamikaze suicide planes pounded the fleet supporting the Americans ashore. Buckner unimaginatively plunged forward in repeated frontal attacks. As his Army divisions wore down, he plugged into the right flank of his line the under-employed Marines, first the 1st Marine Division and then the 6th Marine Division.

On 18 June, LtGen Buckner came up to a 1st Division observation post to watch the newly landed 8th Marines jump off in the attack, and a

Jubilant soldiers and Marines cheer the victory at Okinawa as the flag is raised on 27 June 1945 over Hill 89. The hill, secured by troops of the 7th Infantry Division on 21 June 1945, housed the subterranean command post of LtGen Mitsuru Ushijima, commander of the Japanese Thirty-second Army. (Photo: USMC)

Japanese shell killed him. MajGen Geiger, as senior officer on the island, took command of the Tenth Army. Three days later he declared Okinawa secured, just before Army Lieutenant General Joseph W. "Vinegar Joe" Stilwell, who had commanded U.S. forces in the China-Burma-India theater, hurriedly arrived to relieve him. Replacements poured in and preparations began for the final invasions—of the Japanese home islands. In August, the atomic bombs and the Japanese surrender made that unnecessary.

This terrible but imperative war cost the Marines 19,733 dead and 67,207 wounded. Strength of the Corps had peaked at 485,053. Of this total, almost twenty thousand were black and about the same number were women.

Until this war the Corps had thought of itself, not completely accurately, as all-white and all-male. During the Revolution a few muster rolls listed an occasional "Negro" but when the Marines were reestablished in 1798 regulations specifically provided that "No Negro, Mulatto, or Indian" be enlisted.

Forced by the Roosevelt administration to take "Negroes," the Marine Corps decided to keep them in segregated units. The first black recruits arrived in August 1942 and were put into a segregated training camp at Montford Point, Camp Lejeune.

One of the few black recruits with previous military experience was thirty-seven-year-old Gilbert H. "Hashmark" Johnson who years before had served six years in the Army's black 25th Infantry. He wangled a discharge from the Navy, where he was serving as an officer's steward, 2d class, to join the Marines as a private. He soon became the field sergeant major in charge of all black drill instructors, personally determined that black recruits would measure up in every way to white recruits.

Below: *Gilbert H. "Hashmark" Johnson became the first black field sergeant major at the segregated training camp at Montford Point, North Carolina. At age thirty-seven, he was one of the few black Marine recruits with previous military experience. Before joining the Corps he had served in the Army's 25th Division and with the Navy as a petty officer in the steward branch. (Photo: USMC)*

Bottom: *Black Marines served under white officers and initially received their recruit training from white non-commissioned officers. Black NCOs gradually replaced white NCOs, but under the regulations of the time, no white Marine was to serve under a black NCO and there were no black officers. (Photo: Sgt Roger Smith, USMC)*

Right: Black Marines during World War II were limited to two defense battalions, numerous ammunition and depot companies, and duty as officers' stewards. Full integration did not come until the Korean War. (Photo: USMC)

Below: Edgar H. Huff, one of the first blacks to enlist in the Corps, followed in the footsteps of "Hashmark" Johnson, rose rapidly through the ranks, and by the time of his retirement in 1972 was a senior sergeant major, much respected by blacks and whites alike. (Photo: USMC)

Frank E. Petersen became the first black Marine Corps pilot in October 1952. He retired in 1978, a lieutenant general in command at Quantico, Virginia. (Photo: SSgt T. L. Burton, USMC)

"Hashmark" was promoted to sergeant major of the Recruit Training Battalion, and his place as field sergeant major was taken by another of the early volunteers, Edgar R. Huff, a physical giant of a man. When Huff retired in 1972 he was the senior sergeant major in the Marine Corps.

Two defense battalions, the 51st and 52d, were eventually formed and sent to the backwaters of the Pacific. Some black Marines were assigned to a commissary branch as stewards. Most, though, were used as service troops. Fifty-one depot companies and twelve ammunition companies were formed. Most went overseas. These companies found employment in shore parties at such places as Saipan, Guam, Tinian, Peleliu, Iwo Jima, and Okinawa, earning the gradual, begrudging respect of white Marines until by war's end "Montford Point Marine" became a badge of honor. Full integration would not come, however, until the Korean War.

In October 1952, Second Lieutenant Frank E. Petersen arrived from flight training as the Marine Corps' first black pilot. He flew over 350 combat missions in two wars, flying F4U Corsairs in Korea and F-4D Phantoms in Viet Nam. Petersen became the first black Marine general in 1979. Other promotions followed. When he retired in 1988 he was a lieutenant general and in command at Quantico. By 1998 nearly 7 percent of the Corps' officers and 17 percent of its enlisted were black, and black Marine generals were no longer a novelty.

The Marine Corps was the last of the services to open its ranks to women in World War II. During the last months of World War I some 305 women had been enlisted for clerical duties and coyly called "Marinettes." A Women's Reserve was authorized in November 1942 but not publicly announced until February 1943. The goal of a thousand women officers and 18,000 women enlisted, all volunteers, was set and nearly met. By the end of the war 820 officers and 17,640 enlisted "WMs" were serving in noncombatant billets, mostly clerical, and not west of Pearl Harbor. Their numbers, said General Vandegrift, by then the commandant, made possible "putting the 6th Marine Division into the field." All but a cadre went home at the war's end. Not until 1948

Left: *A column of Woman Marines marches past a column of combat-ready male Marines at Camp Lejeune, North Carolina. The nearly twenty thousand women who served in the Corps during World War II freed enough men from non-combatant service to form the 6th Marine Division. (Photo: USMC)*

Below: *Margaret A. Brewer became the first woman Marine Corps brigadier general in 1978. As such she was director of public affairs. (Photo: USMC)*

Carol A. Mutter, promoted to lieutenant general in 1996 and assigned as deputy chief of staff for manpower and Reserve affairs, was the first woman of any U.S. service to achieve three-star status. (Photo: USMC)

was the integration of women into the regular Marines authorized.

The first woman Marine general was Margaret A. Brewer, promoted to brigadier general in 1978, but with her duties limited to those of director of public affairs. By 1998 the number of women on active duty hovered at around 5 percent. One of those women was Lieutenant General Carol A. Mutter, then serving as deputy chief of staff for manpower and Reserve Affairs, the first woman in the U.S. armed services to achieve three-star rank.

After the Japanese surrender, the III Amphibious Corps, with the 1st and 6th Divisions, sailed in late September 1945 through a mine-filled Yellow Sea to North China, and the V Corps, with the 2d and 5th Divisions, arrived in Japan for occupation duty. The stay in Japan was brief; the Marines found the Japanese curiously courteous and compliant.

North China was less peaceful. III Amphibious Corps headquarters and the 1st and 11th Marines occupied Tientsin where a garrison of fifty thousand ceremoniously surrendered. The 5th Marines went into Peking (seldom called Peiping and never then called Beijing) and found the Legation Guard barracks still intact. Another fifty thousand Japanese surrendered there. To the north, working out of Peitaiho, the 7th Marines (with Japanese help!) guarded the railroads and coal mines. The 6th Division occupied Tsingtao, the old German city at the tip of Shantung peninsula. The Marines found and released interned Allied civilians and accomplished other good works.

Officially, the Marines were in North China to disarm and repatriate

The Marine detachment on board the battle-ship USS Missouri *stands at parade rest as dignitaries gather for the official Japanese surrender in Tokyo Bay on 2 September 1945. LtGen Roy S. Geiger was the sole senior Marine officer invited to attend. (Photo: 1stLt David D. Duncan, USMCR)*

Bottom left: *The 1st Provisional Marine Brigade, stripped out of the peacetime skeleton of the 1st Marine Division, arrived in Korea in August 1950. Acting as a "fire brigade," it moved from place to place patching up with counterattacks the punctures the North Koreans tore in the Pusan perimeter's defenses. (Photo: David Douglas Duncan)*

Bottom right: *Marines, wounded in the rough country of the Pusan perimeter, had to be carried down to roads by Korean porters or "cargadores" pressed into service. (Photo: David Douglas Duncan)*

the Japanese. But a greater reason was to hold the northern cities against the Chinese Communists (and possibly the Russians in Manchuria) until Chiang Kai-shek's Nationalist army could come north from south and central China. The Marines contended with road ambushes and blown railroad tracks and occasional raids against their supply points. Small Japanese detachments, guarding bridges and such, fought and died. The Communists seemed wary of the Marines, but renewed their war against the Japanese with zeal.

Eventually, all the Japanese were packed up and sent home, and from a top strength of fifty-five thousand, III Amphibious Corps reduced itself battalion by battalion, squadron by squadron, until in June 1949 the last Marine battalion departed Tsingtao. The Chinese Communists meanwhile went briskly about the business of defeating the Nationalists.

Postwar demobilization had been swift. The number of Marine divisions went down from six to two; the number of aircraft wings, from five to two. The units that remained were skeletons with very little meat on their bones. Strength of the Corps had plummeted to barely seventy-five thousand by the summer of 1950, when the Korean War erupted.

Land of the Morning Calm

In the first days of the war that began on the Korean peninsula on 25 June, Gen MacArthur, head of American forces in the Far East, asked for an air-ground Marine brigade immediately and "his" 1st Marine Division (he remembered the Marines he commanded at Cape Gloucester) at war strength for the landing at Inchon he was already planning. The 1st Provisional Marine Brigade reached the endangered Pusan Perimeter in time to earn the accolade of "fire brigade," then hurried north by sea to join the rest of the 1st Marine Division—fleshed out with reserves and regulars pulled from posts and stations—as it churned through the Yellow Sea toward Inchon.

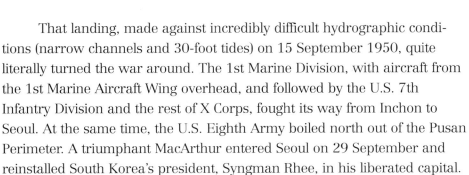

That landing, made against incredibly difficult hydrographic conditions (narrow channels and 30-foot tides) on 15 September 1950, quite literally turned the war around. The 1st Marine Division, with aircraft from the 1st Marine Aircraft Wing overhead, and followed by the U.S. 7th Infantry Division and the rest of X Corps, fought its way from Inchon to Seoul. At the same time, the U.S. Eighth Army boiled north out of the Pusan Perimeter. A triumphant MacArthur entered Seoul on 29 September and reinstalled South Korea's president, Syngman Rhee, in his liberated capital.

MacArthur then sent the Eighth Army rushing north, through quickly captured Pyongyang, North Korea's capital, on toward the Yalu River, Korea's border with Red China. The X Corps reembarked from Inchon in its amphibious ships and circled around the peninsula to land on North Korea's east coast. The 1st Marine Division went ashore at Wonsan on 26 October, and its regiments and battalions fanned out to block the escape of the remnants of the shattered North Korean Army.

Americans and South Koreans began to take Chinese prisoners, who were at first dismissed by MacArthur's Tokyo headquarters as "volunteers." (Beijing would later use the same euphemism.) Major General Oliver P. Smith, commanding the 1st Marine Division, was much concerned over the scattering of his division. He privately informed General Clifton B. Cates, the Marine Corps commandant, that he was going to bring his regiments within supporting distance of each other, even if it meant defying X Corps' commander, the mercurial Army Major General Edward M. Almond.

The Marines in early November advanced northwest of Hungnam against those Chinese "volunteers" to a place known chiefly for the presence of the Chosin reservoir and hydroelectric plant. By the middle of November (even here, the Marines managed to celebrate Thanksgiving with turkey), the Chinese seemed to have faded away to the north. A completely confident MacArthur ordered a "win the war" offensive—by Eighth Army on the west side of Korea's mountainous spine and by X Corps on the east.

MajGen Smith had the 5th Marines and the 7th Marines outside the mountain village of Yudam-ni. The 1st Marines were strung out to the rear—with battalions at Hagaru-ri, Koto-ri, and Chinhung-ni—to keep open the main supply route to the port of Hungnam. The pleasant autumn

Left: Marines, once delivered by stretcher bearers to a road, could then be taken to the rear in jeep trailers. (Photo: David Douglas Duncan)

Right: Capt Francis "Ike" Fenton, commander of Company B, 5th Marines, in Korea's early fighting, shows in his eyes the strain of battle. (Photo: David Douglas Duncan)

Marines go up scaling ladders over the stone seawall that edged Inchon harbor. MacArthur's master stroke, the amphibious assault at Inchon on 15 September 1950, by its deep envelopment turned the war around. The landing was made under almost insurmountable hydrographic conditions by the 1st Marine Division, reconstituted on the scene by Marine units arriving from all over the world. (Photo: SSgt Walter Frank, USMC)

Bottom left: Bloody street fighting and distraught civilians caught in the maelstrom characterized the liberation of Seoul, South Korea's capital, in the last week of September 1950. (Photo: David Douglas Duncan)

Bottom right: Marines on 6 December 1950, before breaking out to the south from Hagaru-ri, watch a Marine "Corsair" strafe and bomb what had been an Army tent camp and is now infested with Communist Chinese. Temperatures at the Chosin Reservoir dropped to 25 degrees below zero at night. (Photo: Sgt Frank C. Kerr, USMC)

weather had turned bitter cold. On 26 November, word reached the Marines that the Eighth Army on the other side of the Taebek mountains had been heavily hit. On the 27th, the Marines at Yudam-ni tentatively attacked to the west, met strong resistance, and fell back. That night, three Chinese divisions struck the Marines at Yudam-ni. Another division hit Hagaru-ri and still another Koto-ri. Some snow had fallen and temperatures at night were going as low as minus 25 degrees Fahrenheit. Winter uniforms, hurriedly issued to the Marines, were inadequate, particularly the footgear. The Chinese IX Army Group dedicated at least eight divisions to the destruction of the 1st Marine Division. The Chinese died in huge numbers, but still they came on.

At thinly held Hagaru-ri, southeast of Yudam-ni, engineers scraped a 2,900-foot runway into the frozen earth—an airhead that had to be held. Further south at Koto-ri, 1st Marines headquarters, itself beleaguered,

sent north a patched-together column that included the Royal Marines' 41 Independent Commando, a company each of Marine and Army infantry, two companies of Marine tanks, and a division headquarters "train" with too many vehicles. Chinese ambushes shredded the column; only a fraction of it got through to Hagaru-ri.

On 1 December the 5th and 7th Marines started back from Yudam-ni. That same day the airstrip at Hagaru-ri became operational, and Marine and Air Force transports began to bring in supplies and take out the wounded. Five hundred Marine replacements, many barely recovered from earlier wounds, arrived by air and were fed into the perimeter.

On 3 December the head of the column from Yudam-ni reached Hagaru-ri, fourteen miles of fighting withdrawal in three days. The breakout to the south through the incredible cold continued—shepherded by Marine close-support aircraft—first eleven miles to Koto-ri, then on to Funchilin pass, and ended with all the division in Hungnam by 12 December. Of the fifteen thousand Marines who had gone up onto the plateau, 730 had died, nearly four thousand more were wounded, many had pneumonia, and nearly all suffered from frostbite, some so badly as to require amputation. Ships took the Marines to Pusan. They went into camp in the "Bean Patch" at Masan to spend Christmas, lick their wounds, and get ready to fight again.

In North Korea on New Year's Eve, the Chinese attacked and went on to recapture Seoul and Inchon. The 1st Marine Division shook down new troops with counter-guerrilla operations behind the front in January, and then, rejuvenated, the division took its place in the center of the line under IX Corps. On 21 February the Marines attacked from Wonju as part of Operation Killer, and in three days had their objective, Hoengsong, eight miles to the north. This buttoned-up style of attack continued in March with Operation Ripper.

On 9 April President Truman replaced General MacArthur with

Surrounded on all sides by Communist Chinese troops, the 1st Marine Division moves south from Koto-ri on 8 December 1950, covered by intermittent flights of Marine aircraft overhead and its flanks protected by rifle companies leap-frogging from crest to crest of the bordering hills. (Photo: Sgt Frank C. Kerr, USMC)

Ill-equipped for a winter campaign, Marines at the Chosin Reservoir suffered almost as much from cold and frostbite as they did from Chinese bullets. There was seldom a chance to heat their canned "C" rations. (Photo: David Douglas Duncan)

Above: *Two U.S. Marines (left) meet two British Royal Marines on the frozen Chosin battlefield. Task Force Drysdale, a mixed force named for its British commander, LtCol Douglas B. Drysdale, RM, included the 41 Independent Commando, Royal Marines, re-armed with American weapons. (Artist: Sgt Ralph Schofield, Marine Corps Art Collection)*

Right: *Marine tanks lurch around a blown bridge south of Koto-ri on 9 December 1950. The icy hills largely confined the use of tanks to the single road that led south from the reservoir. (Photo: Sgt Frank C. Kerr, USMC)*

Facing page, top: *The feet nonchalantly protruding from the body of the truck and tied together at the ankles belong to the frozen bodies of dead Marines. Marines do not leave their dead behind. (Photo: David Douglas Duncan)*

Lieutenant General Matthew B. Ridgway. The 1st Marine Division had reached Hwachon Reservoir when, on 21 April, the Chinese spring counter-offensive hit the Eighth Army. A gap opened to the Marines' left until the 1st and 7th Marines filled it. The Chinese attacked again in mid-May. This time a gap opened on the Marines' right flank and again they took care of the situation. The Eighth Army went on the offensive, and the 1st Marine Division found itself once again in the Hwachon Reservoir sector. By 20 June the division had reached the edge of a deep circular valley which would come to be called "the Punchbowl." Then the United Nations Command stopped its offensive and peace negotiations began.

When these negotiations stalled, the Eighth Army returned to the

attack. The 1st Marine Division was ordered to take the rest of the Punchbowl and this it did in a month's hard fighting, winding up with eleven miles of front on the north side of the depression. In late March 1952 the division departed the Punchbowl sector and moved to the left flank of the United Nations line to hold the thirty-five miles of front covering the approaches to Panmunjom, where the peace talks were taking place in desultory fashion.

On both sides, the lines entrenched and solidified into something

At the end of the march from the Chosin Reservoir, Cpl Charles Price on 13 December 1950 sounds "Taps" over the graves of Marine dead temporarily buried at Hung-nam, North Korea. (Photo: Cpl W. T. Wolfe, USMC)

Marines' initial use of helicopters in combat came in Korea, first for liaison and reconnaissance, then for medical evacuation, and finally for movement of men and supplies. ("Landing Zone, Korea," Col H. Avery Chenoweth, USMCR (Ret), Marine Corps Art Collection)

horribly reminiscent of the Western Front of World War I. Big offensives gave way to localized actions, bruising for those who fought them but with little effect on the grease-pencilled lines on the big-picture situation maps. On 27 July 1953, a cease-fire went into effect, and the long armistice (but not peace) began. In three years of war, 4,267 Marines had been killed and 23,744 wounded. Only 227 Marines had been taken prisoner. The 1st Marine Division stayed on in Korea for nearly two more years before coming home to Camp Pendleton. The 3d Marine Division, reactivated during the war, came out to Japan and Okinawa.

Viet Nam, Divided and Divisive

In the post-Korean 1950s, Marines continued to be busy around the globe. Marine Corps strength stayed at about 175,000. In 1955 Marines with the Seventh Fleet assisted in moving three hundred thousand refugees from north to south Viet Nam, a straw in the wind little noticed at the time. Other Marines helped evacuate Nationalist Chinese from the Tachen Islands to Taiwan. During the 1956 Suez Canal crisis, involving the Israelis and Egyptians, French and British, a battalion from the Sixth Fleet landed at Alexandria to lift out some fifteen hundred civilians.

President John F. Kennedy reviews Marines graduating from sea school in San Diego, California, in 1963. These Marines would serve in time-honored fashion on board the major ships of the Navy. (Photo: Courtesy of command museum, MCRD, San Diego)

Back home that same year, traditional Marine "boot" training was endangered when a drill instructor at Parris Island marched his platoon into swampy Ribbon Creek one night and six of them drowned. There were investigations, recriminations, and a court martial for the drill instructor, but boot camp survived—with more careful oversight.

The largest Marine operation in these years came in July 1958 when four battalions, organized into a brigade-size 2d Provisional Marine Force, converged on Lebanon to dampen down a threatened Syria-backed revolt.

During the Cuban Missile Crisis of October 1962, Marines from both the east and west coasts were positioned to invade Cuba if called upon. Other trouble spots in the Caribbean included Venezuela and the Dominican Republic. After the 1961 assassination of Dominican dictator Rafael Trujillo, a one-time Marine Corps protégé, the Marines quieted local unrest with a bloodless air–ground demonstration. But by April 1965, President Lyndon Johnson was so sure of an imminent Communist

Bottom left: A Marine in an armored vest and with an M-14 rifle stands guard at Hotel Embajador, Santo Domingo, used as a collection point for American and other foreign nationals wishing to leave the troubled island in April 1965. (Photo: Sgt N. B. Call, USMC)

Bottom right: A Marine UH-34 helicopter evacuates American nationals from the Dominican Republic during the April 1965 intervention ordered by President Lyndon Johnson. (Photo: Sgt N. B. Call, USMC)

In restoring order to Santo Domingo, capital of the Dominican Republic, Marines set up checkpoints to examine passing traffic for weapons and other contraband. ("Checkpoint Charlie," John Groth, Marine Corps Art Collection)

It could have been Cape Gloucester, or change the helmets to campaign hats and it might have been the Philippines, but these Marines, members of Company C, 3d Marines, are wading through the waters of the Song Cu De river 14 miles north of Da Nang, Viet Nam, on an eight-day patrol in 1966. (Photo: LCpl Finnell, USMC)

takeover of the little Dominican Republic that he piled Army and Marine Corps troops, plus some token representation from other Latin American countries, onto the island. The Marine landing force ballooned into the 4th Marine Expeditionary Brigade (MEB). The Army air-landed a brigade of the 82d Airborne Division. Some street fighting occurred, and nine Marines were killed and another thirty wounded.

In East Asia, Marines began to exercise in Thailand in 1962 in response to civil war in neighboring Laos—another straw in the quickening wind that soon would blow to typhoon strength. In April of that year, as part of an operation called "Shu-Fly," a Marine helicopter squadron arrived in the delta south of Saigon (and later moved to Da Nang) to provide lift for the "ARVN"—the Army of the Republic of (south) Viet

Marines patrol the Marble Mountain area south of Da Nang. John Groth, celebrated artist and friend of Ernest Hemingway, covered many conflicts, including four for the Marines: World War II, Korea, the Dominican Republic, and Viet Nam. ("Marble Mountain Patrol," Marine Corps Art Collection)

Nam. The 9th Marine Expeditionary Brigade made a much publicized landing at Da Nang on 8 March 1965, the first significant investment of U.S. ground forces in the war between the two halves of Viet Nam. At first, the 9th MEB was tied into a defensive posture around the Da Nang air base (northernmost of the three jet-capable fields in South Viet Nam). New arrivals found it hard to take seriously a war fought against "little guys in black pajamas."

The build-up was swift. The headquarters of the 3d Marine Division and 1st Marine Aircraft Wing arrived in Da Nang shortly thereafter and together formed the III Marine Expeditionary Force (III MEF). "Expeditionary" was changed to "Amphibious" when someone decided that "Expeditionary" might remind the Vietnamese of the bad old days of French colonialism. The 3d Marine Expeditionary Brigade (still styled "Expeditionary") landed on 7 May on a barren stretch of beach fifty-five miles southeast of Da Nang and was absorbed into III MAF. Construction began of a combat base called "Chu Lai," which featured an airfield

that combined aluminum matting with carrier-type arresting gear.

Additional battalions and squadrons, regiments and aircraft groups continued to arrive. III MAF's "Tactical Areas of Responsibility" steadily expanded, and Marine operations became more aggressive. In June, Major General Lewis W. Walt, a combat hero in World War II and Korea, took dual command of both III MAF and the 3d Marine Division. By late summer 1965, four Marine regiments—the 3d, 4th, 7th, and 9th Marines—were in-country.

American forces fought their first regimental-size action on 15 August, when, in an operation known as "Starlite," the 7th Marines converged on the 1st Viet Cong Regiment located on the Van Tuong peninsula fifteen miles south of Chu Lai. Nearly a thousand Viet Cong were killed, but the Marines learned how porous could be a cordon thrown around "entrapped" Viet Cong.

As the hostilities gained momentum, a difference emerged between

Top left: *A sergeant cook from the 9th Marines serves up a cold drink in a Viet Nam hamlet south of Da Nang in February 1966. This was part of a recurring cordon-and-search operation called "County Fair," wherein Marines cooperating with South Vietnamese forces would attempt to flush out Viet Cong from rural villages and restore the confidence of the people in the South Vietnamese government in far away Saigon. (Photo: Cpl Martinez)*

Top right: *Almost like going "over the top" in World War I, Marines of the 4th Regiment scramble up a shell-scarred hill two miles south of the De-Militarized Zone or "DMZ" that separated North from South Viet Nam. In the summer of 1966, North Vietnamese regulars came across this border in strength. (Photo: Cpl Mahoney, USMC)*

Marines of Company K, 5th Marines, operating well south of Da Nang, hurry a wounded comrade to a landing zone where he will be lifted by helicopter to a field hospital. Most Marines, so evacuated, would eventually recover from their wounds. (Photo: Cpl Curry, USMC)

Navy hospital corpsman Andre A. Bougie fights to staunch the bleeding of a wounded Viet Cong in his black pajamas, with his conical straw hat nearby, during a 1st Marine Division operation in March 1967. (Photo: LCpl McClory, USMC)

Army and Marine war-fighting strategies. The Marines used their coastal bases as enclaves and pushed out their boundaries as a shield; behind it the Marines endeavored to expunge the Viet Cong infrastructure so that the South Vietnamese government could assert control of the districts and villages. The Army—personified by General William C. Westmoreland, commander of what was still called the "U.S. Military Assistance Command, Viet Nam," with headquarters in Saigon—stressed "search and destroy" missions, which would go out into the jungled hinterlands to find the Viet Cong and, increasingly, the North Vietnamese.

Marines, remembering Haiti, Santo Domingo, and Nicaragua, saw an effective gendarmerie as the key to controlling the countryside. In this new-style war, however, there could be no "white" commanders of "native"

The violent battle for Hue city, Viet Nam's ancient capital, was fought by battalions of the 1st and 5th Marines, the same regiments that fought the battle for Seoul, Korea, seventeen years earlier. The broken Tet cease-fire in 1968 signaled massive North Vietnamese and Viet Cong attacks throughout the length of South Viet Nam. ("Valor at Hue," Tom Freeman, courtesy of U.S. Naval Institute and U.S. Naval Academy Museum)

An M-60 machine-gun team from 1st Battalion, 5th Marines, entwined in belts of ammunition, "hose down" a street in Hue in February 1968. (Photo: Sgt J. C. Pennington, USMC)

troops. What the Marines had to work with, on a totally cooperative basis, were the "Ruff-Puffs"—Regional Forces at the province and district levels and Popular Forces in the villages and hamlets. This led to what came to be called "Combined Action," specially trained Marine squads paired off with Popular Force (and sometimes Regional Force) platoons.

Even so, the "shield" was far from impervious. On the night of 27 October 1965, Viet Cong infiltrators destroyed or damaged nearly all the Marine helicopters at Marble Mountain air facility near Da Nang and played havoc with the flight line of A-4 Skyhawks to the south at Chu Lai. Other raids and stand-off rocket attacks continued and a completely satisfactory counter was never found.

In March 1966 the headquarters of the 1st Marine Division followed its regiments into Chu Lai. By then the war had developed a rhythm. Marine battalions moved forward in "clearing" operations, sometimes being diverted to go to the rescue of beleaguered ARVN forces and sometimes, under pressure from Saigon, going out into the western rain forest to try to find the elusive enemy, whether they be Viet Cong or North Vietnamese.

The "Buddhist Revolt" that spring gave the Marines' war a hard jolt. South Vietnamese forces in the five northern provinces, torn to pieces by religious and political differences, stopped the war against the Viet Cong in order to fight one another. North Vietnamese regular forces crossed over into northernmost Quang Tri province and threatened to overwhelm the ARVN forces and endanger Hue. The 3d Marine Division echeloned to the north. And the battleground became the strip between the Demilita-

Facing page: A wounded Marine, from Company H, 1st Marines, is lowered from a University of Hue rooftop on 2 February 1968. (Photo: USMC)

rized Zone ("DMZ") on the North Viet Nam border and the east-west Route 9 which ran from Dong Ha to Laos. The North Vietnamese enemy was uniformed, well-equipped, well-trained, and adequately supported by artillery. When pressed too hard, he would break off from battle and fade back across the DMZ or into Laos.

The 1st Marine Division, to the south, continued to fight a "paddy"

Life on the combat base at Con Thien in 1967 was life on a bull's-eye, as miserable and dangerous as the Western Front in France fifty years before. (Photo: David Douglas Duncan)

A Marine C-130 "Hercules," hit by a North Vietnamese mortar shell, burns on the airstrip at Khe Sanh. The Marines holding Khe Sanh were supplied by round-robin air delivery. (Photo: David Douglas Duncan)

war against the nearly invisible Viet Cong, masters of anti-personnel mines, sapper attacks, ambushes, and intimidation of villagers. Westmoreland invested U.S. Army troops in the embattled northern five provinces, brigade by brigade. The U.S. Army took over in Quang Tin and Quang Ngai provinces, and the 1st Marine Division moved northward into Quang Nam for the defense of Da Nang (those perfidious rockets continued to hit the airfield) and into Thua Thien to defend the approaches to Hue.

Tet, the Chinese New Year, began on 27 January 1968. The Viet Cong announced that they would observe Tet with a week-long cease-fire, and then celebrated the cease-fire with rocket attacks up and down South Viet Nam. Ground attacks followed. Their forces approaching Da Nang were easily thrown back; those that infiltrated into Hue had much more success.

Because Hue had some of the aspects of a sacred open city, the ARVN garrison was minimal and there were no American defenders. By midnight on 30 January the North Vietnamese had control of the city. An understrength Marine battalion was sent in the next morning to reconnoiter. It reached the southern half of the city, made a tentative crossing of the Perfume River, reached the walls of the Citadel, Hue's ancient fortress, and then withdrew south of the river. On 4 February another battalion was added and the force put under command of the 1st Marines. In five days of street-to-street fighting, the southern half of the city was cleared. In the northern part, the ARVN built up a force that attacked the North Vietnamese center of resistance in the Citadel. A Marine battalion was put in on the ARVN left flank and the fighting continued until 2 March.

Marines rush a casualty to a UH-34D helicopter (called a "Huss" by Marines) that has just touched down on an "LZ" or landing zone. It is a critical moment—to get the helicopter off the ground before the enemy can bring mortar or small-arms fire to bear. (Photo: David Douglas Duncan)

Men of Company B, 4th Marines, feel their way across a stream near the DMZ in December 1968. Fighting in Viet Nam followed a circular pattern—repetition after repetition. Each month brought a fresh supply of Marines for whom the war was new. (Photo: Sgt Mike Padillo, USMC)

A helmet full of water scooped up while crossing a stream can give a momentarily cooling shower. So thought PFC Harvey C. Henderson patrolling somewhere between Ca Lu and Khe Sanh in April 1968. (Photo: SSgt J. A. Reid, USMC)

At the same time, the battle for Khe Sanh, near the northwest corner of South Viet Nam, began on 20 January 1968, when Marine patrols encountered a North Vietnamese battalion entrenched in the overlooking hills. Comparisons were immediately made with Dien Bien Phu, site of the climactic French defeat in 1954.

On 5 February at Khe Sanh, the North Vietnamese assaulted the 26th Marines on Hill 881 South. The Marines met the attack with artillery and air. Next day the enemy overran the Special Forces camp at nearby Lang Vei. Determined to win a decisive victory at Khe Sanh, Westmoreland directed that a torrential rain of bombs and rockets, called "Operation Niagara," be dropped on the North Vietnamese attackers. By the end of March the North Vietnamese had disappeared into the hills.

The "relief" (hardly needed in Marines' minds) of the "siege" of Khe Sanh—named "Operation Pegasus" to emphasize its airborne nature—began on 1 April. The Army's 1st Air Cavalry Division (and an airborne battalion of ARVN) hop-scotched forward, while a column of Marines and ARVN came west along Route 9.

The enemy was not yet finished. At the end of April he launched a division-size attack against the defenders of Dong Ha. Heavy fighting continued through most of May. To the south, the "paddy" war continued with all its deadly monotony. Place names such as "Arizona Territory" and "Dodge City" came into the Marine Corps vocabulary.

Marine troop withdrawals began in July 1969, and by the following

The Viet Cong took the bridge at Cam Le leading into Da Nang on 23 August 1968, but then lost it, along with their lives, to two companies of Marines. (Photo: Sgt M. S. Lafferty, USMC)

Above: *Marines from the 3d Engineer Battalion sweep a road west of Con Thien to ensure it is safe for the tanks of the 3d Tank Battalion to come up. In Viet Nam, both anti-tank and anti-personnel mines, usually employed in combination, were a constant menace. (Photo: LCpl C. E. Woodruff)*

Left: *Marines from 3d Battalion, 1st Marines, search out a village south of the DMZ in 1968. Villagers were seldom cooperative; sometimes a grandmother or a school boy with a grenade could prove deadly. (Photo: Sgt M. J. Coates, USMC)*

February, all of the 3d Marine Division was gone, and the bob-tailed 1st Marine Division was left with just one infantry regiment, the 1st Marines. The residue was organized briefly into the 3d Marine Amphibious Brigade, and by July 1970 all elements of the brigade had left. But the war was not yet quite over for the Marines.

In a March 1972 Easter Offensive, the North Vietnamese swept down across the DMZ and pushed aside the ARVN defenders. The division-strength South Vietnamese Marine Corps, with its U.S. Marine advisors,

Top: *Navy chaplain LtCdr R. W. Crum holds 1969 Easter services in the field for Company K, 7th Marines. Navy chaplains—brave, dedicated men—took religious solace to where the danger was. (Photo: SSgt A. J. Sharp, USMC)*

Above: *The ruins of a church near Da Nang form an unintentional memorial. (Artist: Col Houston "Tex" Stiff, USMC (Ret), Marine Corps Art Collection)*

moved into the breach. The 9th Marine Amphibious Brigade at sea took station off coast. A Marine aircraft group rushed its F-4 Phantoms to the Da Nang air base and another group, with A-4 Skyhawks, moved into Bien Hoa. The Vietnamese Marines, side-by-side with the Vietnamese Airborne Division, finally stopped the North Vietnamese north of Hue.

The success of 1972 would not be repeated in 1975. Early in the year, the North Vietnamese launched a general offensive, coming across the borders on a broad front. The South Vietnamese, numerically superior but widely dispersed, were rolled up in a series of numbing defeats. This time no American combat support came to their aid. In the old III MAF battleground, Hue and Da Nang fell without a fight.

In neighboring Cambodia, the Khmer Rouge encircled Phnom Penh, the capital. On 12 April 1975, President Gerald Ford gave the order to evacuate the few remaining Americans and any foreign nationals who chose to leave Phnom Penh. A helicopter-borne force of three hundred Marines threw a protective cordon around the soccer field chosen as the evacuation site. In a little over two hours, Marine helicopters shuttled 278 persons to safety.

Two weeks later, the 9th Marine Amphibious Brigade, ever-present offshore, executed the key role in the evacuation of Saigon. Working from landing zones at both Tan Son Nhut air base and the U.S. embassy in Saigon, Marine helicopters took out 1,373 Americans and 5,595 Vietnamese and foreign nationals on 29 and 30 April. Two Marines died in the process. On May Day, the North Vietnamese marched triumphantly through Saigon.

Strength of the Marine Corps reached 317,400 during the Viet Nam conflict, compared to the all-time peak of 485,053 in World War II. Top strength in Viet Nam itself was 85,755, more Marines than fought at either Iwo Jima or Okinawa. This longest of American wars cost the Marines 13,067 dead and 88,633 wounded. One in four of the names on the Viet Nam memorial wall in Washington, D.C., is that of a Marine.

Right: *American flags were allowed to fly over South Viet Nam only after much political discussion. This flag flies above Hill 119 southwest of Da Nang while a CH-53 "Sea Stallion" brings in a "water buffalo" water trailer. (Photo: Cpl W. A. Barger, USMC)*

Following two pages:
A Marine wears a royal straight flush on his helmet, perhaps a hand he drew, perhaps just a wish—or a prayer. The average age of the young Marines fighting in Viet Nam was nineteen. Most served a two-year enlistment—a year of it in Viet Nam. (Photo: David Douglas Duncan)

The year of service in Viet Nam—really thirteen months—is checked off month by month on this helmet cover. Marines serving in a rifle squad had over a hundred percent chance of being wounded or killed. Wounds were of two kinds: those that permitted immediate return to duty and those that required hospitalization. (Photo: David Douglas Duncan)

Below: *When the Marines departed, as here at Observation Post Round Up, southwest of Da Nang, in February 1971, they took with them everything of value and bulldozed the rest into the emptied bunkers and trenches. (Photo: USMC)*

New Missions, New Problems

The Corps brought problems home from Viet Nam: drug abuse, alcoholism, racial friction, absences without leave, and sub-marginal performance on the part of many. Boards were appointed to examine the Corps' size, organization, and future roles. Recruiting standards were stiffened. Much-publicized cases of recruit abuse caused an examination once again of recruit training methods and supervision. A concentrated (and ultimately successful) campaign was launched against drug use.

Turning back to Europe, Marine brigades were sent to exercise in Norway and northern Germany and prepare for a commitment to

reinforce NATO's northern flank. A brigade's worth of supplies and equipment was prepositioned "in the rock" in Norway. To meet contingencies elsewhere in the world, the Corps embraced a "maritime prepositioning" concept. Marines would move by air to a troubled area and connect up with ships preloaded with the wherewithal to fight.

Strategic planners, mindful of the need for a continuing flow of oil, foresaw a high probability of a major confrontation in the Middle East growing out of Islamic unrest and the longtime belligerency of Iran and Iraq. The Marines activated the headquarters of the 7th Marine Expeditionary Brigade at Twenty-nine Palms, California, to prepare for the eventuality of a desert campaign.

Below: *Marine Reservists train in two AH-1W "Sea Cobra" attack helicopters at Twenty-nine Palms, California, in 1994. Earlier, the 7th Marine Expeditionary Brigade's use of the desert training site proved invaluable in the Persian Gulf War. (Photo: Rick Mullen)*

A Marine CH-46 "Sea Knight" helicopter operates off the USS Nassau in the Red Sea, across the Arabian peninsula from the Persian Gulf. (Photo: Rick Mullen)

Desert Shield and Desert Storm

A "tanker war" began in the Persian Gulf in 1984; first, the Iraqis went after Iranian tankers and then the Iranians retaliated by going after the tankers of Iraq's Arab supporters. In July 1987 a Kuwaiti tanker under U.S. registry, the *Bridgetown*, hit an Iranian mine. The U.S. Navy's Middle East Force, part of U.S. Central Command—now under General George B. Crist, the first Marine general to command a unified command—employed anti-mine helicopters carried in amphibious assault ships for mine detection and clearance. A Marine air-ground task force provided an amphibious raid capability. Soon Marines, with attack helicopters overhead, were "boarding" suspect Iranian oil platforms. In August 1989, Iran agreed to a cease-fire. But the pause before more intense hostilities was short.

Bottom left: *A vehicle dangles beneath a heavy-lifting Marine CH-53E "Super Stallion" during Desert Shield, the build-up for Desert Storm. (Photo: Rick Mullen)*

Bottom right: *Marines run to keep fit during Desert Shield in December 1990. (Photo: Greg E. Mathieson)*

Iraq dictator Saddam Hussein's invasion of Kuwait on 2 August 1990 triggered the movement of the 7th Marine Expeditionary Brigade from California to the Persian Gulf as part of a massive U.S. build up called "Desert Shield." Marines of the brigade moved by air to Saudi Arabia and married up with their combat equipment and supplies transported by sea to Al Jubayl. On 25 August, the brigade commander reported to General H. Norman Schwarzkopf, Central Command's commander-in-chief, that

Members of the 1st Marine Division in newly issued desert camouflage uniforms assemble before the Desert Storm phase of the Persian Gulf War. (Photo: USMC)

A Marine CH-46 "Sea Knight" picks up a load from the USS Iwo Jima *in the Persian Gulf. (Photo: Rick Mullen)*

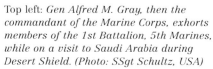

Top left: *Gen Alfred M. Gray, then the commandant of the Marine Corps, exhorts members of the 1st Battalion, 5th Marines, while on a visit to Saudi Arabia during Desert Shield. (Photo: SSgt Schultz, USA)*

Top right: *A Navy ordnance man, on board the USS* Iwo Jima, *prepares to load Mark 82 500-pound bombs onto a Marine CH-53E helicopter for delivery ashore to waiting Marine Corps fighter-bombers. (Photo: Rick Mullen)*

Right: *Marines scan the desert horizon while manning a venerable but dependable caliber .50 M-2 Browning machine gun, effective against personnel and unarmored vehicles. (Photo: Greg E. Mathieson)*

his brigade, with a strength of more than fifteen thousand, was prepared to hold a line forty miles north of Al Jubayl in Saudi Arabia.

The 7th MEB grew into a powerful I Marine Expeditionary Force, commanded by Lieutenant General Walter E. Boomer. Ashore were the 1st Marine Division and the 1st Marine Aircraft Wing; the 4th Marine Expeditionary Brigade remained afloat. By the first of November, some forty-two thousand Marines, a quarter of the Corps' active duty strength, was in the Gulf.

Plumped up with Marine Corps reservists, most of the II Marine Expeditionary Force, notably the 2d Marine Division and the remaining aircraft groups from the 2d Marine Aircraft Wing, started for the Gulf at the end of 1990, later to be followed by the 5th Marine Expeditionary Brigade.

Central Command's plan for a war-winning offensive, to be called "Desert Storm," assigned LtGen Boomer's Marine force the mission of a frontal assault against the Saddam Hussein line, while the majority of the

U.S. and coalition forces swung wide to the west in what Schwarzkopf would call his "Hail Mary" attack.

Desert Storm's aerial campaign began before dawn on 16 January 1991; all the world watched on cable television. The 1st Marine Aircraft Wing, which had one-quarter of the fixed wing tactical aircraft in the theater, did its share of "big picture" attack but was more concerned with preparing the battlefield for I MEF's imminent ground operations.

On the night of 29 January, Saddam Hussein sent two armored columns across the border in a puzzling attack. The fight coalesced in the deserted town of Al Khafji. After an initial success against light Arab screening forces, the Iraqis were chased back into Kuwait with the help

Sgt Charles Grow paints the LAV "Marietta" flying both the national and Marine Corps colors during Desert Storm. The Marine Corps' wheeled light armored vehicles played a role in desert fighting comparable to 19th-century light cavalry or dragoons. (Marine Corps Art Collection)

Above left: *Burning Kuwaiti oil wells make an awesome backdrop of smoke and flame for Marine tanks stopped for an overnight bivouac. (Photo: Greg E. Mathieson)*

Above right: *President George Bush, accompanied by Army Gen H. Norman Schwarzkopf, congratulates Marine commanders at the national victory parade in Washington on 8 June 1991. (Photo: Greg E. Mathieson)*

of Marine ground and air. Boomer and his Marines began to suspect that the Iraqis were not as tough as their reputation would have it.

The ground attack began on 24 February. Boomer planned to have the 1st Marine Division break through the Saddam Hussein line in the vicinity of the Al Wafrah oil fields. The 2d Marine Division was to continue the attack, possibly linking up with an amphibious landing against the Kuwaiti coast. The attack's success exceeded the most optimistic expectations, including Schwarzkopf's. A torrent of demoralized Iraqi soldiers surrendered. Marines moved past the burning oil fields, onto Al Jaber air base, and then to Kuwait International Airport. Forces afloat feinted a landing, but there was no need for an amphibious assault. On the morning of 27 February, reconnaissance Marines entered Kuwait City, reached the U.S. embassy, and then stood politely aside to allow a composite Arab battalion to occupy the city. The next day President Bush called a halt.

The ninety-two thousand Marines in the Gulf, afloat and ashore, made Desert Storm by far the largest operation in Marine Corps history. Marine casualties were twenty-four killed, ninety-two wounded.

Still in desert battle garb, Marines of the 1st Marine Expeditionary Force, back from the Persian Gulf, pass in review before their commander-in-chief, President Bush, just as the Marines of the 4th Brigade had done before President Wilson on their return from World War I. (Photo: Greg E. Mathieson)

Grapes of Wrath and the Milk of Human Kindness

Marine Corps involvement in the security of U.S. embassies and consulates abroad goes back to the nineteenth and early twentieth centuries. After World War II, the assignment of a squad of Marines to embassies as a security guard was sanctioned by formal agreement with the State Department. Often these embassy Marines found themselves on the front lines. A sergeant was killed in Cambodia in 1971. The Marine guard at Khartoum held the embassy in 1973 after the ambassador had been kidnapped and murdered. Marines defended the embassy on Cyprus in 1974 while the Turks and Greeks battled each other. In 1979 the Marine guard held off rioters in Islamabad; one Marine was killed. Two Marines were wounded when terroritsts attacked the embassy in San Salvador in 1979.

Islamic demonstrators attacked the embassy in Teheran in February 1979 and kidnapped several Marines. That November, the Iranians stormed the embassy, and thirteen Marines were among the sixty-five Americans taken hostage. An anguished President Jimmy Carter directed their rescue.

The result was the bungled "Desert One" effort by a mixed team that included Marine pilots flying Navy helicopters. Three Marines were killed. After 444 days, Iran, with a nose-thumbing gesture, released the hostages on 20 January 1981, the day of President Ronald Reagan's inauguration.

Terrorist action against U.S. embassies continued throughout the 1980s. Three Marines were wounded in Costa Rica when a mine

A Sunday morning truck bomb, equivalent to six tons of TNT, leveled the Marines' four-story concrete headquarters at Beirut International Airport on 23 October 1983. Two hundred forty-one Americans were killed, 220 of them Marines. (Photo: USMC)

Rescue workers search for victims and clear the debris of the Beirut barracks bombing. (Photo: USMC)

detonated under their vehicle. Four Marines were among thirteen persons killed at a sidewalk cafe in San Salvador.

A sordid incident in Moscow in 1986 sullied the proud reputation of the "State Department Marines." Several Marines were found guilty of allowing Soviet citizens into classified spaces of the embassy. A court-martial convicted a Marine sergeant of espionage.

The 32d Marine Amphibious Unit landed in Lebanon in June 1982 to evacuate American citizens wanting to leave in the face of an Israeli invasion. In August, 32d MAU landed again to shepherd the evacuation of Palestinian Liberation Organization fighters trapped in Beirut by the Israelis. The 32d MAU returned yet again in late September after the Lebanese government asked for a multi-national force to help restore order. This time the Marines moved onto Beirut International Airport for what would be a long and eventually painful stay.

One Marine amphibious unit would periodically relieve another, and Marines ashore would patrol, although against what was not clear. Sometimes they took casualties from in-coming artillery and mortar shells. In March 1983 five Marines on patrol were slightly wounded. In April a truck-bomb attack against the U.S. Embassy killed sixty-three persons, seventeen of them Americans including one Marine.

As American foreign policy tilted more strongly in support of the weak Lebanese government, rocket and artillery attacks against the airfield by Syrian-backed factions multiplied. The Marines began counterbattery fire in late August, both with their own guns and naval gunfire. Marine casualties inched up, one or two at a time.

When not patrolling, filling sandbags, stringing barbed wire, and digging bunkers, a good number of the Marines at the airport regularly slept in a four-story concrete headquarters building judged strong enough to resist anything short of direct rocket and artillery fire. Early on Sunday morning, 23 October 1983, a yellow Mercedes truck forced its way through wire barriers and penetrated the lobby of the headquarters building. The explosion, estimated at the equivalent of six tons of TNT, brought down the building, killed 241 Americans, 220 of them Marines, and wounded more than a hundred more. Almost simultaneously, two miles away, a smaller but similar truck bomb rammed its way into the underground garage of the eight-story building that housed the Marines' French counterparts, killing fifty-eight French soldiers. The Marine Corps would doggedly replace its losses and continue its vague mission.

During the intervention on the island of Grenada in 1983, a Marine officer shows a puzzled Grenadian how to eat an "MRE"— "meal-ready-to-eat"—the current combat ration, scientifically formulated by civilians who don't have to eat them. (Photo: Sgt Christopher Grey, USMC)

Concurrent with the Lebanon tragedy came a happier intervention. President Reagan, convinced that there was about to be a Communist takeover of the tiny Caribbean island of Grenada, sent in an overwhelming force on 25 October 1983 to "restore order and democracy" and to rescue the thousand or so Americans thought to be on the island. While the Army's Ranger and Airborne force captured a nearly completed jet airfield at the southern end of the island, Marines from the 22d Marine Amphibious Unit moved easily across the remaining seven-eighths of the island. Several Marine helicopters, diverted to Army missions, were lost. In all, three Marines died and fifteen were wounded.

Marines played only a small part in the 1989 intervention in Panama aimed at deposing drug-dealing dictator Manuel Antonio Noriega. As relations with Noriega's government deteriorated, the company-size Marine Corps Security Force, which had replaced the Marines at the old Marine Barracks, grew to battalion strength. A Marine was killed in skirmishes against shadowy intruders. The death of a Marine lieutenant at a Panamanian checkpoint was the last straw that caused President George Bush to order a massive intervention by a predominantly Army joint task force. D-Day was 20 December, and in the week-long operation that followed another Marine was killed and three more were wounded.

The Persian Gulf War of 1991 segued into a relief operation called "Provide Comfort" for the displaced Kurds in northern Iraq. Army Lieutenant General John M. Shalikashvili commanded the effort with Marine Brigadier General Anthony C. Zinni as his deputy. The 24th Marine Expeditionary Unit joined the international force on 16 April and stayed on until 15 July.

Simultaneously, a disaster-relief expedition began on 29 April in Bangladesh. A horrendous cyclone flooded the coastal areas causing a death toll approaching 150,000. Food, shelter, clothing, medical supplies,

Marine CH-46 "Sea Knights" hover over a Kurdish refugee tent city in northern Iraq during Operation Provide Comfort in 1991. (Artist: Col Peter "Mike" Gish, USMCR (Ret), Marine Corps Art Collection)

Left: *Catholic Marines of the 24th Marine Expeditionary Unit, deployed to northern Iraq, take communion during a field mass conducted in May 1991 by Navy Chaplain William D. Devine. (Photo: PH2 Dante M. DeAngelis, USN)*

Below left: *Two Marine helicopters approach the Marine command post at Zakhu, Iraq, during Operation Provide Comfort, the allied effort to aid Kurdish refugees. (Photo: PHC Bruce Wallace, USN)*

A Marine, M16A2 rifle at the ready, walks the boundary of the refugee tent camp set up near Zakhu. Iraqi troops stood aside and did not interfere. (Photo: PH3 William A. Savage, USN)

and potable water were desperately needed. Elements of the III Marine Expeditionary Force, with Major General Henry C. Stackpole as joint task force commander, rushed to the rescue in what came to be called "Operation Sea Angel." All services did their part.

In Somalia what began as a humanitarian mission to rescue Americans and other foreigners turned into an anti-terrorist campaign. Marines of the I Marine Expeditionary Force landed there in December 1992. By early May 1993 most of the Marines had left, but two Marine expeditionary units arrived off the Somali coast again in October to help protect the U.S. forces still ashore, and another arrived in March 1994 to cover the final withdrawal. The Good Samaritan mission cost the Marines two killed and fifteen wounded.

In July 1994 the United Nations sanctioned an intervention to oust

Marine AH-1W "Sea Cobras"—more frequently called "Whiskeys"—lift off from the USS Tripoli *on their way in to Mogadishu, Somalia, in December 1992. (Photo: PH1 Joseph Doxey, USN)*

Marines of Task Force Somalia prepare to search a building in Mogadishu in January 1993. The multi-national relief effort, Operation Restore Hope, ended in tragedy and disappointment. (Photo: PHCM Terry C. Mitchell, USN)

the dictator of Haiti, Lieutenant General Raoul Cedras. So the point would not be missed, the operation was code-named "Uphold/Support Democracy." (No one seems to have checked as to when Haiti had last experienced democracy.) The main event was the landing of the XVIII Airborne Corps under Army Lieutenant General Hugh Shelton, the future

chairman of the Joint Chiefs of Staff, at Port-au-Prince on 19 September. The sideshow landing of a special Marine air-ground task force at Cap-Haitien in the north—the stamping ground of "Old Breed" Marines such as Butler and Hanneken—came a day later. Except for shooting up a detachment of Haitian military police that drew weapons against a Marine patrol (ten Haitians were killed), all went smoothly. The Marines left on 1 October.

Since their small beginnings in 1775, the Marines have grown, expanding with wars and contracting with peace, looking backward to tradition and forward to innovation, adapting and surviving as an elite organization in an increasingly egalitarian society. When changing times have called for their service, a few good women have joined the ranks of the "few good men." Weapons have proliferated with accelerating sophistication, but every Marine has remained, at heart, a rifleman. Mottos—"with courage," "always faithful," and "first to fight"—give voice to an indelible creed. As the calendar continues its march toward the 21st century, it appears that there will be no lack of employment opportunities, hostile or humanitarian, for Marines in their time-honored expeditionary role.

A Marine holds back a curious but friendly crowd in Mogadishu. What began as a humanitarian mission turned into a peace-keeping effort with Marines taking part in a United Nations force attempting to deal with warring Somali factions. (Artist: Col Peter "Mike" Gish, USMCR, Marine Corps Art Collection)

THE Iwo Jima Flag-Raising AND THE Monument

NEW GEORGIA·BOUGAINVILLE·TARAWA·NEW·BRITAIN·1944·MARSHALL·ISLANDS·MARIANAS·ISLANDS·PELELIU·1945·IWO·JIMA·OKINAWA

© Felix W. de Weldon
Sculp. 1945-1954

THE
Iwo Jima
Flag-Raising
AND
THE
Monument

Lieutenant Colonel Jon T. Hoffman, USMCR

Early on the morning of 23 February 1945, the fourth day after the assault landing on Iwo Jima, Lieutenant Colonel Chandler W. Johnson, commander of 2d Battalion, 28th Marines, ordered First Lieutenant Harold G. Schrier to take forty men and secure the top of Mount Suribachi. Johnson handed the lieutenant a small American flag to raise over the summit. The patrol, climbing cautiously, reached the windswept crater of the extinct volcano by mid-morning. Schrier, Platoon Sergeant Ernest I. Thomas, Jr., Sergeant Henry O. Hansen, Corporal Charles W. Lindberg, and Privates First Class Louis C. Charlo and James Michels quickly rigged the flag to a length of Japanese pipe and raised the colors. Staff Sergeant Louis R. Lowery, a combat photographer for *Leatherneck* magazine, who came up with the patrol, recorded the scene. Two enemy soldiers emerged from hiding; others threw grenades from a large cave. The Marines disposed of the opposition, and Lowery, trying to get out of the line of fire, tumbled down a rocky slope and broke his camera. Both he and his film survived the fall.

The Stars and Stripes flying over Iwo's highest point brought cheers from the thousands of men on the beaches below. Ships sounded

Five Marines and a Navy corpsman of the 28th Marines, 5th Marine Division, on 23 February 1945 raise the second American flag to fly atop Suribachi. Photographer Joe Rosenthal did not think he had taken a good shot, but this picture stirred the patriotism of the nation and brought him the Pulitzer Prize. (Photo: Associated Press/Joe Rosenthal)

Facing page: *With Mount Suribachi looming over them, Marines cross the sandy terraces of the Iwo Jima beachhead against withering Japanese fire. Designated a D-Day objective, Suribachi would be taken only after four days of heavy fighting. (Photo: PFC Robert R. Campbell, USMC)*

Previous spread: *The Marine Corps War Memorial at Arlington, Virginia, overlooks the Potomac. Honoring the Marine dead of all wars, the massive six-figure sculpture is one of the most frequently visited sites in the Washington capital area and has gained the status of a national shrine. (Photo: Eric Long)*

113

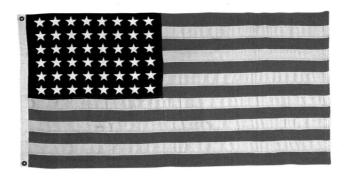

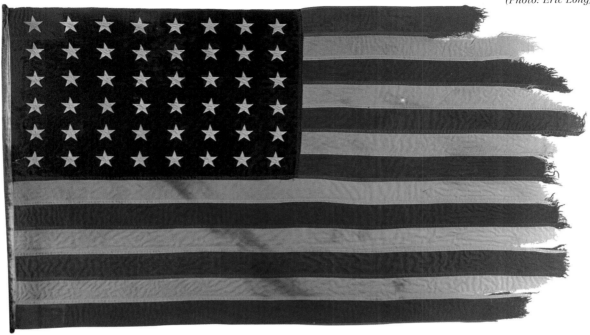

horns and whistles and many a man choked up. Secretary of the Navy James V. Forrestal, present as an observer, saw the national colors waving over this heavily fortified Japanese island on the path to Tokyo and predicted: "The raising of that flag on Suribachi means there will be a Marine Corps for the next five hundred years."

Johnson realized that his flag (just 54 x 28 inches) was too small to be seen all across the island, so he sent a lieutenant to obtain a larger flag from one of the landing ships. An officer of LST 779 gave the Marine the flag (96 x 56 inches) that the ship flew on Sundays and holidays. When Johnson received the folded colors, he passed them to Private First Class Rene A. Gagnon, a runner about to head up Suribachi to deliver radio batteries to Schrier. Gagnon climbed with four other men of Company E—Sergeant Michael Strank, Corporal Harlon H. Block, and Privates First Class Franklin R. Sousley and Ira A. Hayes—who were laying communications wire to the top. They passed Marines sealing caves and blowing up bunkers to silence the remaining opposition on the slopes. Three photojournalists—Staff Sergeant William H. Genaust, Private First Class Robert R. Campbell, and civilian Joe Rosenthal of the Associated Press—had heard that a flag was to be raised and they set out to record the event. Half way up they met Lowery coming down. Lowery told them of the first flag-raising.

When the three photographers reached the summit, they found five Marines and a Navy corpsman clustered along a length of pipe,

Above: *The Rosenthal photograph inspired the nation and became the subject of numerous artistic and adaptive interpretations. Noted illustrator Howard Chandler Christy, who had done many posters for both World Wars, combined in his painting elements of the first flag-raising with those of the photograph. (Marine Corps Art Collection)*

Left: *The flag-raising became the theme for the 7th War Bond Drive. Later, for the Victory Bond Drive, a life-size sculpture of the flag-raising went on national tour. Felix de Weldon would always insist that while the photograph inspired his sculptures, they were not copies of the photograph. (Marine Corps Art Collection)*

preparing the larger flag to replace the first one. They carefully wrapped the ensign around one end of the pipe to keep it from touching the ground. All three photographers moved into position just in time to capture the moment. As the pipe rose, the strong wind caught the flag, unfurled it, and snapped it out to full extension. The men nearest the base steadied the pole and then reached upward to jam it down into the ground, while the others gathered rocks to pile around it. Genaust's movie camera captured those few seconds of action in color, while Campbell, shooting from another angle, caught, in a single black-and-white still image, both the smaller flagpole being lowered to the ground and the new one going up. Rosenthal, standing near Genaust, clicked his shutter at what he considered to be "the peak of the action," but he felt that the shot was "mediocre." He asked the Marines and corpsmen in the vicinity to stand near the flag, and a group, imitating the classic Japanese *banzai* pose, shouted and raised

116

their helmets and weapons in triumph. But no one there felt that the moment had any great significance.

Rosenthal delivered his film to a ship that afternoon. From there, it went by seaplane to Guam, where it was developed. The pool photo editor passed the flag-raising photo by radio to the States. The simple, dramatic image made the front page all across the country and stirred the hearts of nearly all who saw it. Among the few who were not moved were the editors of *Life*, the leading picture magazine of the day. They were certain it had been posed and did not use it. *Time-Life* war correspondent Robert L. Sherrod seemed to confirm their doubts when he filed a dispatch asserting that the famous picture was a "phony" staged by Rosenthal after he missed out on the original flag-raising. The photographer's own caption added to the confusion by saying that it "signal[ed] the capture of this key position," thus appearing to indicate that this had been the first flag to go up. The Associated Press queried Rosenthal, ascertained the facts, and got Sherrod's erroneous story quashed, but not before a radio program had quoted from it.

Toward the end of March, *Time* published a brief article explaining the two flag-raisings and noting that Rosenthal's "unposed" work was already "the most widely printed photograph of World War II." At this time, *Life* finally published the picture and the story of the two flags. The public cared nothing for the details and continued to swoon over Rosenthal's compelling shot. The picture became the centerpiece of the Seventh War Bond Drive and won the Pulitzer Prize. The Post Office quickly issued a stamp of the scene that would soon sell in record numbers.

President Roosevelt himself ordered that the flag-raisers be brought back to the States. It was not easy to obey FDR's command. Immediately after taking the picture, Rosenthal had tried to identify the men who raised the second flag, but 1stLt Schrier shrugged him off—the platoon had more important things to do in the midst of battle. Now the word went down the chain of command to find them. The first identified was Gagnon. Working from the photograph, he in turn named Strank, Hansen, Sousley, and Pharmacist's Mate 2d Class John H. Bradley, a Navy corpsman who had gone up the mountain with Schrier's patrol. Gagnon did not want to reveal the name of the final Marine, who had asked for anonymity, but he eventually disclosed that it was Hayes. Only three of the six would return alive to the States. Sergeants Strank and Hansen were killed in action on 1 March, and PFC Sousley, on the 21st. Bradley was still hospitalized with shrapnel wounds in his legs. In May, Gagnon, Hayes, and Bradley (recovering from his wounds) were hosted by the White House and Congress before participating in the Seventh War Bond Drive.

Although the Corps was satisfied that the flag-raisers had been correctly identified, the mother of Cpl Block was sure that her son was in the photograph. Mrs. Block got in touch with Hayes in the summer of 1946, and he supported her contention that it was Block, not Hansen, at the base of the flagpole. The Marine Corps established a board to investigate the matter. It reviewed the photographic evidence

As a young man, famous artist Tom Lovell served in the Marine Corps during World War II. His interpretation of the flag-raising, done while he was on active service, is particularly realistic in its execution. (Marine Corps Art Collection)

The Flag-Raisers

The six men who raised the second flag over Suribachi personified the stereotypical American cross-section one might find in a Hollywood movie of that era.

There was Ira A. Hayes, a Pima Indian from a reservation in Arizona and a former Marine paratrooper with combat experience at Bougainville.

Michael Strank was the son of Czech immigrants who lived and worked in the coal fields of Pennsylvania. The rugged sergeant had enlisted in 1939 after Nazi Germany had swallowed his parents' homeland and fought on Bougainville with the Raiders.

Harlon H. Block was drafted in 1943 after a year of working in the Texas oil fields. He volunteered for parachute duty and served in the same battalion as Hayes on Bougainville.

Franklin R. Sousley, a boyish-looking nineteen-year-old draftee, had grown up on his grandfather's small Kentucky farm.

Rene A. Gagnon, a New Englander of French-Canadian extraction, had been rejected by the Navy for low blood pressure, but with schooling from a friendly civilian doctor, had succeeded in passing the Marine Corps physical.

John H. Bradley, "a solid guy with a sense of humor," had completed his apprenticeship to a Wisconsin funeral director when he enlisted in the Navy to become a corpsman.

Sgt Strank, Cpl Block, and PFC Sousley were killed in action. (Combat cameraman Staff Sergeant William H. Genaust also died in the last stages of the battle.) Pharmacist's Mate 2d Class Bradley was wounded. The Marine Corps never made awards to the men for raising the flag, though several of them received decorations for other acts of courage. PFC Hayes received a letter of commendation, and Strank merited a posthumous Bronze Star. The Corps conferred a Navy Cross on Bradley for aiding Marines under fire. He was, in fact, treating Sergeant Henry O. Hansen, a member of the original patrol, when a sniper's bullet killed the sergeant.

Hayes fared worst in postwar life. The quiet young man had grown up in a close-knit tribal community of two hundred and was troubled by the unwanted limelight of the bond tour and subsequent publicity. He became a problem drinker, unable to hold a job, and died of alcohol and exposure near his home in 1955, barely two months after the unveiling of the Marine Corps War Memorial.

Gagnon flirted briefly with a Hollywood career, after playing in The Sands of Iwo Jima with Hayes and Bradley, and then settled down to a position with an airline for nearly two decades. The end of his life was unhappy. A newspaper printed an unflattering Memorial Day interview in 1978 that got him fired from his job as a motel desk clerk. A year later he died of a heart attack while working as a maintenance man for an apartment complex.

Strank, Hayes, and Gagnon now lay buried in Arlington National Cemetery not far from the monument they inspired. Bradley returned to his hometown and his former business, setting up his own funeral home. He died in 1994, the last of the flag-raisers.

—JTH

Facing page: *In the foreground are two Marines who led the patrol that raised the flags over Iwo: 1stLt Harold Schrier and PlSgt Ernest "Boots" Thomas. To their rear are three men who photographed the event: Marine motion picture photographer SSgt William Genaust, Associated Press photographer Joe Rosenthal, and Marine combat photographer PFC Robert B. Campbell. Both Thomas and Genaust would die before the violent battle came to a close. (Photo: USMC)*

and the recollections of the survivors and in the end accepted Hayes's firm assertion. Cpl Block, like Hansen and Strank, had died on 1 March in the regiment's attack on Nishi Ridge.

The War Memorial

The flag-raising photograph inspired an enlisted Seabee stationed at Patuxent Naval Air Test Center in Maryland. Felix de Weldon was a particularly talented member of the Navy's construction corps. Born in Vienna, Austria, in 1907, he had trained as a sculptor and archaeologist and come to the United States in 1937, already an internationally known artist. Now, he saw the aesthetic potential in Rosenthal's photograph and over two intense days he created a small wax model for the grand statue he envisioned. The Navy Department set De Weldon to work on a life-size version made of plaster and coated to look like bronze. The three surviving flag-raisers posed for the sculptor, who used photographs to create likenesses of the others. De Weldon presented his completed work to President Harry S Truman in June 1945, and it was unveiled in front of the Navy Department Building on Constitution Avenue on 10 November. A twin went on national tour as part of the Victory Bond Drive.

The Marine Corps appreciated the possibilities of De Weldon's design as the basis of a permanent memorial to honor all Marines who had given their lives for their country since the organization of the Marines in 1775. In July 1947, Congress authorized the monument for the national capital. And three years later, the Marine Corps War Memorial Foundation, an independent corporation charged with raising funds and overseeing the erection of the memorial, contracted with De Weldon for a bronze casting of the scene that would be four times life size. The estimated cost was $350,000. In October 1950, while Marines battled new enemies in the snowy mountains of North Korea, General Clifton B. Cates, the commandant of the Marine Corps, made a ceremonial first contribution to the memorial fund and appealed to all Marines to raise the money themselves for their monument.

De Weldon began work at his cavernous studio in Washington, D.C., on a full-size plaster model. First he created the heads, five feet tall from the neck to the top of the helmet. The surviving flag-raisers sat again for their likenesses, with De Weldon working in clay and then casting the plaster renderings. He followed the same technique in constructing equipment and weapons to scale. The sculptor next created a pseudo-skeleton of steel, over which he modeled the bodies in the nude to depict realistically muscles straining to lift the pipe. Only then did he overlay the figures with uniforms, studying the texture of real cloth under a microscope to capture the details and carefully recreating the effect of wind and wear.

With the full-scale model finished, De Weldon broke it down into manageable pieces for shipment to a New York foundry. He carefully cut the statue into 108 parts that moved north in sixty-five truckloads. From the plaster sections, the foundry created molds and then poured the molten bronze. Artisans welded the pieces together around a bronze

framework, joining most of them into three large sections to form the bodies of the six flag-raisers.

As De Weldon's work progressed, the War Memorial Foundation and the Corps set their sights on a piece of land on the Virginia side of the Potomac River. This twenty-seven-acre parcel, known as the Nevius Tract, was adjacent to Arlington National Cemetery. From there, one could look across the water and down the Mall to see the Lincoln Memorial, the Washington Monument, and the Capitol all in a line. There was competition for this scenic plot, but ultimately the Fine Arts Commission and friends in Congress and the executive branch ensured

The Marine Corps War Memorial, at the edge of Arlington National Cemetery, looks across the Potomac to monuments to two great American war leaders, the Lincoln Memorial and the Washington Monument, and in the distance, the dome of the Capitol. The memorial, with its four-times-life-size figures, stands close to the south end of the Memorial Bridge. (Photo: USMC)

TMIHIEL BLANC·MONT·MEUSE – ARGONNE ✕ NICARAGUA 1926–1933

The 100-ton bronze statue was an engineering as well as an artistic triumph. Here, standing by the ladder, sculptor Felix de Weldon supervises the lifting of a carbine to its place in the finished sculpture. It took three years to create the full-size plaster model and turn it into bronze castings. Piece by piece, the bronze castings were hung from an internal steel skeleton or armature. (Photo: USMC)

that the Marines landed on the Nevius Tract and took it well in hand, though they would have to share it with The Netherlands carillon and were forbidden to place their memorial in direct line with the landmarks along the Mall.

The Marines found fund-raising as difficult in its own way as flag-raising had been. The foundation collected nearly $200,000 through the end of 1951, but the price of the monument soared because of wartime inflation and unforeseen additional expenses, such as the cost of landscaping the grounds. When General Lemuel C. Shepherd, Jr., took office as the commandant of the Marine Corps in January 1952, he continued Cates's policy of relying almost entirely on Marines as the source of money. He also asked retired Major General Merritt "Red Mike" Edson, a World War II Medal of Honor recipient, to assume the presidency of the foundation and infuse it with renewed vigor. With Shepherd's strong backing, Edson and the foundation raised more than a half million dollars in the next two years, most of it from newly minted Marine officers and enlisted men as they passed through training at Quantico, Parris Island, and San Diego.

Shepherd and Edson officiated at a ground-breaking ceremony for the memorial on 19 February 1954, the ninth anniversary of the Iwo

Jima landing, wielding the same shovel that had been used in similar rites for the Jefferson and Lincoln memorials. That fall, construction workers swarmed over the site, building access roads and pouring an octagonal concrete base sixty-six feet long, forty-six feet wide, and ten feet high. Inside they sealed a time capsule, which contained a print of the Rosenthal photograph, books about the Corps, a copy of "The Marines' Hymn," two vials of Iwo Jima sand, and other memorabilia. A mound of rough dark granite six feet high atop the base simulated the broken summit of Suribachi.

A trio of huge flatbed trucks delivered the three main segments of the statue and the remaining nine separate parts. Cranes lifted the pieces into place and workmen crawled inside to bolt and weld them together. With the last connection made, a man wriggled out through a trapdoor in a figure's cartridge belt and permanently sealed the exit.

By special act of Congress, the foundation imported, duty-free, polished black Swedish granite to face the pedestal. Artisans carved the battle honors of the Corps into the stone in four-inch gold-leafed Roman letters, forming a single band, or frieze, around the entire base. (General Shepherd personally reviewed the list; a southerner by birth, he decreed that the Civil War be called the War Between the States.) On one side, Marine Corps emblems flanked the inscription: "In honor and memory of the men of the United States Marine Corps who have given their lives to their country since

In creating his statue, Felix de Weldon, striving for absolute authenticity, met with the three surviving flag-raisers and used as his models Marines, properly uniformed and equipped, from Marine Barracks, Washington. (Photo: USMC)

Above: *Adm Chester Nimitz's much-quoted tribute to the Marines at Iwo Jima is incised within a wreath on the front of the base to the monument. (Photo: USMC)*

Right: *Wreaths are placed on the steps of the monument by many honored guests at ceremonies as well as by other visiting dignitaries. (Photo: USMC)*

10 November 1775." The opposite side displayed a wreath surrounding Fleet Admiral Chester W. Nimitz's famous tribute to the men who fought on Iwo Jima: "Uncommon valor was a common virtue."

Finally, landscapers planted two hundred trees and laid out the adjoining grass parade ground. The completed memorial, awe inspiring in size and beauty, rose seventy-eight feet from the ground to the tip of the flagpole. The bronze statue itself weighed one hundred tons. Final cost of the project was $850,000—paid for entirely by donations, with 96 percent of the total coming from Marines.

On 10 November 1954—the 179th anniversary of the Corps—thousands of Marines and their friends gathered to dedicate the memorial. President Dwight D. Eisenhower delivered the main address. Gagnon, Hayes, Bradley, Rosenthal, Schrier, Lindberg, Michels, and Lowery were among the guests.

Today the monument is the scene of frequent ceremonies large and small. On each birthday of the Corps, the Marine Corps Band, the Drum and Bugle Corps, and the drill unit of Marine Barracks, Washington, D.C., take to the parade ground to mark the occasion. The annual Marine Corps Marathon begins and ends in the shadow of the memorial. Many Marines use the majestic setting as a backdrop for reenlistment or retirement celebrations. The fiftieth anniversary of Iwo Jima in 1995 brought out the largest crowd since the monument's dedication, as the nation turned its eyes there and remembered the bloody battle that inspired De Weldon.

The flag-raising that thrilled a nation has continued to spark controversy as well. Some people have even seen conspiracies in the vastly uneven treatment of the two groups that placed the Stars and

The Marine Color Guard stands in front of the monument, flanked by Marines from the Washington barracks. The staff of the Marine colors is festooned with the many streamers marking the Corps' campaigns and battles. The monument site is the scene of many ceremonies, including weekly parades on Tuesday evenings during the summer season and a solemn observance marking the Marine Corps Birthday each 10th of November. (Photo: USMC)

Stripes on Suribachi. Gagnon was once quoted to the effect that the Corps had purposely "covered up" the first raising because the later one was better for public relations. A 1993 book by two art historians gave the impression that the second raising was a fraud that gave rise to "a national myth." And Sherrod begrudged the Rosenthal photograph its due, referring to it disparagingly in 1980 as "the salon painting of World War II."

The Marine Corps Drum and Bugle Corps, "The Commandant's Own," performs on the steps of the monument. This musical aggregation, in its bright scarlet coats, considers itself the lineal descendants of the Corps' original fifers and drummers. (Photo: USMC)

During the Korean War, one Army officer was reported to have complained that the famous photograph prompted Marines to raise a flag over every captured town or piece of terrain. Colonel Lewis B. "Chesty" Puller, the storied recipient of an unprecedented five Navy Crosses for valor in combat, put a quick end to that gripe. He reputedly growled in reply that the best fighter was "a man with a flag in his pack and the desire to put it on an enemy strongpoint."

Parade Blue, Battle Green

Parade Blue, Battle Green

Lieutenant Colonel Charles H. Cureton, USMCR

I n the beginning, Marines wore distinctive uniforms so they would not kill each other on the battlefield—for much the same reason a football team wears highly distinctive jerseys and helmets. But since modern weapons have changed the battlefield, these warfighting distinctions have been put away, and at work Marines now clothe themselves in camouflage, whether jungle green or desert brown.

Marines still retain the earlier distinctions in their dress uniforms that let them stand out in any parade. Dark blue dress coats with a standing collar that has the remnant of a leather stock around the neck. Lighter blue trousers with blood-red stripes down the sides. Mameluke sword for officers.

No uniform is more immediately recognizable than Marine "blues," but whether blue, green, or khaki, Marines are set apart by their uniforms. The uniforms and insignia Marines wear today proudly link them with Marines of the past.

In the beginning, Continental Marines wore green coats, their lapels at first "faced" with buff-white, and buff-white waistcoats and breeches. The "facings" were soon changed to a more striking red. But there was little to distinguish Marines from Continental soldiers or state militia except the fouled anchor on their buttons.

A Marine legend has it that green was chosen for the coat to show that Marines were riflemen, a practice common with rifle units in European armies. But the Continental Marines were musketeers, not riflemen. Green seems to have been chosen simply because green cloth was plentiful in Philadelphia at the time. A prominent group of Philadelphia militia called "the Associators" wore similar uniforms.

The same pragmatic reasoning ruled when the U.S. Marine Corps, as such, was established in July 1798. Its first uniforms were made from

Portrait of 1stLt Charles R. Broom in winter dress was painted about 1813. Hair was no longer worn in a queue or powdered. His sword sling bears a gilt brass plate with an eagle-and-anchor design on its face. Broom was commissioned in 1813, served at Sacketts Harbor on Lake Ontario during the War of 1812, was breveted a lieutenant colonel in 1834, and died in 1836. (Artist unknown. Marine Corps Art Collection.)

clothing contracted for Major General "Mad Anthony" Wayne's army legion but never issued. The coat was of dark blue broadcloth faced red. Brass naval buttons were substituted for army buttons and red waistcoats replaced white—and the Marines had their uniforms. And that is why Marines today wear dress blue uniforms.

Early enlisted men wore short coats called "coatees" with blue shoulder straps edged in red, and blue pantaloons with outer seams edged with red. They were worn with a red waistcoat, white cotton shirt, and black leather stock. Each Marine topped off with a black woolen hat trimmed with yellow, turned up on the left side with a leather cockade. Sergeants wore a red feather plume on their hat, a yellow silk epaulet on each shoulder, and carried a brass-mounted sword. Corporals were distinguished by a single epaulet on the right shoulder.

Officers wore a long dark blue coat with scarlet facings. Waistcoats were scarlet and breeches were dark blue. Rank was distinguished by one or two gold epaulets. Black hussar boots and a black cocked hat called a "chapeau" completed the officer uniform.

The term "Leatherneck" comes from the leather stock that both enlisted men and officers wore. Sailors came to call Marines "Leather-necks," among other less complimentary names, and the nickname has stuck. Post-Civil War Marine regulations dropped the stock–but not quite. In place of the stiff leather stock, a strip of black glazed leather was attached to the inside front of the dress uniform's collar. The Marines' modern dress uniform has a cloth tab that lays behind the front of the collar—the last reminder of the leather stock.

About 1804, the Marine Corps adopted new uniforms patterned after those being worn by the British in the Napoleonic Wars—a single breasted coatee for enlisted men and a double-breasted coat for officers. The colors stayed the same: blue faced with red. The lapels of the officers' coat were now worn buttoned across the chest instead of buttoned back as on the 1798 uniform. The coats were trimmed with gold "lace," as braid was called. When Marine junior officers complained of the coat's cost, the commandant, showing that sense of humor expected of senior officers, replaced it with a single-breasted uniform that was even more expensive.

Enlisted uniforms were equally impressive, but their trimmings were of pale yellow wool tape instead of gold lace. The remainder of the enlisted uniform consisted of white breeches, black cloth gaiters, and a leather cylindrical cap called a "shako" with a brass plate bearing an eagle and the motto "Fortitudine" meaning "with courage." Privates and musicians wore a red plush plume and a yellow cord braided hat band and tassel. Sergeants were even more elegant with the red feather plume, epaulets, and sword.

Another feature of the 1804 uniform was the wide scarlet silk net sash worn by officers. It was possible to determine whether an officer was on duty, off duty, or officer of the day simply by the presence of the sash and how it was worn. Sashes went out of American military fashion after the Civil War. The Marine Corps made two exceptions: The commandant continued to wear a distinctive buff-yellow sash and junior officers, acting as officer of the day, still wore a crimson sash over their shoulder. The red cummerbund worn with the present day officers' evening dress uniform is all that remains of the once ubiquitous sash.

Senior noncommissioned officers wore sashes until 1875. Two patterns were specified: a red worsted sash for orderly sergeants and first sergeants, and an officer-style crimson silk net version for the sergeant major, quartermaster sergeant, and leader of the band.

Officers were initially allowed swords of any style just so long as they were yellow-mounted. In 1825 Quartermaster Elijah Weed ordered Mameluke-hilted swords from England. Except for the period from 1859 to 1875, Marine officers have carried this sword ever since.

In 1804, Marine officers stopped wearing naval buttons and began using a button that had an eagle with wings extended in flight and an anchor grasped at an angle. It took about twenty years before enlisted Marines had a similar button. It has scarcely changed since.

In the beginning, Marines wore black leather shoulder belts from

This Marine captain is an aide-de-camp to the president of the United States as indicated by the gold aiguillette on his right shoulder. Aides to general officers wear the aiguillette on the left shoulder. Beginning in 1798, officers wore a red and, later, a crimson silk sash around their waist. The sash was discontinued from general use in 1875, but a vestige survives today in the red cummerbund worn with evening dress. (Photo: Greg E. Mathieson)

Buttons worn by officers and enlisted Marines today are virtually the same, other than the change in the number of points on the thirteen stars from six to five, as when first adopted in 1804.

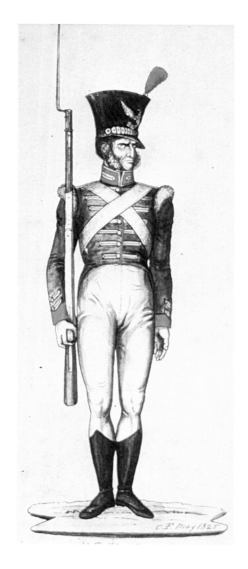

A Marine private painted about 1824 by Marine Lt Charles R. Floyd shows the uniform prescribed three years earlier. Enlisted uniforms changed frequently during the first half of the nineteenth century, but the tall bell-crown cap endured until just before the Civil War. (Marine Corps Art Collection)

which to hang their Army-pattern accouterments. But the black belts did not last as well as belts made of white buff leather. The Corps began changing to white buff leather belts in 1806, and white belts have been prescribed for enlisted dress uniforms ever since.

Officers after 1821 wore waist belts of black leather for field duty, and white waist belts for dress and parade. In the 1870s, the dress belt was adorned by the addition of gold lace. This belt was standard until into the 1930s and continues to be worn by the principal officers of the Marine Band.

Musket slings were rarely used by early Marines. Barracks Marines on guard duty didn't need them, and when shipboard Marines went aloft to the "tops" of sailing warships, their muskets were bundled together, placed in a basket, and hauled up by rope. When Marines served ashore on lengthy land campaigns, such as in the Seminole War in the late 1830s and the Mexican War, 1846-1848, the quartermaster acquired leather slings from the Army, along with canteens and haversacks.

Chevrons were introduced in 1821 as a means of determining rank. The commandant prescribed a system of "angles" to be worn on the sleeves of the dress uniform, by junior officers as well as NCOs. They were large, similar in size and form to the present-day chevrons worn by West Point cadets. Chevrons for officers went out in 1834.

President Andrew Jackson insisted that the Marine uniform be changed from dark blue to the green worn during the Revolutionary War. To try to comply with his wish, the 1834 uniform regulations changed the uniform from blue and red to green and white and divided officer uniforms into three basic categories, "dress," "undress," and "service." Enlisted men had "uniform" dress and "fatigue" dress.

Problems arose. First, there was not enough green broadcloth available on the American market to meet Marine Corps needs and the

In this portrait, 2dLt Addison Garland is wearing the uniform specified in 1834 that returned the Corps to the Revolutionary War colors of grass green faced with buff-white. Trousers were dove gray with a buff-white stripe on the outside seam. Garland was commissioned in 1834, reached the grade of major in 1861, and died in 1864. (Artist unknown: Marine Corps Art Collection)

The red-edged cuff flap and three buttons on the enlisted Marine blue dress coat are all that remain of the elaborate cuff decorations adopted in 1839. (Artist: LtCol Donna J. Neary, USMCR. Marine Corps Art Collection)

quartermaster was forced to buy the material from Great Britain, America's enemy in two wars, at higher cost. Second, the green dyes of the period were terrible. Complaints about the new uniforms poured into headquarters. Some barracks commanders claimed that the coats lost their original color after only one day's use. At sea the effects of sun, rain, and salt water on the coats were even worse – some turned yellow, others a strange blue-green. The commandant, Colonel Archibald Henderson, absorbed the complaints and said nothing until President Jackson left office. In 1839 the commandant simply returned the uniform to its by now traditional dark blue and red.

The cuff on the sleeve of the present day enlisted dress coat began with the 1834 design, only it then had a real purpose. Its function was to allow the cuff to be unbuttoned so the hand could fit through the tight sleeve, and it was designed to distinguish the various rank groups with a system of gold "lace" or worsted loops. The three buttons still on the cuff once held the now discarded loops of lace.

For generations Marine drill instructors have solemnly told recruits that the scarlet stripe on the blue trousers of Marine officers and noncom-missioned officers are "blood stripes" in honor of Marines killed in storming Chapultepec in Mexico City in 1847. Interesting but not true. The wearing of stripes on the trousers began in 1834, following the Army's practice of having trouser stripes the color of the facings. Col Henderson

prescribed buff-white stripes for officers and sergeants. When in 1839 the uniform changed back to dark blue coats faced red, officer trouser stripes became dark blue edged in red. Ten years later officer stripes changed to red and in 1859 the uniform regulations prescribed a scarlet welt inserted into the outer seam for officers, and a scarlet cord for staff noncommissioned officers and musicians. After more variations were tried, finally, in 1904 the simple and striking all-scarlet stripe was adopted.

The 1839 regulations also brought in light blue trousers for enlisted Marines and line officers, dark blue trousers for staff officers. General officers still wear dark blue trousers. White trousers were

In this contemporary Huddy and Duval print, the lieutenant on the left, his rank indicated by the two loops on his cuff, wears the 1839 winter dress uniform with light blue trousers. His tall cap with plume and brass plate is at his right elbow. The captain on the right, with three loops on his cuff, is in summer dress with white trousers. His assignment to the staff is indicated by his aiguillette and chapeau. Both carry the Mameluke-hilted officers' sword. (Marine Corps Art Collection)

Top right: *This plate from the uniform regulations of 1859 shows two staff officers (in chapeaus) and two line officers (in French-style caps) in summer full dress. Combining white trousers with the dress coats for summer wear began in 1821 and continues today. During winter months, staff officers wore dark blue trousers and line officers light blue. (Marine Corps Historical Library)*

Bottom right: Officer undress uniforms adopted in 1859 included the French-style kepi *or cap with the crown tilted rakishly to the front. Such caps, usually associated with the Civil War, served both the Army and Marine Corps for half a century. (Marine Corps Historical Library)*

During the Civil War, ColComdt John Harris wore this dress coat and chapeau, now in the Marine Corps Museum at the Washington (D.C.) Navy Yard. The undress coat of the time was nearly identical but with plain cuffs and shoulder knots instead of epaulets. (Photo: Eric Long)

worn during the summer—and were reinstated in recent years.

French Second Empire influences were strong in the 1859 uniform regulations. The stylized four-leaf quatrefoil knot, as French as its name, was placed on the top of officers' service and dress caps. It has endured, buttressed by the myth that John Paul Jones's Marines chalked crosses on the tops of their hats in boarding fights at sea so their comrades high in the fighting tops would not mistake them for the enemy. The 1859 service cap copied the French *kepi*, and similar caps continued in use in both the Army and Marine Corps into the 1890s.

The style of the modern enlisted dress uniform originated with the 1859 regulations. That version was very simple, consisting of a dark blue, knee-length frock coat, single breasted with seven Marine buttons down the front, and a red welt inserted in the bottom seam of the collar. In the 1890s, the coat was restyled and given a collar edged all around in red, a red-edged cuff flap with three buttons, and red-edged shoulder straps. In 1904 red edging was added to the front and skirts of the coat. Pockets and a cloth waist belt were added in 1946.

The 1859 regulations also brought in the sword still carried by

Marine noncommissioned officers. The design is based on the 1850 Army foot officers' sword, which Marine officers carried from 1859 to 1875.

In 1868, Brigadier General Commandant Jacob Zeilin convened a board of officers to decide upon a cap ornament to replace the bugle horn that had been adopted in 1859. Starting with a silver globe of the Western Hemisphere "surmounted by a Silver eagle . . . with wings extended," the familiar eagle, globe, and anchor emblem emerged and was approved by Secretary of the Navy Gideon Welles on 30 November 1868. In May 1875, new uniform regulations made this the sole emblem of the United States Marine Corps.

The 1875 and 1892 regulations introduced a series of uniforms that showed both British and German influences. (France had gone down to defeat in the Franco-Prussian War.) The system of cuff lacing adopted in 1875 originated with the British Army and its use by Marine officers was unique among the American services. Essentially, the sleeves of company grade officers were decorated by what was called an "Austrian" knot, with braid added in increasing amounts to indicate successive grades from second lieutenant to captain. Field grade officers' cuffs followed a similar pattern but with a wide band of gold lace in the shape of a chevron instead of the Austrian knot. The pointed cuff on today's

Enlisted dress and undress uniforms as illustrated in the 1859 uniform regulations show a strong French Second Empire influence. Today's enlisted blue uniform is directly descended from the uniform worn by the private on the right. (Marine Corps Historical Library)

This sword adopted in 1859 for both officers and noncommissioned officers was a close copy of the Army model 1851 foot officers' sword. Marine officers returned to the Mameluke sword in 1875, but NCOs continue to wear the 1859 model sword on ceremonial occasions. (Photo: USMC)

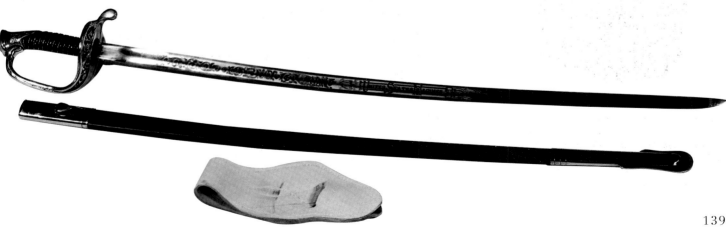

Top left: *Officers as they appear in the 1875 uniform regulations, from left to right: full dress, undress, and fatigue. French influences continue, but with the fall of the Second Empire in the Franco-Prussian War and the ascendancy of the British Empire elsewhere, British influence begins to dominate. (Marine Corps Historical Library)*

Top right: *Enlisted Marines in their 1875 uniforms. From left to right, a private in undress blues with "pillbox" hat; a private ready for guard mount with white gloves and white belt; and a lordly first sergeant with double-breasted coat, epaulets, pompom on his cap, and wearing the 1859 model sword. (Marine Corps Historical Library)*

Marine Corps uniforms originated with the field grade officers' chevron but without the lace and tracing braid.

"Mess dress" was another British Army uniform introduced into the Marine Corps in 1875. In the early nineteenth century British officers in India began wearing short jackets at dinner, white linen in summer, blue cloth in cooler weather. The white mess jacket disappeared from Marine Corps usage in the 1980s, but the blue jacket survives as evening dress.

The fatigue coat of 1875, called a "patrol jacket" by the British, became the Marine undress coat for officers until replaced in 1908 by the present-day blue uniform. The hat was regulation from 1898 until 1912 (in 1904 the emblem moved from side to front), and the canteen is of the pattern used from 1875 until 1912. (Marine Corps Museum, Washington. Photo: Eric Long)

The 1875 mess dress and kepi are worn by 2dLt William Freeman Zeilin, son of BrigGenComdt Jacob Zeilin. Present day officers' evening dress uniform is much the same. The photograph was taken about 1878 by Mathew Brady's rival, Alexander Gardner, and is in the form of a carte de visite, *the photographic calling card that became popular during the Civil War. (Original: Marine Air-Ground Museum, Quantico)*

The full dress uniform worn by the Marine Band of today does not differ much from that of 1875. (Photo: Greg E, Mathieson)

Also copied from the British, was an elegant dark-blue, single-breasted officers' coat, trimmed with black mohair hussar-style braiding, called by the British a "patrol jacket" and by the Marines a "fatigue coat." It remained in use until 1908 when it was replaced by the present-day officers' dress coat. The hussar-style braiding survives in the full-dress uniform worn today by the Marine Band.

Most present day service and dress uniforms are little changed from designs adopted in 1904, when clothing intended for work and field duty replaced the nineteenth century's conspicuous blue, red, white, and yellow with drab-colored material. The 1904 khaki summer service dress was based on late nineteenth century British uniforms which had seen considerable use in India, Egypt, and South Africa. The design adopted by the Marine Corps (and the U.S. Army) consisted of a khaki

Above: *Marines fighting in the Philippine Insurrection (1899-1904) usually wore the soft field hat, khaki trousers and leggings, and blue wool flannel shirts. Wool flannel, once soaked with sweat, was thought to be cooler than cotton. Mustard-colored flannel shirts came later and were worn by Marines as late as the Korean War. (Photo: USMC)*

Below: *Boys as young as fourteen could enlist as musicians in the nineteenth century. This boy trumpeter and boy drummer, in their white summer spiked helmets, served in the USS* Massachusetts *about 1892. (Photo: USMC)*

cotton coat, single-breasted with five buttons down the front, standing collar, shoulder straps, pointed cuffs, and four pockets—one on each breast and one on each skirt.

There were no stylistic differences between the 1904 summer service coat and the dark blue undress officers' coat adopted in 1908 or the forest green winter service coat adopted in 1912.

Adoption of earth-toned service uniforms was occurring all over the world as a practical response to dramatic late-nineteenth-century technological improvements in weaponry that made the wearing of conspicuous uniforms on the battlefield the province of the ontologically challenged. Officer service dress included breeches or trousers, russet leather puttees or boots, and a field or "campaign" hat. Khaki "frame" caps included the eagle-globe-and-anchor emblem in bronze in front and the quatrefoil on top.

Marine second lieutenants, as well as their counterparts in the American and British armies, did not yet have rank insignia for their service uniforms. The uniform itself was sufficiently distinctive to show that the wearer was an officer, but one had to know that the lack of grade insignia on the shoulder straps indicated the rank of second lieutenant. Not until the massive military expansion of World War I did the gold bar come in as a less cerebral way of telling the rank of second lieutenants.

The first model of what would become the "Smokey the Bear" hat associated today with Marine drill instructors entered Marine Corps service in 1898 when Lieutenant Colonel Robert W. Huntington's First Battalion of Marines received brown linen campaign suits and campaign hats following

the seizure of Guantanamo, Cuba. Those Marine hats were identical to the contemporary Army 1885 model, tan in color, and creased "fore and aft." Officers' hats carried a gold-and-red hat cord. The Corps emblem in bronze was worn by both officers and enlisted men on the left side of the hat. In 1904, the emblem device shifted to the front. The 1885 model hat remained in use until 1912 when it was replaced by the "Montana" peaked campaign hat. This much-loved hat remained in general use until 1942 when it fell victim to wartime economies. In 1961, the hat reappeared as "Hat, Service, Campaign," but authorized only for rifle and pistol team members, permanent range personnel, and drill instructors.

The enlisted service coat of 1904 differed from the officer version in two important respects: The skirts had no lower pockets and the collar was devoid of insignia. Instead of breeches, enlisted men wore khaki trousers tucked into canvas leggings. A more practical summer uniform for extremely hot weather was created by substituting a wool shirt, first blue and then mustard-colored, for the coat.

"Forest green" was introduced with the 1912 winter service uniform, and five years later Marines wore this uniform in France. The color contrasted strongly with the Army's newly adopted olive drab. Then, beginning in January 1918, Marines in France were issued Army olive drab uniforms, supposedly to simplify the supply situation and to prevent easy identification of Marine units by the Germans. Despite this mandated change, all Marine officers and many Marine enlisted continued to wear their green uniforms.

Marines' service in France in First World War I resulted in a host of uniform changes. An admiring Franklin D. Roosevelt, then the assistant secretary of the Navy, visited the Marine brigade after the battle of Soissons and authorized, on the spot, collar insignia for enlisted Marines. Initially manufactured in France, the badge was a circular Army-pattern collar

Above: *Marines ashore in Shanghai, China, for a Memorial Day parade in May 1913 wore the summer service khaki uniform introduced in 1904. All wear the old-style campaign hat, creased "fore and aft," except for the officer commanding the center platoon who wears new, stiffer hat with four dents, forming the so-called "Montana peak." Today the same hat is worn by drill instructors and designated rifle range personnel. (Photo: USMC)*

The dress helmet was adopted in 1882 and lasted until 1904. Helmets of majors and above officers were plumed; helmets of junior officers and enlisted Marines had spikes. This helmet was worn by Col Henry Clay Cochrane and is now in the Marine Corps Museum at the Washington Navy Yard. (Photo: Eric Long)

SgtMaj Henry L. Hulbert, in about 1910, wears his special full dress uniform. Hulbert received his Medal of Honor, the ribbon of which is worn around his neck, for heroism in Samoa in 1899. In March 1917 he was one of the first to be promoted to the new warrant officer grade of "Marine gunner." In July 1918, in France, he was commissioned a second lieutenant and was a first lieutenant when he was killed in action at Blanc Mont on 4 October 1918. (Photo: USMC)

Yellow stripes on a red background have been used for enlisted insignia since the 1820s. Chevrons for the dress uniform became much smaller after World War I. Crossed rifles used with most chevrons signal the tradition of every Marine a rifleman.

disk, but with the eagle, globe, and anchor instead of the Army's branch symbols. In 1920 the disk was replaced by a simplified version of the officers' emblem, gilt for the blue uniform, bronze for the khaki and green.

During the closing weeks of fighting in late 1918, the American Expeditionary Forces commander, General John J. Pershing, authorized the creation of shoulder patches for his divisions, corps, and armies. Men of the 4th Marine Brigade wore the badge of the Army's 2d Infantry Division, an Indian head within a white star upon a variety of different shaped and colored backgrounds denoting the size and nature of the unit. The 5th Marine Brigade, which arrived late in the war, wore a patch with a "V" on a silhouette of the Marine Corps emblem.

Army-style wound and overseas service chevrons were authorized and continued to be worn by Marines on the lower coat sleeve of their winter service coats until 1920. A World War I uniform embellishment that survives to this day is the red-and-green fourragere representing multiple awards of the Croix de Guerre to the 5th and 6th Marine Regiments; it is still worn by those regiments.

Pershing admired greatly the British Sam Browne belt and he ordered it worn by officers in the AEF. Marine officers called the Sam Browne a "Peter Bain," after a favorite manufacturer. It was worn until 1942 when it was replaced by a cloth belt as a wartime economy. After the war it returned on a limited basis for parade and ceremonial use.

Admiration for the comfortable roll collar worn by British officers caused a shift from the standing-collar to the roll-collar coat for both enlisted and officers in 1928. Ten years later the enlisted summer service coat was abolished, and the khaki shirt (sometimes cotton, sometimes wool), field scarf (as Marines called their necktie), and trousers remained as "intermediate weather summer service dress." Not until 1972 did khaki uniforms cease to be worn altogether. Their vestiges are the khaki tie, the khaki service belt, and khaki shirts.

In 1963, the green kersey used for enlisted service uniforms since 1912 was discontinued and replaced by wool serge of a slightly lighter shade of green. Buttons and collar devices changed from bronze to black. Leather items, such as cap visors, shoes, and sword belts, went from cordovan brown to black.

After 1922, regulations stipulated medals for dress, ribbons and badges for undress. During World War II the blue uniform was made optional for officers. It returned as a required uniform in 1948, slightly modified and with a blue cloth belt instead of the leather "Peter Bain."

Before World War I officers wore a lightweight white summer uniform, made of cotton and unlined. It kept the standing collar which continued in use until, after much debate, it went off the uniform list in the early 1990s. By then the blue uniforms were being made of a lighter weight "all season" fabric, and in the summer the blue coat was authorized for wear with white trousers by both officers and enlisted.

"Special full dress" of 1904 is a uniform that no longer exists. It was discontinued for enlisted in 1912 and for officers in 1922. Traces of it can still be found in the oak leaf embroidery on the visors of field grade and general officer caps and on the cuffs of their evening dress. The gold

lace stripes worn on officers' evening dress trousers, and the shoulder knots worn by the Marine Band, also originated with the special full dress uniform.

Divisional and other unit shoulder patches came back into use during the World War II and were discontinued again in 1948. Shortages of service uniforms in 1943 for Marines recuperating in Australia after the battle for Guadalcanal caused a temporary issue of brownish olive drab Australian battle jackets. The Marines wore their jackets pressed open to show their khaki shirts and ties. The jacket was then copied in both green and khaki and became known as the "Vandegrift" jacket after the commander of the 1st Marine Division, much as a trimmer version of the British battle jacket was called the "Eisenhower" jacket in the Army.

The "unification" battle after World War II and a perceived need to level the differences between officers and enlisted created a recommendation that all services and all ranks be put into the same uniform (a recommendation adopted by Canada for its armed forces). In the United States the recommendation was equally distasteful to the Army, Navy, the new Air Force, and the Marines. For a time, though, Marine officers were required to maintain a complete set of enlisted green and khaki uniforms.

Women first enlisted in the Marine Corps during World War I and again during World War II. In the latter the designer Mainbocher developed a line of feminine Marine clothing that was as fashionable as it was distinctive. By the 1970s, as the role of women changed in society and as the Marine Corps expanded its recruitment of women, their uniforms

Mainbocher designed the subdued elegance of the winter service uniform worn by World War II Woman Marines. The lighter weight forest green material used the same buttons and emblems as those used on men's uniforms. Regulations decreed that women's lipstick match the scarlet cord on her service cap. (Marine Corps Museum, Washington. Photo: Eric Long)

moved closer to the mainstream of male Marines' clothing. Fabrics and colors and many items are now the same for all Marines. Women's service and dress uniforms, however, retain certain feminine features—buttoning on the left, fitted shirts, different service caps, and, of course, different undergarments.

Two considerations provide the basic criteria for the inclusion or exclusion of Marine Corps clothing items. The "sea bag," the enlisted issue of clothing received at the recruit depots, has to be within a cost ceiling, which now hovers around $1,000. For every new item added, something has to go. This is not so much the case with officers who must purchase their uniforms. Presently, a second lieutenant pays about one month's salary for his minimum uniform requirements.

Watching over this process, rationalizing changes, developing new material, and ensuring continuity has been the Permanent Marine Corps Uniform Board. It was established in the nineteenth century and revived in 1952 by the then commandant, General Lemuel C. Shepherd. Among the Uniform Board's innovations have been the "woolly-pully" service sweater taken from the British, and the all-weather "trench" coat and the "tanker" jacket. All these have been subsequently adopted in close copies by the Army, Navy, and Air Force.

Ancestors of today's combat or "utility" uniforms date to the War of 1812 period when gray jackets were provided for fatigue duties. From 1898 to World War II, khaki sufficed for the tropical climates where most Marines served. For dirty work, such as vehicle maintenance, blue denim overalls and jacket were provided. In 1941, the denim uniform was phased out in favor of a sage-green herringbone twill (HBT) utility jacket and trousers. A mechanic's cap, adopted in 1943, preceded the utility cap now used by both the Marine Corps and the Navy. Utility uniforms of various designs in both sage-green and camouflage were worn during World War II. With the wide popularity of the photograph of the flag-raising on Iwo Jima, the utility uniform became synonymous with the Marine Corps in the eyes of much of the American public.

This Marine rifleman in Viet Nam in 1967, as seen by combat artist Isa Barnett, looks much like the Marine of World War II and Korea. (Marine Corps Art Collection)

Facing page, bottom left: *On the 4th of July, 1944, PFC Raymond L. Hubert pauses in the fighting on Saipan to sit on a 16-inch shell that has failed to explode while he empties coral sand from his "boondocker" shoes. His fighting uniform is reduced to his helmet with camouflage cloth cover and his tattered green "herringbone twill" utility coat and trousers. A crucifix hangs at his throat next to his "dog tag" identification disks. (Photo: SSgt A. B. Knight, USMC)*

Facing page, right: *Marines on Iwo Jima hunker down in the volcanic sands in the shadow of Mount Suribachi. In World War II, the green utility uniforms and camouflaged helmet covers became as familiar a Marine Corps image, signifying battlefield prowess, as the parade ground "dress blues." (Photo: USMC)*

During the Persian Gulf War, all services wore the "chocolate chip" desert camouflage uniform. Name patches and minute differences in insignia were all that distinguished Marines from soldiers. (Photo: Greg E. Mathieson)

In the late 1950s, the Army-developed "green sateen" uniform replaced the HBT. It, in turn, was replaced by the Army's green poplin jungle uniform for Marines serving in Viet Nam. This uniform, with its four bellows pockets, was patterned after the Army's 1941 parachutists' jump uniform. A camouflage pattern "Southeast Asia" uniform replaced the green poplins in the latter stages of the Viet Nam War. Meanwhile the green sateens remained the standard utility uniform outside of Viet Nam. The practice of laundering the sateen uniform with starch to achieve a crisp appearance made for the daily ritual of "breaking starch" (often with a knife, bayonet blade, or foot)—the signature of a "squared away" Marine.

The Uniform Board favored the cargo-carrying four-pocket coat over the two-pocket sateen uniform. In 1978, the Marine Corps was the first service to begin general issue of jungle utilities. This pattern was replaced in 1982 by the "woodland camouflage" utility uniform designed for all services. A desert "chocolate chip" version of the woodland utility uniform was worn during the Persian Gulf War and, in time, was replaced by a predominantly tan pattern.

There is little likelihood that the Marine dress and service uniforms will undergo significant changes in the near future. Some uniforms may go out of use, as happened to the white summer dress, but the current service and dress uniforms have become so much a part of the Marine image, and so steeped in the Marine heritage, that altering or doing away with them will not occur without a great deal of soul searching.

Utility and specialist clothing are another matter. Functional garments constantly evolve as new materials, color patterns, chemical and biological resistant capabilities, infrared signature protection, and other features relating to battlefield survivability and personal comfort become available. Yet, even with utility clothing, every garment represents a piece of Marine Corps history. The Marine emblem with "USMC" stamped on the pockets of utility coats is as evocative to Marines as the emblems they wear on their dress and service uniforms. Whether romanticized or not, how Marine uniforms came to be is not as important as the history they have come to embody.

THESE 1983 UNIFORM plates, following in the tradition of the uniform plates of the nineteenth century, were developed jointly by the History and Museums Division and the Permanent Marine Corps Uniform Board of Headquarters, U.S., Marine Corps, and were executed by the distinguished military artist, LtCol Donna J. Neary, USMCR, then a captain. Each figure is the portrait of an actual Marine. The plates show the full gamut of Marine Corps uniforms as they were at that time. Regulations provided that a set of these uniform plates be posted in each Marine barracks and installation as a guide to the proper wear of uniforms. Changes have been few since 1983: A "tanker jacket" has been added as an informal outer garment; the summer white dress uniforms and white mess jacket are no longer worn.

PLATE I, OFFICERS' SERVICE UNIFORMS.

PLATE II, ENLISTED SERVICE UNIFORMS.

PLATE III, OFFICERS' BLUE DRESS UNIFORMS.

PLATE IV, ENLISTED BLUE DRESS UNIFORMS.

PLATE V, EVENING DRESS UNIFORMS.

PLATE VI, MESS DRESS AND WHITE DRESS UNIFORMS.

PLATE VII, U.S. MARINE BAND (THE PRESIDENT'S OWN).

PLATE VIII, MARINE BARRACKS CEREMONIAL UNIFORMS.

PLATE IX, AVIATION CLOTHING.

PLATE X, FIELD UNIFORMS.

PLATE XIII, DESERT BATTLE UNIFORMS

Muskets
to Missiles

Muskets to Missiles

Colonel Brooke Nihart, USMC (Ret)

Marines fought the British in the battle for New Orleans on 8 January 1815 using smoothbore muskets modeled on the French Charleville. Best shots on the field, however, were not the Marines but Kentucky and Tennessee backwoodsmen armed with Pennsylvania rifles, slow-loading but deadly accurate. Marine prowess with the rifle would come much later. ("The Battle of New Orleans," Col Charles Waterhouse, USMCR (Ret), Marine Corps Art Collection)

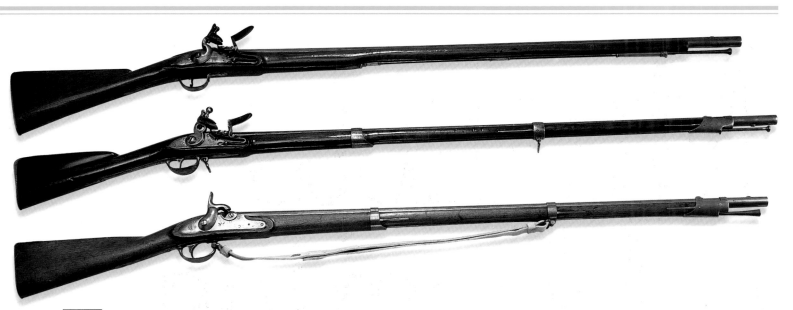

The foot soldier's—and the Marine's—weapon from the American Revolution through the War of 1812 was a smoothbore flintlock musket. It began as any one of several models of the .75 caliber British "Tower" or "Brown Bess" musket ("Tower" was for the Tower of London where the muskets were made and stored and "Brown Bess" for the color of the stock). Continental Marines preferred the "short sea service" version, when they could get it, since it was handier in the confines of a ship. To protect against salt water corrosion at sea, the fittings of muskets were of brass, and the barrels and locks were tin-plated whenever possible.

Through the efforts of Benjamin Franklin and Silas Deane, the American representatives in Paris, the colonies received large numbers of French .69 caliber Charleville muskets, and by the last years of the war they more or less replaced the Brown Bess.

With independence, national arsenals were established at Springfield, Massachusetts, and Harpers Ferry, Virginia. The first musket they produced was the M1795, a copy of the M1763 Charleville. The arsenals closely followed French developments and copied each change through the U.S. M1842 musket. Marines used them all.

For the most part, Marines have used the same weapons as the U.S. Army in order to be assured of the availability of the weapon and its ammunition. However, when a more effective weapon became available, the Marines have always been ready to test it and, if found suitable, to adopt it.

Marines did not use rifles in the Revolution and did not become known as expert rifle marksmen until many years later. Close range combat of the day did not require the longer range and precision (nor justify the cost) of the rifle. A trained man could get off only two to three shots a minute with the cheaper smoothbore; but the more expensive rifle took even longer to load. The musket's range of one hundred yards or less made it effective against massed formations in land combat. For sea-going Marines, in the fighting tops or in boarding parties, the action was at fifty yards or less. At that distance, a trained man could be expected to hit a man-sized target.

To board an enemy ship or in a final assault on land, Marines

Top to bottom: *Three Marine basic weapons of the muzzle-loading smoothbore period: the .75 caliber British "Tower" or "Brown Bess," the French .69 caliber Charleville, and the .69 caliber Springfield M1816 converted to percussion-lock from flintlock. (Marine Corps Museum. Photo: Eric Long)*

Below: *A Continental Marine of 1776 with a Charleville musket, a drum emblazoned with a rattlesnake and "Don't tread on me," Grand Union flag in background. (Artist: MGySgt Wendell A. "Tex" Parks, Marine Corps Art Collection)*

Previous spread: *A Marine in desert camouflage fires the Swedish AT-4 anti-tank rocket launcher. This hand-held weapon, with its 300-meter effective range, was used successfully by Marines against Soviet-type armor in the Persian Gulf War. (Photo: Greg E. Mathieson)*

Top: *Continental Marines, returning from a raid on New Providence, Bahamas, suffer first casualties as they engage a British ship with muskets and assist in manning the broadside cannon. ("The First Casualties," Col Charles Waterhouse, USMCR (Ret), Marine Corps Art Collection)*

Above: *LtColComdt Archibald Henderson's Mameluke-hilt M1829 officers' sword commemorated Marines' service against North African pirates. Essentially the same sword, with its brass scabbard first changed to nickel-plated and then to chromium-plated, is carried today by Marine officers on ceremonial occasions. (Marine Corps Museum. Photo: Eric Long)*

relied on the Brown Bess's bayonet and on a short, brass-barreled flintlock blunderbuss. In the confusion of combat, the latter's flared muzzle made it easy to reload with a charge of powder followed by a handful of buckshot, rocks, nails, or whatever nastiness was available. The blunderbuss evolved into the shotgun, and in the 1847 attack on Mexico City, Marine Major Levi Twiggs carried his favorite double-barreled shotgun. For the trench assaults in France in World War I, Marines adopted repeating shotguns, and used them again in the close combat of jungle fighting in World War II and Viet Nam.

The seven-barrel topman's musket, built first by a London gunsmith named Nock, gave Marines another competitive edge in close ship-to-ship combat. A Nock flintlock fired all seven barrels at once and the effect against an enemy's fighting top, officers and helmsman on the quarterdeck, or a gun crew was devastating. The recoil against the Marine firing the Nock was less deadly—but nevertheless painful.

The slow firing muskets made edged weapons a necessary last resort. For close combat, enlisted men's muskets were fitted with bayonets, officers carried a brace of pistols and a sword, and boarding parties from the ship's crew brandished cutlasses and short pikes. The sword for officers was not prescribed until 1829 when the Mameluke sword was authorized. It had become popular with Marines from their service in the Mediterranean against North African pirates. A similar sword is still today a Marine officer's ceremonial sword.

The inventive genius of America blossomed during the first half of the nineteenth century, and much of it centered around firearms manufacture. The Hall breech-loading rifle, developed at

the Harpers Ferry armory, was used briefly by Marines in the Seminole wars of the 1830s. Samuel Colt's revolver was first produced at about this time, and a Colt revolving rifle was tried by the Marines. Ignition of both, as well as the M1842 musket, was by percussion cap. Neither the Hall nor Colt rifle had the power of the musket, and powder gases leaking at the breech made their use uncomfortable at best. Colt's revolver, held at arm's length to fire, was more successful. A Navy model six-shooter in .36 caliber was adopted for Marine officers in the 1850s.

In 1859, the Marines who entrained from Washington for Harpers Ferry to put down John Brown's rebellion were armed with the .69 caliber M1842 percussion musket, even though it had already been made obsolete by the .58 caliber M1855 rifled musket. In 1861, the Marines from the Washington Barracks fought at Bull Run with the M1855, although many units on both sides continued to use smoothbores during the first two years of the Civil War.

Left: John Paul Jones and his Marines—armed with short sea-service Brown Bess muskets—head from the Ranger *for a raid against Whitehaven on the British coast. ("The Invasion of Britain," Col Charles Waterhouse, USMCR (Ret), Marine Corps Art Collection)*

Right: A Marine of the 1830s with a Hall breech-loading rifle, brass eagle cap plate, and a twenty-four star flag in the background. (Artist: MGySgt Wendell A. "Tex" Parks, Marine Corps Art Collection)

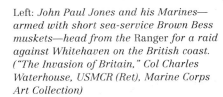

Marines from Marine Barracks Washington, commanded by 1st Lt Israel Green and armed with .69 caliber M1842 percussion-cap muskets and fire-ladder battering rams, attack abolitionist John Brown and his band barricaded in the fire engine house at Harpers Ferry Armory on 17 October 1859. (Woodcut from Harpers Illustrated Weekly)

The Marine Corps quartermaster, Major William B. Slack, pleaded for rifled muskets for the expanding Corps but was forced to accept old smoothbores until supplies of rifles, now the new simplified M1861 .58 caliber rifled musket, caught up with demand. Ships' detachments got the rifled muskets while Marine barracks in Navy yards made do with the old .69 caliber smoothbores. Eventually, when government arsenals and private contractors tooled up for full production, the Marines got the further improved M1863 rifles.

The Civil War inspired American inventors to produce breech-loading and even repeating rifles firing metallic cartridges. Many designs were tried by the Navy and some saw use by Marines. Most favored were the Sharps .52 caliber single shot using a special paper cartridge and the Spencer seven-shot repeater firing a .52 caliber rimfire copper cartridge. A tube containing seven cartridges was inserted into the butt of the Spencer's stock. Cartridges were fed into the breech by a lever which was also the trigger guard. The steel parts of both the Sharps and the Spencer were tinned to protect against salt water corrosion at sea.

Breechloaders were easy to load and fire rapidly, and repeaters were designed for even more rapid firing. The repeaters created an argument still heard today: Troops so armed, it was asserted, would waste ammunition. However, First Lieutenant John Green, who tested the Sharps for the Marine Corps, reported to Civil War Commandant John Harris that the ease of loading, even while moving forward—without the Marine taking his eye off the target—resulted in considerable tactical advantage.

Despite the effectiveness of the breechloaders, the muzzle-loading rifled musket stayed in service for several years after the Civil War. Post-war military budgets discouraged the greater expense of the more complicated breechloaders and their ammunition, and the heavier bullet and greater powder charge of the .58 caliber musket packed a stronger punch at longer ranges.

Erskine S. Allin, the master armorer at the Springfield Armory, converted huge stocks of muzzleloaders to breech loading. The result was the "trapdoor" Springfield, named for its upward hinged breechblock. It ultimately was made in .45 caliber with a brass center-fire cartridge powered with 70 grains of black powder. The trapdoor continued in .45 caliber through a number of improvements until the M1884 which armed Marines until the 1890s.

Below: *A Civil War Marine, with an M1861 rifled musket and a brass cap plate with a hunting horn with the letter "M" on a United States shield, stands before a thirty-six star flag. (Artist: MGySgt Wendell A."Tex" Parks, Marine Corps Art Collection)*

Above: *The Dahlgren 12-pounder boat howitzers or landing guns of the Civil War period were cast in bronze in the foundry and mounted on carriages in the shops of the Washington Navy Yard; some were smoothbore, some rifled. (Marine Corps Museum. Photo: Eric Long)*

Above: *Marines in the Civil War used the Springfield M1861 .58 caliber rifled musket. They also used M1842 smoothbores, later improvements on the M1861, and Sharps and Spencer breechloaders. (Marine Corps Museum Collection. Photo: Eric Long)*

During this same period, the first successful machine gun, also the result of American inventive genius, appeared. The Gatling gun was invented by Richard J. Gatling in 1862, and Admiral David D. Porter reportedly used a few to drive Confederate riflemen from the banks of the Mississippi. Its ultimate success had to wait for the mass production of metallic cartridges.

Gatlings were produced in subsequent years in many models and calibers. Typically, they had ten barrels around an axle and a breech

mechanism that loaded cartridges from a hopper or magazine. A hand crank revolved the ten barrels and fired them sequentially. The Gatling passed many Navy tests and was finally adopted in .45 caliber as the M1876. The ten barrels were encased in a bronze jacket and the gun was mounted on a light steel-wheeled carriage for ease in landing.

Another weapon that was adopted for some ships' Marine detachments was the Remington-Lee bolt-action five-shot .45 caliber rifle. It was fed by a Lee vertical detachable box magazine, and the name Lee, taken from the magazine, would have a long life. The box magazine was adopted by the British for their Lee-Enfield rifles which continued in service through the Korean War.

Smokeless powder was developed by 1880 and permitted small-caliber high-velocity rifles with longer range. Marines first used smokeless powder in the M1895 Winchester-Lee 6mm (.236-inch)

straight-pull five-shot rifle. A Browning machine gun, also called the M1895 and using the same 6mm cartridge, came into service at the same time. These two weapons, plus the M1876 3-inch landing gun, were used by Lieutenant Colonel Robert W. Huntington's First Marine Battalion in the seizure of Guantanamo Bay, Cuba, in the Spanish-American War.

Above: *A Marine of the Spanish-American War in dress uniform with a large brass eagle, globe, and anchor helmet plate; armed with a Winchester-Lee M1895 rifle; and in the background a forty-five star flag. (Artist: MGySgt Wendell A. "Tex" Parks, Marine Corps Art Collection)*

Right: *Capt McLane Tilton poses with Medal of Honor winners Cpl Charles Brown and Pvt Hugh Purvis of Marine detachment, USS* Colorado, *after 1871 landings in Korea. Tilton was not permitted to arm his men with new breechloaders offered by the Remington company before leaving the states and continued to use Civil War–era muzzle-loaders which he referred to as "old muzzle-fuzzles." (Photo: USMC)*

Below: *Accuracy and range were capabilities shared by the Krag-Jorgensen M1892 (top) and the Springfield M1903, both .30 caliber. The former was designed by Norwegian Army Captain Krag and Danish armorer Jorgensen and was used by those two armies. Adopted by the U.S. Army, it was made at Springfield Armory. The M1903 was adapted from a design of German Paul Mauser and was manufactured at both Springfield Armory and Rock Island Arsenal. (Marine Corps Museum. Photo: Eric Long*

Marines in the 1900 defense of the Peking legations and the China relief expedition—known popularly as the Boxer Rebellion—carried a mixed bag of rifles. The Legation Guard, made up of two ships' detachments, used the 6mm Winchester-Lee. The 1st Marine Regiment, coming from the Philippines, had the .30 caliber Krag-Jorgensen made at the Springfield Armory. Ships' detachments, organized into a second Marine regiment, used the older .45 caliber trapdoor Springfields and five-shot Remington-Lees. Ammunition resupply was a quartermaster headache.

During the Philippine Insurrection that followed the Spanish-American War, the trusty Krag-Jorgensen was immortalized in the clear but brutal phrase: "Civilize 'em with a Krag." The Marines lagged behind the Army in skillfully using the accurate .30 caliber Krag. This was

The Lewis light machine gun, invented by Col Isaac N. Lewis, USA, was rejected by the Army but accepted by Britain and Belgium on the opening of World War I. The Marines adopted it in 1915 and used it in Caribbean wars but not in France. Weighing only 27 pounds, it was fed by a 47-round drum or pan. (Marine Corps Museum. Photo: Eric Long)

brought out painfully when Marines finished low at early National Matches. After that, serious marksmanship training began for all Marines, and the Corps' rifle team soon became competitive.

By 1912 the Corps was fully armed with the new Springfield M1903 rifle firing the .30-'06 improved cartridge. "Oh Three" and "Thirty Ought Six" entered the Marine vocabulary. The Springfield '03's accuracy was superb, and Marines, both in combat and match shooting, would be well served by this peerless bolt-action rifle for the next thirty years.

The opening guns of World War I spurred further modernization, and when America joined the war in April 1917, rifle marksmanship was the Marines' primary training goal. Group photographs of World War I Marine companies show almost all the men wearing the marksman badge, with many displaying sharpshooter and expert rifleman badges. The payoff came on 4 June 1918 in the Marines' first real battle. The Germans advanced through the wheat field in front of Belleau Wood, and Marine riflemen stopped them at up to eight hundred yards with aimed rifle fire. Gunnery sergeants called out the range, the men set their sights, and the command "Commence firing" was given, just as if on a rifle range. On that day, the accuracy of the Springfield '03 and the Marines' skill in its use became legend.

The 4th Marine Brigade took the excellent drum-fed Lewis machine gun to France but never got to use it. The guns were badly needed to arm Army Air Service planes, or so the story went. The U.S. 2d Army Division, to which the Marine Brigade was assigned, was given French Hotchkiss heavy machine guns and Chauchat automatic rifles, both firing the French 8mm cartridge.

A Marine recruiting poster, circa 1910, shows a Marine field music with his bugle and a Marine at port arms with an M1903 rifle. An M1905 long bayonet is attached to his belt. Both Marines are in "blues," which were still being worn as a service as well as a dress uniform. (Marine Corps Art Collection)

The Chauchat, a French weapon made in a bicycle factory, was the Marines' squad and platoon automatic rifle in World War I. It weighed only 17 pounds and fired the French 8mm cartridge. Marines said it could be fired from the hip as accurately as from the shoulder—that is, "spray and pray" for a hit. (Marine Corps Museum. Photo: Eric Long)

When the United States went to war, American gun designer John Moses Browning was ready with two exceptional automatic weapons: the water-cooled M1917 Browning machine gun and the M1918 Browning automatic rifle or "BAR." Although the last twelve of the forty-three American divisions sent to France were armed with these weapons, the Marines didn't get theirs until just after the 11 November Armistice. The BAR would be a Marine Corps favorite infantry weapon until after the Korean War.

After World War I, the Marines returned to their not-very-peaceful peacetime duties: little wars in Haiti, Santo Domingo, and Nicaragua, and peacekeeping in China. The post-World War I years were a time of experimentation and some rearmament. The Marines were the only American forces actually in combat during this period. They quickly adopted the .45 caliber Thompson sub-machine gun (a favorite with G-men and gangsters of the era) and gave one to the corporal of each eight-man rifle squad. There was also one Browning automatic rifle in each squad, plus one man designated the rifle grenadier. In effect, the squad comprised two four-man fire teams; the BAR and rifle grenadier

Top left: *The Browning heavy machine gun M1917 replaced the French Hotchkiss at the end of World War I. Weighing 41 pounds with a 61-pound tripod and cradle, it was water cooled and fired .30 '06 cartridges from a 250-round fabric belt. The heavy Browning, a Marine favorite, was still being used in World War II and the Korean War. (Photo: USMC)*

Top right: *The Hotchkiss heavy machine gun used in France, shown here mounted for anti-aircraft fire, was heavy at 70 pounds with a 70-pound tripod, and was fed by brass strips holding 30 cartridges. (Photo: USMC)*

Above (top to bottom):
The Browning automatic rifle M1918 was an important and enduring invention by John Moses Browning. Replacing the Chauchat at the end of World War I, the BAR weighed 16 pounds, fired from a 20-round magazine, and for many years was the squad automatic weapon. In World War II a bipod was added for increased accuracy. (Marine Corps Museum. Photo: Eric Long)

The Thompson sub-machine gun M1921 was tested and eagerly adopted by the Marines as soon as it was available. Used with good effect in the Caribbean, it fired the .45 caliber pistol cartridge from a 20-round magazine or a 50-round drum. The M1928 TSMG with a straight stock forearm became the standard as a rifle squad close assault weapon. The M1 TSMG, a simplified version, was made for World War II. (Marine Corps Museum. Photo: Eric Long)

Marine Reserve Capt Melvin M. Johnson, Jr. fires the light machine gun version of his 9.5-pound semiautomatic rifle. The Johnson LMG weighed 13 pounds and was fired from a 20-round magazine. Both guns were used by Marine parachute and some raider units early in World War II. (Photo: USMC)

team provided a base of fire and the team with the Thompson were to "close with and destroy the enemy."

In the late 1930s, the Springfield Armory's designer John Garand developed the eight-shot rifle that became the M1. While the M1 was still in the experimental stage, one Marine battalion on each coast field-tested it. Meanwhile, Marine Captain Melvin M. Johnson, Jr., invented a competing rifle. The Johnson was accompanied by a light machine gun (LMG) version which had the same recoil action, making possible identical mechanical training for its users. The M1 was adopted for general use by both the Army and the Marine Corps. The Johnson went into limited production and was used by Marine parachute units because both the rifle and LMG could be broken down into a short package convenient for a parachutist to carry during a drop.

The U.S. rifle M1—also known as the "Garand" for its inventor, John Garand— armed Marines from 1942 until the early 1960s. It was self-loading or semiautomatic, weighed 9.5 pounds, and fired from an 8-round clip. (Marine Corps Museum. Photo: Eric Long)

At the beginning of World War II, Browning automatic rifles became M1918A2s, which gained 2.5 pounds in weight with the addition of a bipod (often discarded during close-in combat). Rifle squads increased from eight to twelve men but continued to have only one BAR. By mid-war a squad numbered thirteen Marines with a squad leader and three four-man fire teams, each with a BAR.

There were not enough Thompson submachine guns to meet the needs of the rapidly expanding Marine Corps. As a wartime expedient, Harrington & Richardson Arms developed and produced the Reising SMG submachine gun for the Marines. Unfortunately, on Guadalcanal, this cheap and easily manufactured weapon jammed often from the dirt of battle and rusted readily in salt air and tropical humidity. The Reising was relegated to stateside guard duty. Later in the war, both Thompsons and Reisings were replaced by M3 submachine guns—"grease guns"— inexpensively stamped out of sheet steel.

After Guadalcanal, the 1st Marine Division gave up its venerable Springfields '03s and rearmed with M1 Garands for Cape Gloucester and later campaigns. All units of the 2d Marine Division were armed with the M1. A lightweight shoulder weapon, the M1 carbine, replaced

the .45 caliber M1911 pistol carried by weapons crews and company grade officers. By the end of the war a fully automatic version was issued as the M2 carbine. Despite its convenience, Marines never liked the carbine.

Heavy machine guns were still Brownings, now the slightly improved M1917A1 with a new tripod and cradle and with more precise adjustments in elevation and traverse. They were employed by the battalion weapons companies, each of which had a four-gun (later six-gun) platoon. A new light machine gun, designated the M1919A4, was also a Browning, mechanically identical to the M1917 but air-cooled rather than water-cooled and thus weighing but thirty-one pounds. It fired from a low-profile tripod, and a platoon of four (later six) guns was included in each rifle company.

Antitank grenades were fired from spigot-type launchers that could be attached to rifle muzzles; they provided a short-range capability against tanks and bunkers. The 2.36-inch rocket launcher (nicknamed "bazooka") was a lightweight sheet-metal tube that fired an antitank projectile up to two hundred yards. By the time of the Korean War, it would be replaced by the more powerful, longer range 3.5-inch rocket launcher.

The disliked .30 caliber M1 and M2 carbines were found to be

Top: *The Browning M1919A4 light machine gun on a Camp Lejeune training exercise in May 1943. The gun's low profile enabled the gunner to give close support to rifle platoons in the assault. (Photo: USMC)*

Bottom: *The Browning M1917A1 heavy machine gun, improved with a stronger receiver and a more accurate cradle attaching the gun to the tripod, was used in both World War II and Korea. It supported the attack with long-range fires and in defense thickened front-line fire power. (Marine Corps Museum. Photo: Eric Long)*

Top left: *A Marine at Camp Pendleton, California, mounts an M1919A4 light machine gun on its low tripod during exercises in 1959. He wears the camouflage-cloth helmet cover that has identified Marines since World War II. (Photo: ActGySgt L. L. Toolin, USMC)*

Top right: *The assistant gunner of a 3.5-inch rocket launcher at Twenty-Nine Palms, California, in 1956 taps the gunner on his helmet to let him know that the rocket is loaded and ready to fire. (Photo: USMC)*

Right: *A Marine fires his bipod-mounted Browning automatic rifle, M1918A2, from a trench-line position in the final defensive phase of the Korean War. (Photo: USMC)*

Below: *A Marine stands to fire his Browning automatic rifle at a Japanese position on Iwo Jima. Mount Suribachi can be seen in the background. ("The BAR Man," Col Charles Waterhouse, USMCR (Ret), Marine Corps Art Collection)*

useless in the extreme cold of North Korean winters, as any oil in the mechanism congealed and froze. They were replaced by pistols for junior officers and M1 rifles for most weapons crews. Tank crews and some others continued to carry M3 submachine guns. One irony of the Korean War was that many Thompson submachine guns, which had been American gifts to the Chinese Nationalists, were captured from the Chinese Communists and put back into U.S. service.

In the early years of Viet Nam, Marines used the M14 rifle, an improved version of the M1 Garand. It was replaced in 1967 by the M16, a lightweight 6.3-pound weapon firing a high-velocity 5.56mm (.223 caliber) cartridge from a 20- or 30-round magazine. It could be fired either semi-automatic or full automatic. The rationale was that modern close infantry combat did not require the range of the .30 caliber weapons, and the lighter weight of the M16 and its ammunition enabled a man to carry and fire much more ammunition in the assault.

For longer range, the 7.62mm (.30 caliber) M60 machine gun replaced the esteemed Brownings, but they would be found wanting. By 1969 the new M79 grenade launcher was supplanted by the even newer M203 grenade launcher attached to the M16 rifle—adding three pounds to its weight. But the M79 launcher, called the "blooper," continued to be a favorite with Marines in Viet Nam. Both fired a 40mm grenade.

The M60 machine gun was never deemed fully satisfactory by its users despite efforts by both the Marine Corps and the Army to correct its many deficiencies. In the 1980s the M60 was replaced by the Belgian Fabrique Nationale 7.62mm MAG-58 general purpose machine gun, re-designated as the M240. At the same time the 5.56mm Fabrique Nationale squad automatic weapon (SAW) came in as the fire team

Above: *Twenty-one-year-old Sgt H. D. Vines fires his M79 grenade launcher or "blooper" at a Viet Cong-infested tree line during the "paddy war" near Da Nang in 1968. The M79 projected its 40mm shell out to 400 yards with accuracy and was a favorite weapon in paddy and hedgerow fighting. (Photo: LCpl Robert Sanville, USMC)*

Left: *Marine sniper LCpl Bryant White fires a Remington M40 rifle cal. 30 with a Redfield telescope on a cool evening in 1968 near the so-called De-Militarized Zone separating North from South Viet Nam. Snipers claimed kills at over 1,000 yards. (Photo: PFC E. E. Hildreth, USMC)*

automatic. A new crew-served weapon also appeared in these years, the 40mm Mark-1940 automatic grenade launcher. It fired the same grenade as the M79 and M203 but with a greater propelling charge. All these weapons were used in the Gulf War.

The 9mm Beretta pistol replaced the M1911 Colt .45 in the 1980s because it was easier to shoot and the large stock of .45s was worn out. Recently, special operations units brought back the old but respected Colt .45 because of its greater stopping power.

Non-lethal weapons have been developed for use in peacekeeping operations, including such imaginative devices as projected netting and "sticky bombs" to entangle opponents.

Top: *With the M48 tank commander providing covering fire with his .50 caliber Browning machine gun in the tank's cupola, members of the 9th Marines engage the North Vietnamese near Dong Ha in 1968. (Photo: Cpl J. McCullough, USMC)*

Above: *For nearly one hundred years the coveted Expert Rifleman qualification badge has remained virtually unchanged except for the type of crossed rifles. After recruit training, Marines continue to shoot annually to re-qualify. The highest level of qualification is expert followed by sharpshooter and marksman. Only 2 percent fail to qualify and 35 percent make expert. (Artist: LtCol Donna J. Neary, USMCR)*

Right: *Marine recruits or "boots" undergo preliminary marksmanship training at Parris Island in 1967. Much "dry-shooting"— position, sighting, and aiming exercises—is conducted before shots are actually fired. (Photo: MSgt R. H. Mosier, USMC)*

Marines at Quantico's Weapons Training Battalion improved the M16 rifle into the M16A2 with a heavier barrel for greater accuracy and faster twist rifling to stabilize the longer, heavier, bullet in a new Belgian-designed cartridge. The new bullet gave both increased long-range accuracy and greater penetrating power. Full automatic fire was eliminated in the M16A2, but a change lever shifts the single-shot mode to a three-round burst that is more likely to assure hits in the confusion of close combat. An interim rifle under consideration is the Close Quarter Battle (CQB) weapon based on the M16, but is more compact, has a shorter barrel, selective fire, and is capable of being fitted with accessories such as a sound suppresser and various sighting options.

Other small arms in development are the Objective Individual Combat Weapon (OICW) and an Objective Crew-Served Weapon (OCSW). The first is expected to weigh fourteen pounds and is intended to replace some M16 rifles; it will fire the same 5.56mm cartridge, and will also shoot a 20mm explosive shell. The crew-served weapon will fire either a 20mm or 25mm round. These weapons will have electronic ranging and imaging sighting systems. They will not be fielded until at least 2006.

Newer, more capable 60mm and 81mm mortars, the M224 and M252, have replaced older models. The M30 4.2-inch mortar has been dropped and a new 120mm mortar is under consideration.

Marines of the 3d Light Anti-Aircraft Missile Battalion aim their Redeye heat-seeking missile at an aircraft target in 1972 at Twenty-nine Palms, California. The Redeye was later replaced by the Stinger, which was effective against aircraft at any angle, not just in a tail-chasing attack. (Photo: Sgt G. Smith, USMC)

A Marine mortarman drops a shell into the tube of an M29 81mm mortar at a firebase near "the Rockpile" in Viet Nam in 1969. Mortars are often called the infantry battalion commander's own "artillery." (Photo: Cpl G. N. Zimmerman, USMC)

The Javelin—a medium-range, man-portable, fire-and-forget homing missile—will supplant the TOW and M47 Dragon as the infantry battalion antitank weapon early in the twenty-first century. To replace the M198 155mm howitzer, a new lightweight 155mm is being developed by Textron and Vickers for operational testing by the Army and Marines. Procurement is scheduled for year 2000.

As the history of Marine Corps development and use of weapons continues, Marines will select or develop the best weapon for the tactical task at hand and use that weapon with skill. Marines with eye- or image-intensified-sighted rifles and automatic weapons backed up by such sophisticated weapons as telescope-sighted sniper rifles, homing missiles, artillery, armored vehicles, and Marine close air support can be counted upon to dominate the battlefield well into the twenty-first century.

The Heavy Weapons

Marines have been well acquainted with artillery from the beginning. In the Revolution they helped man shipboard guns and for awhile after the battle of Princeton were detailed to General George Washington's artillery.

In the early days, artillery supporting Marine landing parties was usually manned by Navy bluejacket crews. Then, late in the nineteenth century, the Navy turned from sail to steam and from wood to steel, and warfare at sea changed radically.

Early in the twentieth century, Marine ordnance was getting heavier, more powerful, and harder to land from the sea. When the Advance Base Brigade came ashore in 1914 at Veracruz, Mexico, it landed its M1902 3-inch guns with harness but no horses. Draft horses had to be requisitioned from more-or-less willing Mexicans.

The 4th Marine Brigade sailed to France in World War I without either artillery or tanks. An artillery regiment, the 10th Marines, was organized at Quantico but never got to France. Instead, the Marines were supported by French artillery and the U.S. Army's 12th Field Artillery using French M1897 75mm guns—the famous fast-firing Mademoiselle soixant quinze. And they were augmented by both U.S. Army and French tank units. During the war, copies of the French Renault light tank were made in the U.S. but did not get to France in time to fight.

After World War I, each Marine brigade included a chemical company armed with the Army's 4.2-inch rifled mortars, which at that time fired only smoke and gas shells. In World War II, the "four-deuces" were supplied with high-explosive shells and each Marine regiment had a 4.2-inch mortar company.

In the 1920s, the Marine Corps began to foresee and to plan for war with Japan.

The Marines expected this would include crossing the coral reefs surrounding Japanese-defended Pacific atolls. Inventor Walter Christie developed amphibious tracked vehicles, one of which mounted a French 75mm

Above: Marines assault Fort Chojijin from the Han River in Korea on 10 June 1871. Painter John Clymer took artistic license in showing the M1876 landing gun five years before its adoption. The Dahlgren 12-pounder boat howitzer probably was used. (Marine Corps Art Collection)

Above: Marines at Quantico in the 1920s man a French M1897 quick-firing 75mm gun. The famous "French Seventy-Five" had a 9,000-yard range and was fired in batteries of four guns. (Photo: USMC)

Top right: The U.S. 7-ton light tank M1917 copied the French Renault FT-17 and was armed either with a machine gun or an M1916 37mm gun in its rotating turret. Marines in the 1920s and '30s had a five-tank platoon of these with each of the brigades at Quantico and San Diego. (Marine Corps Air-Ground Museum. Photo: Eric Long)

gun. Trials by the Marines were not fully successful but the idea remained attractive. By then, the 10th Marines was armed with French M1897 75mm guns and long-range M1918 155mm GPF guns—both drawn by Caterpillar tractors. And each of the Marine brigades based at San Diego and Quantico had a platoon of American-built French Renault light tanks.

In 1930 the Army developed a 75mm howitzer that could be carried by mule in the mountains. The howitzer broke down into two-man loads, and it occurred to the Marines that this was the way to land field artillery, man-handled from beached ships' boats. The wooden-spoked artillery wheels were replaced by pneumatic-tired wheels, and once ashore small Marmon Harrington high-speed tractors pulled the pack howitzers. Small two-man, five-ton tanks, CTL-3s, also made by Marmon-Harrington and mounting two machine guns, replaced the slow, aging Renaults. And the 81mm Stokes-Brandt mortar with an 1,800 yard range succeeded the short ranged, erratic 3-inch Stokes mortars of World War I. "Eighty-ones" were to serve unchanged through World War II and Korea.

In World War II, Marine infantry regiments had a weapons company with three platoons of 37mm antitank guns towed by 1/4-ton trucks (better known as "Jeeps"), and one platoon of armored M3 half-tracks mounting French 75mm guns. The 37s and 75s proved powerful enough to deal with the lightly armored Japanese tanks. The 37s fired shotgun-like canister and were often used in defense. Both 37s and 75s were used to attack Japanese bunkers.

Top: Marines land an M1 75mm pack howitzer from an LCVP (Landing Craft Vehicle Personnel) in stateside training early in World War II. With the introduction of landing craft with bow ramps the pack howitzer could be pulled ashore on its wheels rather than being broken down into two- or four-man loads. The pack howitzer, with a 17-pound high explosive shell, had a range of 9,500 yards. (Photo: USMC)

Below left: The M1 81mm Stokes-Brandt mortar, a French improvement on the World War I Stokes, initially had a range of 1,800 yards, later increased to 3,300 yards. It broke down into three one-man loads. (Marine Corps Air-Ground Museum. Photo: Eric Long)

Below right: The M2 4.2-inch rifled mortar, familiarly known as the "four-deuce," weighed 320 pounds and had a 4,400-yard range. It was used extensively in the Korean War. (Marine Corps Air-Ground Museum. Photo: Eric Long)

Above: An M-4 Sherman tank busts Japanese bunkers with its 75mm gun as Marines wait to mop up on Guam in August 1944. The Marine on the extreme right has lashed to his pack a trophy of war, a Japanese "Samurai" sword. (Photo: USMC)

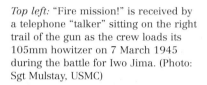

Top left: "Fire mission!" is received by a telephone "talker" sitting on the right trail of the gun as the crew loads its 105mm howitzer on 7 March 1945 during the battle for Iwo Jima. (Photo: Sgt Mulstay, USMC)

Bottom right: The M4 Sherman medium tank weighed 30 tons and was landed by LCM-6 and LCM-8 ramped landing craft. Armed with either a 75mm gun or a 105mm howitzer it was far superior to the few Japanese tanks encountered in the Pacific. (Marine Corps Air-Ground Museum. Photo: Eric Long)

Previous spread: Marines strain and grunt as they man-handle an M2 105mm howitzer into firing position on Okinawa in June 1945. With a range of 12,000 yards, the 105 was the standard Marine division light artillery piece from the last battles of World War II through Viet Nam. (Photo: Sgt West, USMC)

Top right: To give the "four-deuce" mortar better mobility, Marines mounted the tube on a pack howitzer recoil mechanism and carriage, thus creating the M98 107mm "howtar." (Photo: Sgt Thomas H. Bland, Jr., USMC)

Middle right: Automatic launchers mounted on Marine one-ton trucks fire Navy 4.5-inch barrage rockets against Japanese defenders of Iwo Jima on 28 February 1945. (Photo: SSgt Robbins, USMC)

Right: A Marine 90mm anti-aircraft gun in action in January 1943 on Tulagi in the Solomons. These guns were used initially by defense battalions and later by separate AAA battalions. At Munda on New Georgia in 1943 a Marine battalion of 90s was credited with shooting down an entire squadron of Japanese twin-engined bombers. (Photo: USMC)

Early in the war, a Marine artillery regiment consisted of three battalions of 75mm pack howitzers and a battalion of 105mm howitzers. For the final campaigns of 1945, the 105mm howitzer replaced the 75mms, and the 155mm howitzer replaced the 105s. Amphibious corps and force artillery battalions were armed with 155mm howitzers and 155mm long-range guns. Barrage rockets were also used; automatic gravity-fed launchers were mounted on one-ton trucks and fired 4.5-inch Navy rockets. These launchers were also mounted on LSMRs (Landing Ship Medium Rocket) for beach saturation just before the first wave of Marines reached the beach.

The 1st Marine Division landed on Guadalcanal with a company of M3A1 Stuart light tanks armed with a 37mm gun and two machine guns and weighing fifteen tons. As the Pacific war progressed, these tanks were replaced with a battalion of M4 medium Shermans with a 75mm gun and two machine guns and weighing thirty tons. The Marines used tanks mainly in tank-infantry teams engaging Japanese machine-gun bunkers. For this purpose M4 Shermans armed with 105mm howitzers replaced the 75mm guns in some units. "Ronsons," which were Shermans equipped with flame-throwers, proved particularly useful against caves and bunkers.

The Korean War, 1950–1953, was fought mainly with World War II

weapons, plus some notable additions and changes. One was the long range 75mm recoilless rifle, which had been developed during World War II and tested briefly in the Okinawa campaign. Man-portable, it fired tank-piercing and high explosive shells with great accuracy.

The 1st Provisional Marine Brigade landed in the Pusan perimeter of South Korea in 1950 with its company of M26 Pershing medium tanks armed with 90mm guns; they proved accurate at long ranges and effective against defensive works and the North Koreans' vaunted Soviet T-34 medium tanks. By the second year of the war, the M26s were replaced by the newer M46 Patton tanks, also armed with 90mm guns.

In the Viet Nam era, the 106mm recoilless rifle, mounted on the "mechanical mule" (a small flat-bed wagon-like vehicle) or the ubiquitous jeep, or in a package of six rifles mounted on the lightly armored and tracked M50 multiple gun carriage, nicknamed "Ontos," continued in use—as did the 81mm and 4.2-inch mortars, 105mm and 155mm howitzers, 155mm guns, and 8-inch howitzers. A new and disappointing addition was the 175mm long-range gun which promised much and delivered little.

At the time of the Persian Gulf War and Operation Desert Storm, the 1st Marine Division still had the M60 tanks with 105mm guns, an upgrade of the Patton. Superior gunnery by Marine crews made them effective against the Soviet armor used by Iraq. The 2d Marine Division employed M1A1 Abrams tanks with 120mm guns, and these proved clearly superior to anything the Iraqis fielded.

The eight-wheeled LAV-25 (light armored vehicle) armed with a 25mm automatic cannon had its baptism of fire in the Gulf War and was effective in reconnaissance and against Iraqi light armor. Also successful against Iraqi armor were the TOW and M47 Dragon, heavy and light wire guided antitank missiles. Marine artillery was 155mm howitzers, both M109 self-propelled, and lightweight long-range M198 towed pieces.

The 155s can now fire, in addition to impact or timed high explosive and smoke shells, the Copperhead laser homing shell and a newer Sadarm fire-and-forget homing shell. The Marine Corps continues to develop and to adopt new weapons to take advantage of new technology and to meet new tactical needs on the battlefield of the twenty-first century.

—BN

Top left: The M20 75mm recoilless rifle, shown here in training, was used effectively in Korea against tanks and bunkers. With a useful range of 1,500 yards, its hollow-charge shell could penetrate 3.6-inches of armor. (Photo: USMC)

Top right: The M50 multiple gun carriage or "Ontos" mounted six 106mm recoilless rifles. The crew had to dismount to reload the 106s and, with its light armor, its battlefield use in Viet Nam was minimal except in street fighting as here in Hue in February 1968. (Photo: Sgt B. A. Atwell, USMC)

Above: Marines received the M1A1 Abrams tank at the last minute in the Persian Gulf War. With its extremely accurate 120mm gun, laser range finder, and computer fire control, the Abrams was far superior to the Soviet-made Iraqi tanks thrown against it. (Photo: USMC)

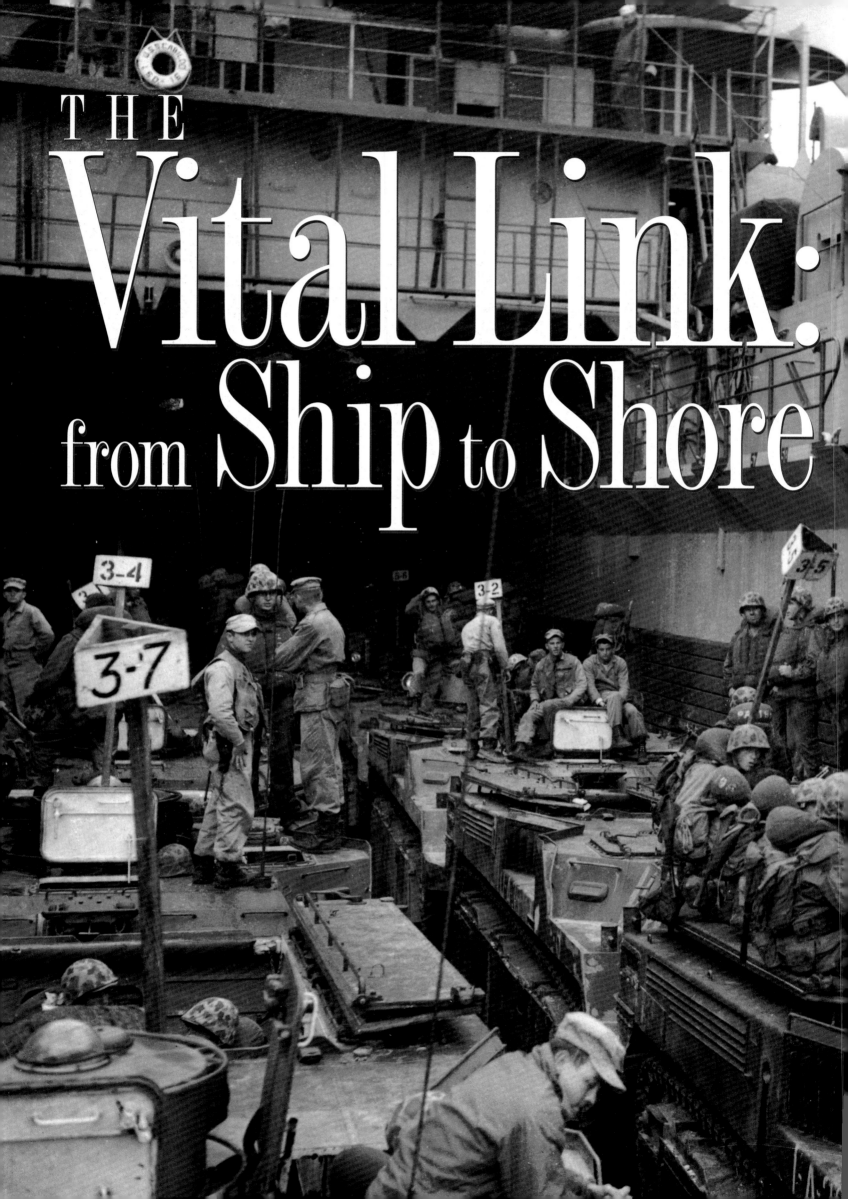

THE Vital Link: from Ship to Shore

THE
Vital Link:
from Ship to Shore

Colonel Joseph H. Alexander, USMC (Ret)

Landing from the sea, Marines climb ashore at Monterey, California, in 1847. Most Leathernecks fought the Mexican War as members of ships' detachments, executing a series of amphibious landings on both coasts of Mexico as well as California. ("Landing in Monterey," Col. Charles Waterhouse, USMCR (Ret), Marine Corps Art Collection)

Amphibious ships and landing craft have become as much the Marines' characteristic stock in trade as their rifles and fighting knives. Today, the Marines, teamed with the Navy, use highly refined amphibious ships and craft to execute difficult landings from the sea, but attaining proficiency did not come easily.

For most of their Corps' existence, Marines simply splashed ashore. A warship's Marine detachment would muster on the quarterdeck and gingerly debark into whatever small boats the ship could launch, then sit—steely-eyed and resolute—while sailors rowed them toward the beach. When the boats grounded in the surf, the Marines would leap overboard with an obligatory curse, wade ashore, and enforce the fleet commander's will against the nearest armed adversaries.

The vastly more lethal weaponry and increasingly sophisticated opponents of the twentieth century brought an end to these primitive ship-to-shore techniques. The Marines and the Navy had to junk the old ways and produce, first of all, a realistic amphibious doctrine and then the modern seagoing and surf-crossing ships and craft necessary to implement that doctrine under fire. The United States' ability to achieve this capability, virtually just in the nick of time, is one of the great success stories of World War II.

The result of the rapid transformation of the fleet "from whaleboats to Alligators" is best reflected in this description of the U.S. landing at Okinawa on April Fool's Day 1945 by historians Jeter A. Isley and Philip A. Crowl:

> Through this din and smoke, vessels carrying the first waves of landing troops . . . dropped their stern anchors, and came to rest fronting a shore line more than seven miles in length. These were strange craft that would have shocked any honest sailor ten years before—ungainly, flat-bottomed, scrofulous with varicolored camouflage paint. They were the tank landing ships (LSTs) and their smaller sisters the medium landing ships (LSMs), both with double doors fitted

Marines wade ashore from an experimental "armored" landing barge during fleet amphibious exercises in Culebra, Puerto Rico, in 1924. The craft proved unseaworthy and impractical. (Photo: USMC)

Previous spread: *Ready for combat, Korean War-era Marines embark in their assigned LVT-3C amphibian tractors in the well deck of a dock landing ship (LSD) prior to an amphibious assault. The LVT-3C was the first "amtrac" to feature steel hatch covers, affording some protection from air-burst shell fragments but also making for a claustrophobic ride to the beach. (Photo: TSgt Shkymba, USMC)*

Salvos of 4.5-inch rockets being fired just ahead of the assault waves at Okinawa on 1 April 1945. The Navy converted numbers of their versatile medium landing ships ("LSMs") from tank haulers to rocket-launching platforms. (Photo: USN)

into their bows almost flush with the water line. As the doors swung open, out swarmed hordes of another singular craft, if such it can be called. This was the tracked landing vehicle (LVT), frequently called the amphibian tractor, one of the truly amphibious vehicles of the war.

Navy and Coast Guard crews manned these amphibious ships and boats. For their own LVTs, Marines trained their own "boatswain's mates," a breed of web-footed Leathernecks adept with boat hooks,

This colorful array of markers helped bring order out of the chaos of amphibious assaults. During World War II and after, assault waves included Navy beachmasters and Marine shore party teams that mark the beach for follow-on waves and combat equipment and supplies. Marine LVT crews, their radios most often rendered inoperative by ocean spray, learned to scan the beaches for flags denoting their assigned unloading points. (Chart: Author's collection)

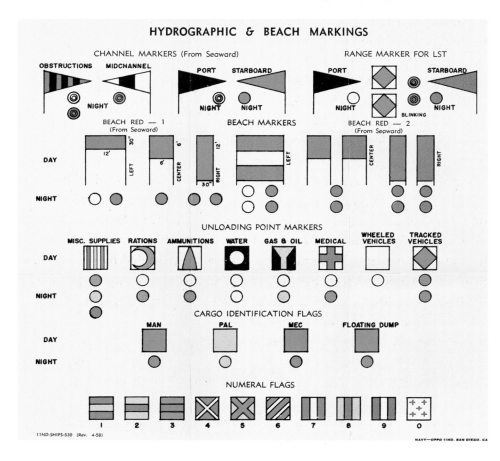

180

heaving lines, and "monkey fists," proficient in signal flags and sema-phore. At higher echelons, on board specially configured amphibious force command ships (called AGCs) circling just off shore, Navy and Marine commanders and their staffs wrestled with the intricacies of the amphibious assault. Two sea services were working in harness, long before it became mandated.

The developing need for specialized amphibious assault ships and craft was clearly demonstrated early in the twentieth century by two amphibious landings at Veracruz and Gallipoli, which occurred one year apart. At the height of the Veracruz crisis of 1914, the Marines assem-bled a force of five thousand troops—more than half the Corps—and deployed them to Mexico on a collection of battleships, cruisers, a pair of designated transports, a collier (a coaling ship), a target ship, and a chartered commercial steamship. In ship's boats towed partway to shore by tugs, the Leathernecks landed without opposition. The fighting, such as it was, did not get underway until later in the day, well inland. Reinforcements and resupplies came ashore, also unopposed.

Gallipoli, the colossal failed effort of the Allies to force Turkey out of the war by means of an amphibious assault against the Dardanelles, occurred a year later, but bore no resemblance to the Veracruz romp. Experimental troop ships and landing craft fared poorly in the face of spirited Turkish fire. In some cases, Allied troops stepped off the ramp of an improvised landing craft directly into interlocking bands of enemy machine-gun fire. Those who survived the bloody landing clustered ineffectively in small toeholds along the shoreline. The campaign atrophied from loss of momentum, disunity of command, and inadequate logistic support. The major powers, observing this debacle, concluded that modern technology had rendered the amphibious landing obsolete.

Oddly, a handful of U.S. Marine and Navy officers came to the opposite conclusion during the interwar years of the 1920s and '30s. But because of the enormous risk inherent in an opposed amphibious assault, its use attracted few other strategic thinkers.

Every modern amphibious operation is by nature a catastrophe waiting to happen. Opposed landings occur in a prohibitive environment (shoal water, breakers, rocky escarpments), involve the risky buildup under fire of combat power from absolute zero—the first lone rifleman on a "hot" beach—and demand uncommon cooperation between stub-born air, naval, and ground commanders. Any "administrative unload-ing" of the tanks and field artillery, so desperately needed by the landing force commander as soon as his Marines are ashore, is impossible. Any combat system that cannot hit the beach at a dead run imperils its crew and risks failure of the entire operation.

The Marines examined Gallipoli in depth, concluded that the campaign violated amphibious warfare's most fundamental principles, acknowledged the requirement for "surf-worthy" landing craft and lighters, and eventually, by 1935, produced a visionary work of doctrine, *The Tentative Manual for Landing Operations.* These were brave, pio-neering concepts, but in the absence of any tactical means of delivering

Walter Christie's promising "amphibious tank," armed with a 75mm gun, emerges from calm water prior to field testing during the 1924 Culebra exercises. The prototype nearly foundered in modest surf, and neither the inventor nor the Marines had sufficient funds for engineering improvements to make it seaworthy. (Photo: USMC)

USS *Henderson,* Old Number One

The Marines have never had ships of their own—that's the Navy's job. But two generations of Leathernecks looked upon the troop transport Henderson (AP 1) with proprietary affection during two world wars and a host of "banana wars" in between. Certainly no other ship ever served the Corps more faithfully, year in and year out, than "Old Number One."

Henderson *was the first transport designed and constructed for the specific needs of Marine expeditionary forces. Named for the fifth Commandant of the Corps, Brevet Brigadier General Archibald Henderson—who held the office for thirty-nine years—the ship was launched in the Philadelphia Navy Yard on 17 June 1916 by Genevieve W. Taylor, Henderson's great-granddaughter. The transport arrived in New York just in time to embark the 5th Marines—"fifteen hundred men and twenty-four mules"— to sail for France with the advance elements of the American Expeditionary Force in World War I.*

Henderson *made nine transatlantic voyages in the remaining sixteen months of the war, typically carrying fresh replacements for the heavily engaged 4th Brigade of Marines and retrieving its sick and wounded. Convoy duty in the North Atlantic proved hazardous. German U-boats torpedoed a nearby Army transport, sinking her in six minutes.* Henderson *escaped the torpedoes but experienced a devastating fire at sea— during which two thousand Marines had to be evacuated—plus several collisions and an outbreak of the deadly influenza epidemic, which afflicted five hundred men on board and killed one in every six. In short, the ship was as much a veteran of arduous expeditionary service as the sunburned "Devil Dogs" who gratefully rode her home following the Armistice.*

Between the world wars Henderson *served as a familiar "troop rotation ship," carrying Marines, their families, and their supplies to and from distant occupation duty in the Caribbean and the Pacific. She was a large transport, bigger (if slower) than even the Haskell-class APAs that served so widely in the last year of World War II and throughout the Korean and Viet Nam wars. Certified capable of transporting 1,695 troops, the ship frequently exceeded that figure, sometimes cramming as many as 2,700 (a small regiment) for short-fused crises in Haiti, Nicaragua, or China. Few Marines complained. The ship fed well and often, the plumbing generally worked, and two huge gyroscopic stabilizers helped minimize seasickness.*

Henderson *carried plenty of lifeboats but no landing craft. She was a great port-to-port ship, but her value diminished as the Pacific war evolved into a war without ports. She remained an AP, never a modified APA, and made her last transport run in September 1943, delivering SeaBees to the Solomons. The Navy then converted her to a hospital ship, renamed her USS* Bountiful *(AH 9), and deployed her to the Central Pacific. Grievously wounded Marines from Saipan, Peleliu, Iwo Jima, and Okinawa came to her, perhaps unaware that many of their fathers had received the same sanctuary after Belleau Wood or Soissons.* Bountiful *carried observers to the atomic test at Bikini Atoll in 1946 and then returned to California for decommissioning. Scrapped in 1947 after thirty-one faithful years of service to the Corps, the ship's gleaming brass bell has ever since adorned the quarterdeck of Henderson Hall at Marine Corps Headquarters.*

—JHA

The USS *Henderson* (AP 1) at sea in 1920s. (Photo: USN)

organized units ashore, or reinforcing them with even the lightest of combat support units, the doctrine remained a pipe dream. Delivering the necessary mass and acceleration ashore against heavy fire would demand entire families of special ships and landing craft that did not exist (indeed, could only dimly be perceived) and lacked powerful sponsors. And there was no funding in the Depression years.

The eight years between publication of the *Tentative Manual* and its validation in the great amphibious assaults of World War II began with bureaucratic indifference to the development of specialized landing craft and ended with frantic, top-level efforts to find such craft for the fleet. U.S. Army Chief of Staff General George C. Marshall said in 1943: "Prior to the present war I never heard of any landing-craft except a rubber boat. Now I think about little else."

The ability of the United States to launch even modest amphibious assaults in North Africa and the Solomon Islands as early as 1942 can be largely credited to the initiative of three men in the prewar years: two civilian engineers and one Marine.

The civilians were New Orleans boat-builder Andrew Jackson Higgins and the gifted Florida engineer, Donald Roebling, Jr, inventor of the tracked amphibian. Between them, they would provide the means for American landing forces to assault every opposed beach in the war.

The Marine was Holland M. Smith, a World War I veteran, now a new brigadier general (and not yet nicknamed "Howlin' Mad"). He took the vision of *The Tentative Manual for Landing Operations* and translated it into prac-

Right: *Marines in motor sailers pass through the fleet and head for the beach in 1924 fleet landing exercises. (Photo: USMC)*

Above: *Navy corpsmen with the newly formed Fleet Marine Force struggle ashore through waist-deep waters of the Potomac River off Quantico, Virginia, in 1934. They are using stretchers to transport heavy medical supplies. (Photo: USMC)*

tical application for the fleet and the landing forces. For years a "voice crying in the wilderness," Smith insisted on realistic training, and he maintained a drumbeat of requests for accelerated development of amphibious ships and landing craft. Holland Smith's performance as an amphibious corps commander in the coming Pacific war would be both decked with glory and clouded by controversy, but his greatest contribution to victory came in these prewar years, by his introduction of new amphibious doctrine, tactics, and techniques to future assault troops of all three armed services.

Nothing came easily to Holland Smith in the early years of his amphibious crusade. While many Washington decision makers foresaw a war with Japan, few accepted Smith's claim that the sheer geography of the Pacific would require amphibious operations on an unprecedented scale. Acquiring an amphibious fleet would be costly and would compete with the higher-priority construction of combatant ships. Some prewar planners suggested the nation's mighty battleships and land-based bombers would demolish enemy-held objectives without the need for forcible landings.

The Marines held a more sanguine view. Someday soon, perhaps in the Caribbean, surely in the Pacific, they would be called to storm island fortresses. Resolutely, the Marines set out in the late 1930s to convince the Navy to develop a sturdy landing boat, one readily launched at sea, powerful enough to carry a decent payload of troops and weapons through riptides and breakers, and capable of self-extraction without broaching in the surf. But at the Bureau of Ships, faced with the requirement to build a two-ocean fleet, the response was tepid. The prototype landing craft, designed halfheartedly on a pauper's budget, proved top-heavy and unseaworthy. This led the Marines to a can-do private entrepreneur, Andrew Higgins, and his bayou-proven "Eureka" boat.

The Marines liked the Eureka boat's high power, shallow draft, and protected screw. The craft sparkled in direct competition with the "Bureau boats"—scooting in to the shallows, unloading troops over the gunwales while maintaining its stern into the surf, then extracting without foundering. But the Marines were tough customers and wanted an armor-protected bow ramp for rapid debarkation of both infantry and small vehicles. The unflappable Higgins made the necessary design changes almost overnight, then astounded the "Bureau" and delighted the Marines by producing the ramped, 36-foot LCVP (Landing Craft, Vehicle, Personnel)—or simply, the

TWO PIONEERING ENGINEERS: *Andrew Jackson Higgins and Donald Roebling, Jr were as dissimilar a pair of engineers as could be imagined. Higgins, the New Orleans boat designer and builder, was lean, driven, aggressive, impulsive, two-fisted, and outspoken. Roebling, the Clearwater, Florida, inventor of the tracked landing vehicle (LVT), was soft-spoken, overweight, reflective, and reticent. Neither was the kind of East Coast technocrat favored by the Navy's Bureau of Ships in the 1930s. Both, however, were sought out by the Marines, who were increasingly anxious to find reliable means of executing the ship-to-shore assault under all hydrographic and tactical conditions.*

During World War II, Higgins designed and built more than twenty thousand craft for the military, including thousands of what became the workhorse—the ramped landing craft for personnel (LCVPs) and combat vehicles (LCMs). Marine General Holland M. Smith was characteristically blunt in a letter to Higgins: "Where the Hell would the Amphibious Force have been without you and your boats?" And in a 1944 Thanksgiving radio address to the American people (five months after the massive D-Day landings on Normandy), General Dwight D. Eisenhower said, "Let us thank God for Higgins Industries . . . which has given us the landing boats with which to conduct our campaign."

Donald Roebling, Jr, whose grandfather designed the Brooklyn Bridge, invented his "Swamp Gator" for humanitarian rescue operations during hurricanes. He had to be convinced that an all-steel, militarized version of his prototype would actually save American lives by allowing a direct delivery of assault troops on often coral-surrounded Pacific islands. Once persuaded, he worked with quiet efficiency to develop the world's first truly amphibious military vehicle—not just a river-crosser or a mill-pond floater, but a craft capable of transiting ocean swells and pounding surf, and once on shore, performing with agility. Roebling unselfishly delivered his design to the government for free. The Marine Corps received its first LVT-1 "Alligator" in 1941. Thereafter, the nation produced fifteen thousand LVTs in seven variants for service in every World War II theater. "Without these landing vehicles," said General Holland Smith after the war, "our amphibious offensive in the Pacific would have been impossible." In 1946 President Harry S Truman presented Donald Roebling the Medal of Merit "for outstanding services to the United States." And in 1997 the American Society of Mechanical Engineers designated the Roebling "Alligator" as an International Historic Mechanical Engineering Landmark.

—JHA

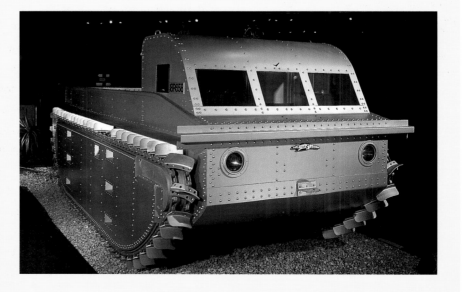

Top: Andrew Higgins's 50-foot ramped tank lighter became the Navy's familiar medium landing craft (LCM). Over the past half-century variations of the "Mike Boat" have delivered tanks, self-propelled guns, and troops to hundreds of beaches. (Photo: USMC)

Bottom: The original Roebling "Alligator" LVT-1, now restored, is on exhibit in the Marine Air-Ground Museum at Quantico. (Photo: Eric Long)

At Guadalcanal in November 1942, a Bureau of Ships version of a tank lighter, launched from USS President Jackson *(AP 37), beaches in a follow-on landing. A hodgepodge of landing craft, some of them carryovers from the 1939–1941 experimental tests, brought the Marines ashore in this first major World War II amphibious operation. (Photo: USMC)*

"Higgins boat." No other invention proved so universally useful in executing the difficult ship-to-shore movement of assault troops.

Andrew Higgins was on a roll. Immediately after solving the Marines' problem of delivering assault troops through the surf zone, Higgins applied the same energy and imagination to the long-standing obstacle of getting tanks ashore early in the assault. The challenge had flummoxed a host of other engineers. Tank lighters had to be big enough to transport both the existing 13-ton "tankettes" and the much heavier tanks under development. Yet the weight of the unladen craft could not exceed the boom capacity of amphibious ships. Further, the landing force needed a craft with a large, hinged, armor-protected bow ramp (larger versions of Higgins's new LCVPs), adequate freeboard to prevent swamping in the breakers, and a laden draft shallow enough to permit unloading the vehicles without drowning their crews.

With a delegation of representatives from the Marine Corps Equipment Board scheduled to examine "a plan" for a tank lighter in late May 1941, Higgins and his team aimed for actual hardware, working around the clock to convert a forty-five-foot Mississippi River towboat into a ramped prototype lighter in an incredible sixty-one hours. For the Marines it was love at first sight. The production version, the fifty-foot LCM-3 (landing craft, mechanized—commonly called the "Mike boat"), would deliver tanks and combat vehicles in every American amphibious landing of the war.

Yet one nagging aspect of the landing craft problem remained unsolved: how to get assault troops ashore against a barrier coral reef?

Good as the Higgins boats were, loaded with troops they drew between three and four feet under the keel. The sandy beach approaches of Guadalcanal, New Guinea, or Bougainville would present few obstacles. But at low tide the fringing reefs around the Central Pacific islands of Betio (Tarawa), Eniwetok, Saipan, Guam, and Peleliu would prove unassailable to LCVP-boated troops.

The Marines did not realize at the time that they already had at hand a most suitable alternate for tactical, ship-to-shore assault over a reef: the humble, logistics-oriented, amphibian tractor, or LVT. The Marines had been drawn to Donald Roebling's full-tracked, amphibious rescue vehicle, the "Swamp Gator," since learning about it in *Life* magazine in 1937. In another marvel of quick adaptation of "off-the-shelf" private sector equipment, the Marines contracted for militarized versions, LVT-1 "Alligators," to be designed by Roebling and built in Dunedin, Florida.

Off Guadalcanal, Marines launched their LVTs, stuffed with essential cargo, by swinging booms from ships. The LVTs executed non-stop runs from ship to inland supply dumps in the jungle, then back to sea. The Alligators were agile in Guadalcanal's swampy goo, and their light armor provided adequate protection for crewmen and the occasional passengers. But few people in 1942 envisioned LVTs as assault craft. Fortunately, Holland Smith was one.

Top left: *Seventeen years after the disappointing 1924 Culebra fleet landing exercises, the prototype LVT-1 Alligator successfully comes ashore in 1941 trial tests at Culebra. (Photo: USMC)*

Above: *Off Guadalcanal in August 1942, Navy deck crews carefully load a Marine 75mm half-track into an LCM-3 medium landing craft secured alongside a transport. Such landing craft were invaluable in getting the tanks and half-tracks of the 1st Marine Division ashore. (Photo: USMC)*

Lower left: *A Marine Corps LVT-1 "Alligator" finds its final resting place on the sea wall at Tarawa in November 1943. Despite the fringing reef and galling fire, these thin-skinned vehicles, field-modified with sheet-iron plates around the cabs, successfully delivered the first three assault waves of Marines. (Photo: USMC)*

The desperate battle by the 2d Marine
Division to wrest Betio Island in Tarawa
Atoll from a determined and well-fortified
Japanese enemy lasted seventy-six hours.
Amphibian tractors, used tactically for the
first time, proved their worth, but there
were not enough of them, and many
Marines had to wade ashore from the
outlying reef. ("The Seawall at Tarawa,"
Col Charles Waterhouse, USMCR (Ret),
Marine Corps Art Collection)

The problem of barrier reefs came to the fore as the Joint Chiefs of
Staff planned the great Central Pacific campaign that would bring the war
to Japan's doorstep. Worried planners asked the Marines to determine
whether their LVT could withstand both plunging surf and coral reefs.
Lieutenant Colonel Victor H. ("Brute") Krulak in far-off New Caledonia got
the call to conduct a field test. Doing so was hairy business. "Personnel
were thrown roughly about," admitted Krulak, who in the test vehicles
endured the ten-foot breakers and unforgiving coral. On the other hand,
he reported, using LVTs as amphibious personnel carriers was "mechanically feasible."

The value of LVTs to deliver assault troops ashore through coral
reefs remained unproven until Tarawa. There, and in the subsequent
Marshalls campaign, the Marines simply field-modified their vehicles by
bolting scrap-iron around the cabs and festooning the vehicles with
machine guns and stern-mounted grapnels to pull away barbed wire.
Design and production of true assault amphibian tractors—factory-built
armor, stern ramps—lagged a half-year behind. LVT-3s and LVT-4s
appeared in large numbers to support the great "storm landings" at Iwo
Jima and Okinawa. Yet some of the most inspirational photographs of
the Pacific war show the thin-skinned original LVTs littering the lagoon of

Tarawa after the battle, riddled with holes, surrounded by their fallen
crewmen—a tribute to the valor of the 2d Marine Division in executing
what is still regarded as the war's most difficult assault.

In this manner, the Marines eventually mastered the ability to project an assault force ashore from the sea against heavy opposition. But
the ship-to-shore movement was just one part of the difficult equation.
The Pacific war began before the Marines and Navy had solved the other
half—the development and construction of specialized ships to deliver
the assault force, along with their landing craft, from advance staging
bases in Australia and New Zealand to the targeted islands.

The Marines' sole transport, the USS *Henderson* was now long in
the tooth. Indeed, the Allies conducted many of their earliest landings
in the South and Southwest Pacific sub-theaters using the small, ancient
World War I vintage flush-deck destroyers converted to high-speed, low-capacity transports (APDs).

The Navy Department rather quickly acquired a dozen well-traveled merchant ships, painted them gray, and renamed them after
legendary Marines (*Doyen, Harris, Zeilin, Heywood, Biddle, Harry Lee,*
etc). The *Heywood*, for example, was the 20-year-old former SS *City of
Baltimore*. Although these improvised transports (designated APs for

auxiliary transports) served well, they were awful—leaky, crowded, poorly ventilated, unsanitary. Worse, in terms of the contested assaults to come, the converted merchantmen had insufficient boats and inadequate booms and davits to debark a landing force for the beach swiftly.

The war was a year and a half old before the original auxiliary transports were converted to APAs, attack transports. The key conversion was not, as some suppose, the upgrading of antiaircraft gun mounts, but the installation of multi-tiered Welin davits that could quickly launch as many as thirty-three of Andrew Higgins's remarkable landing craft. The main armament of an APA became its Higgins boats loaded with armed, impatient Marines.

America's shipyards eventually produced attack transports designed as such from the keel up, ships spacious enough to accommodate a full battalion landing team of Marines and most of their combat cargo. While the APAs (and their sister attack cargo ships, the AKAs) proved adept at launching their boats ("Away All Boats!" was their battle cry), when it came to heavily defended islands, they were dangerously slow in launching tanks and LVTs. Off-loading a Sherman tank by a single boom into a pitching Mike boat alongside was hair-raising and time-consuming. The LVTs, lighter and "floatable," could be swung over the rail and directly into the water faster; but there would be easily a hundred or more to be launched, and no one would risk doing this with troops embarked. Troops often had to load first into boats, then find their LVTs and undertake shaky gunwale-to-gunwale transfers into their LVTs at sea. Surprise and momentum would evaporate, making the beachhead harder to force, and greatly spiking the risk of the entire task force to the inevitable Japanese counterattack.

But two ungainly, special-purpose amphibious ships materialized: the tank landing ship, LST, and the dock landing ship, LSD. Both were

This Marine stares grimly over the gunwale of his landing craft as it approaches the beach on D-Day at Peleliu, 15 September 1944—a murderous day in one of the most obscure corners of the earth. The 1st Marine Division, veterans of Guadalcanal and Cape Gloucester, made the assault against deeply dug-in Japanese defenders. ("Going In," Tom Lea, U.S. Army Art Collection)

Facing page: *Accompanying vehicles, equipment, and supplies for the 1st Marine Division crowd the forward main deck of a Coast Guard LST underway for the assault at Cape Gloucester, New Britain, in December 1943. This was a short run from embarkation points along nearby New Guinea. Rough weather on the longer voyages of the Central Pacific campaigns would limit the amount of cargo that could be loaded on the open decks of these wallowing, flat-bottomed ships. (Photo: U.S. Coast Guard)*

Above: *Even a disabled amphibian tractor had its uses in the Central Pacific fighting. This shot-up vehicle on Peleliu provides defilade protection to D-Day assault elements of the 1st Marine Division. (Photo: Sgt Roemar, USMC)*

Right: *The hungry mouth of an LST, beached somewhere in the South Pacific, awaits its load of combat equipment. Barrage balloons hover protectively overhead to keep attacking aircraft at a respectable height. Seldom in the Pacific war did tactical and hydrographic conditions permit direct beaching of LSTs. (Photo: 1st Lt Richard Kokem, USMC)*

Iwo Jima's steep beach gradient and the absence of a reef made it possible to beach larger landing ships among the wreckage of smaller craft and to continue the flow of vital supplies. (Photo: USMC)

revolutionary in design. The LST had clam-shell bow doors that opened up to reveal a hinged ramp. This rough-riding ship, derisively called a "Long Slow Target," could land directly on many sandy beaches. Despite its "tank" name, the LST served the Marines best as the deliverer of LVTs. Once its ramp splashed down, a good LST could launch its seventeen preloaded LVTs in less than ten minutes, a huge improvement over the single-boom launch and subsequent troop-transfers in the open sea.

The LSD, with its massive stern gate and floodable after well deck, proved invaluable for transporting and launching medium tanks. As many as fourteen Sherman tanks could be preloaded on "Mike boats" (LCMs), and embarked in the flooded well. On D-Day, the LSD would steam to its anchorage, flood the well, lower the gate, and launch the boated Shermans en masse for the beach, all within a matter of minutes.

Other specialized amphibians appeared as the war progressed. Medium landing ships (LSMs) were seagoing amphibians that could transport five tanks for direct delivery on a steep beach—which they did heroically at Iwo Jima. A new family of mid-sized LCIs (landing craft infantry) proved much more useful when modified as rocket-launchers or mortar craft. Additionally, the shallow draft and low free-

board of most of these landing ships and craft made them ideal as close-in hospital ships.

The impact of specialized amphibious ships and landing craft on the conduct of Marine assault operations is best understood by comparing three forcible landings made in the eight months between November 1943 and June 1944: Bougainville, Tarawa, and Saipan.

The 3d Marine Division landed at Cape Torokina, Bougainville, in the upper Solomons, on 1 November. The amphibious task force, a bare-bones collection typical of the South Pacific operations, contained

only attack transports and antique APDs. Since there was no reef here and the Japanese did not occupy fixed fortifications, the wooden Higgins boats worked well in landing the assault troops against a spirited but disorganized opposition. The Marine division commander was anxious to deploy his brand-new Sherman medium tanks but knew the process of single-boom offloading would take too long. He was right. The small task force unloaded critical cargo and within hours scattered to safer waters, just ahead of the first wave of aerial and naval counterattacks. The Shermans never reached the battlefield.

Tarawa, only three weeks later, was significantly different. There the 2d Marine Division commander also wanted his Shermans in early. Plus he worried about the coral reef that fringed the main island of Betio. The difference in amphibious vessels at Tarawa was slight—three LSTs, the very first LSD. But this difference sufficed to provide enough LVTs to get the first three assault waves ashore—over the reef and against murderous fire— and to allow landing of a company of Sherman tanks before noon on the first day.

This was the first true trial-by-fire of the doctrine of amphibious assault. More specifically, Tarawa provided the first use of LVTs as assault landing craft, the first combat deployment of an LSD, and the first Pacific action of the Shermans. One lingering nightmare was the attempt to transfer

An LVT-4, loaded with 2d Division Marines, launches from the bow of a tank landing ship (LST) and heads for the beach at Iheya Island, fifteen miles northwest of Okinawa, in June 1945. The LVT-4 was the first "amtrac" to have a stern ramp, a quantum improvement from making the troops leap over the gunwales on arrival at the beach. (Photo: Sgt F. C. Rogers, USMC)

Facing page bottom: *Medium landing ships (LSMs), each loaded with five Sherman tanks, head for the line of departure, the jump-off point for Iwo Jima and a very long day. The island's steep shoreline made direct beaching of LSMs entirely feasible— if they could survive the Japanese artillery fire. (Photo: Sgt Kiely, USMC)*

1,500 Marines from Higgins boats to LVTs in the open sea at night under sporadic but terrifying fire from major-caliber Japanese coast defense guns. The three-day victory was costly but it would have been impossible without the innovative use of new amphibious ships and landing craft.

For Saipan, seven months later, the amphibious corps commander transferred his assault troops well in advance from their "comfortable" APA transports to the decidedly uncomfortable LSTs, which carried the LVTs. On D-Day the landing ships, some fifty in number, steamed directly for the line of departure, and launched their laden LVTs a mere six thousand yards from the beaches. As hellish as the opposition proved to be, the first troops hit the beach in thirty-five minutes from the time they left their ships—compared with six hours at Tarawa.

Saipan also featured the concentration of specialty craft that would become standard for the remainder of the war—high-speed motor boats to deliver underwater demolition teams, rocket-launching LCIs to saturate the near-shore defenses, dedicated amphibious force flagships, wheeled amphibious trucks ("DUKWs") to deliver field artillery and critical ammo ashore early in the assault, and armored amphibian tractors—the LVT-As, featuring turret-mounted 37mm or 75mm guns—to lead the troop-carrying LVTs all the way ashore.

By 1945 the Fleet Marine Forces and the "Dungaree Navy," the hardworking amphibious sailors, had reduced the complicated choreography of forcible landings to fine art. At Iwo Jima and Okinawa, overwhelming amphibious power delivered a landing force ashore strong enough to sustain awful punishment and still maintain velocity. At H-Hour on Iwo Jima, eight thousand Marines stormed ashore—thirty thousand by nightfall. On the first day at Okinawa, sixty thousand Marines and soldiers landed, with tanks and field artillery. Thousands of amphibious ships and craft made

On 15 September 1950, barely five years after the end of World War II, an LST beaches at high tide on Wolmi-do island in the harbor of Inchon, Korea. In the background, the Inchon waterfront blazes from the pre-landing bombardment supporting the amphibious assault by the 1st Marine Division. (Photo: SSgt W. W. Frank, USMC)

their direct approaches to the target islands under the pounding protection of naval gunfire and carrier air strikes. The same assaults were envisioned for Kyushu and Honshu—had Japan not surrendered.

The spectacle of a thousand or more amphibious ships and landing craft clustered off a congested beachhead vanished with the first fireball over Hiroshima. The "Atomic Age" caused each of the armed services to modify its tactical means of doing business. First, the Marines and Navy dispersed the amphibious assault fleet over an enormous area, and then they adapted the helicopter to the pioneering concept of "vertical assault" from the sea. Troop-carrying helicopters required a new form of amphibious ship—a transport with a flight deck, hangar, and control facilities. Thus was born the Navy's LPH, or landing platform helicopter.

USS Boxer *(LPH 4), a World War II aircraft carrier converted into an interim amphibious assault ship, conducts helicopter landing operations at Vieques, Puerto Rico, in January 1959. The "vertical assault" concept was on its way to becoming a reality. (Photo: USMC)*

The Korean War (1950–53) occurred while the Marines were still experimenting with transport helicopters and before the advent of the first LPHs. The one major amphibious assault of the war, General MacArthur's brilliant strike against the port city of Inchon in mid-September 1950, featured the same amphibious tools as the preceding war: shallow-draft LSTs to negotiate the narrow channel and treacherous mud-flats, plus LVTs and Higgins boats (many with wooden boarding ladders—Inchon had few beaches, mostly seawalls). The veteran-led 1st Marine Division spearheaded the way ashore, fought through the port and east towards Seoul by dawn the next day.

Inchon demonstrated the usefulness of amphibious capability in the emerging Cold War. A series of far-sighted decisions led to the acquisition of a "twenty-knot" amphibious force in time for the first U.S. landings in the Republic of Viet Nam. By 1965, helicopters had become integral to Marine Corps operations, and the fleet included not only LPHs but a number of valuable new hybrids. The LPD or landing platform dock combined an abbreviated flight deck and a somewhat truncated well deck for landing craft. Larger, relatively smoother-riding LSTs were seaworthy enough to receive names (the *Newport* class) instead of impersonal hull numbers.

The urgency of the Cold War demanded long-term forward deployments of small-sized amphibious forces around the world. Most of these deployments involved the commitment of a 2,500-man Marine Amphibious

198

Right: *By the mid-1960s the Navy and Marine Corps had developed a balanced surface and air amphibious assault capability. Typically, Marines would land by amphibian tractors across the beach while transport helicopters took other Marine units to inland objectives, as shown in this demonstration at Onslow Beach, North Carolina, in 1964. (Photo: SSgt C. Chance, USMC)*

Below: *A mine-clearing version of the LVTP-5 (called the "E-1") used its huge bow blade to plow through land mine fields in Viet Nam. It also carried a line charge—essentially a 300-foot cloth "snake" filled with explosives— that could be rocket-launched in front of the vehicle. Detonation of the line charge caused an over-pressure designed to explode the land mines and open a safe lane through which vehicles and troops could pass. (Photo: USMC)*

Bottom left: *An LCTP-5 from the 1st Amphibian Tractor Battalion leads a search-and-destroy mission just south of the Demilitarized Zone in Viet Nam in 1967. More than three hundred amphibian tractors were lost to enemy land mines during the course of the war. (Photo: Cpl L. P. Brown, USMC)*

Bottom right: *The LCM-6, used in Viet Nam and later, is an upscaled version of Andrew Higgins's medium landing craft of World War II, capable of carrying a heavier pay-load of troops or combat vehicles than earlier models. (Photo: PH3 John T. Bullington, USN)*

Unit (MAU—and sometimes MEU when the name shifted to the politically explicit Marine Expeditionary Unit). A MAU or MEU consisted of a Marine infantry battalion landing team, a logistics support unit, and a composite helicopter squadron, all embarked on board a five-ship task group, typically made up of a LPD (flag-configured), a LPH, a LKA (attack cargo), and a pair of LSTs.

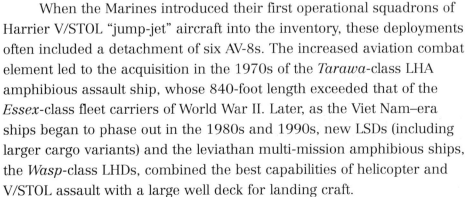

Left: *In this landing exercise on Crete in the Mediterranean in 1967, Marines descend from the deck of USS* Fremont *(APA 44) to a waiting landing craft by the traditional means of a cargo net. (Photo: USN)*

Top right: *LPH 12, well-named the* Inchon, *enters the Gulf of Mexico for its sea trials in May 1970. This amphibious helicopter ship was built at Ingalls Shipyard, Pascagoula, Mississippi. (Photo: Litton/Ingalls Industries)*

Middle right: *The tank landing ship USS* Saginaw *(LST 1188), underway here in 1972. The* Newport-*class dwarfed their World War II predecessors and were the first to have a ramp in the stern instead of the bow. (Photo: USN)*

Bottom right: *The amphibious transport dock USS* Trenton *(LPD 14) underway outside Puget Sound, Washington, in 1971. The new LPDs proved to be highly efficient hybrids, combining both a well deck for landing craft and a flight deck for helicopters. (Photo: USN)*

When the Marines introduced their first operational squadrons of Harrier V/STOL "jump-jet" aircraft into the inventory, these deployments often included a detachment of six AV-8s. The increased aviation combat element led to the acquisition in the 1970s of the *Tarawa*-class LHA amphibious assault ship, whose 840-foot length exceeded that of the *Essex*-class fleet carriers of World War II. Later, as the Viet Nam–era ships began to phase out in the 1980s and 1990s, new LSDs (including larger cargo variants) and the leviathan multi-mission amphibious ships, the *Wasp*-class LHDs, combined the best capabilities of helicopter and V/STOL assault with a large well deck for landing craft.

For all the sophistication of modern amphibious systems, the surface ship-to-shore assault remained the Achilles heel of landing operations. The "cutting edge" of the surface assault continued to be the sluggish amphibian tractor—regardless of the upgrade of its acronym from LVT to AAV (assault amphibious vehicle). Even the seventh-genera-

Above: *A Marine M-60 tank emerges from a workhorse "landing craft utility" (LCU) in a 1974 exercise at Vieques, Puerto Rico. LCUs, widely used in Viet Nam, were larger than some World War II landing ships. (Photo: PH3 Dennis A. McElveer, USN)*

Below: *The LVTP-7, the seventh-generation assault amphibian, became operational in 1972. With its improved cross-country mobility, it was increasingly used as a lightly armored personnel carrier. (Photo: Author's collection)*

Right: *An LVTP-7, redesignated as an AAV-7 (assault amphibian vehicle, 7th model) launches from the well deck of an underway ship. This technique was developed in the 1960s to reduce the exposure of amphibious ships to shore-based enemy fire. (Photo: USMC)*

tion AAV-7 proved no faster in the water than Donald Roebling's 1937 Swamp Gator. Amphibious ships still had to approach dangerously close to enemy coastal precision-guided weapons during launch operations. And there would never be enough assault helicopters or helicopter-deck ships available for a fully heliborne landing.

In the 1980s the Navy fielded a fleet of air-cushioned landing craft, the remarkable, revolutionary LCACs. Their high speed and long legs

"What Amphibious Tanks?"

Marine leaders always worried, with good reason, about the "window of vulnerability" that imperils a landing force just as the initial waves approach the beach. That is the precarious point when naval gunfire and close air support must lift and shift to inland targets and before tanks and artillery can get ashore. Marines dreamed of an amphibious tank that could cover them when they were most naked to their enemies.

But Marines now know there is no such critter as an "amphibious tank." They quickly explain that while certain vehicles like the Soviet Union's PT-76 "amphibious tank" can cross modest rivers, they can by no means survive the surf zone or ocean swells. Amphibious by Marine Corps definition always means sea-going, surf-riding.

Tanks are built for shock action, armor protection, and firepower. They sink in deep water, although fording kits may help them survive premature dunkings from a landing craft close to the beach. In World War II experimental direct drive skirts and enormous flotation devices helped some Sherman medium tanks negotiate from ship to shore, but the losses in deep water were catastrophic, especially at Normandy.

In 1924 the Marines tested engineer Walter Christie's "amphibious tank" during landing operations in the Caribbean. The experimental vehicle mounted a 75mm gun and had worked well during initial trials on the Hudson River. Launched from the deck of a submarine off Culebra, Puerto Rico, the Christie tank chugged impressively towards the beach—then it nearly foundered in the surf zone.

Twenty years later, during the Marshalls campaign, the Marines introduced into combat the first armored amphibian tractors. These LVTA1s mounted 37mm cannon. A later version, the LVTA3, mounting a 75mm howitzer, appeared in time for the Saipan landings. These were ideal vehicles for the ship-to-shore assault (they would have been worth their weight in gold at Tarawa) because they led the troop-carrying LVTs all the way in to the shore, blasting beachfront fortifications from the protection of a low silhouette and an armored turret. After H-Hour the armored amphibians could provide initial close fire support from just offshore until tanks and field artillery could land.

But when the LVTAs moved inland trying to fulfill the tank role, as at Saipan, they suffered heavy losses. Japanese gunners quickly learned to concentrate on the thin vertical hulls, purposefully light to provide reserve buoyancy when afloat. Lieutenant General Louis Metzger, who commanded an armored amphibian battalion in World War II, later observed: "Armored amphibians should never be employed as land tanks but only as assault guns. The difference being that LVT(A)s should always operate behind a screen of infantry and support such infantry by direct fire."

The last Marine armored amphibian vehicle to see combat was the Viet Nam War's ponderous LVTH-6, which mounted a gyro-stabilized 105mm howitzer. The advent of the air-cushioned landing craft in the 1980s closed the "window of vulnerability" for good. Heavy tanks can now be landed within minutes of H-Hour. Today's Marine M1 "Abrams" tanks whiz ashore in high-speed landing craft, arriving soon after the assault waves of riflemen have cleared a landing point. It has been a long road, but Marines are no longer looking for something called an "amphibious tank."

—**JHA**

The last of the "armored amphibians," the LVTH-6, with its gyro-stabilized 105mm howitzer, was designed to provide first-wave direct-fire support to the landing force. In Viet Nam, the LVTH-6 gradually became an expensive self-propelled artillery piece used well inland. (Photo: Author's collection)

abruptly quadrupled the percent of the world's coastline now assailable from the sea. In practical terms, the landing force commander at last had early delivery of heavy tanks, fighting vehicles, and field artillery units.

And yet, superb as it is, the LCAC is not meant to be the final solution for the vulnerable surface ship-to-shore assault. Enemy infantry weapons can damage and destroy the LCACs. They are big, noisy, expensive targets. The target beach or inland objective still needs to be cleared first by a few good riflemen—delivered currently by stealth or by helicopter, and to be delivered in the years to come by something called an AAAV, an amphibious fighting vehicle that for the first time eliminates the displacement-hull gridlock and skims to shore "on plane" at twenty-five to thirty-five knots.

The enormous amphibious task force that assembled off Kuwait in the Gulf War—the largest such force since Inchon forty-one years earlier—contained many Harriers, LCACs, transport helicopters, and bravely upgunned but still slow-as-molasses AAV-7s. A future amphibious force might include fewer ships—some say the combination of LHDs and LSDs could accomplish the whole landing "enchilada." But in place of the Viet Nam–era CH-46 "Sea Knight" helicopters, it will likely feature the MV-22 "Osprey" tilt-rotor assault aircraft.

Technology waxes and wanes, but amphibious warfare remains a

An air-cushioned landing craft (LCAC) skims across the waves at high speed off San Diego, California. The LCAC literally flies just above the surface of the water on a cushion of air at speeds impossible by conventional track or screw propulsion. (Photo: Carl "Tank" Shireman)

dangerous enterprise. Taking that first step on a hostile shore—whether from an improvised whaleboat or a speedy Osprey—will always require an ingrained aggressiveness, an abiding belief in the team that follows, and a certain hell-for-leather exuberance that has marked Marine amphibious assaults since 1776.

Left: *An M-1 "Abrams" main battle tank debarks from an LCAC onto a Southern California beach in 1997. (Photo: Carl "Tank" Shireman)*

Below: *Amphibious warfare requires ship-to-shore proficiency at many levels. These Marine scout-swimmers train in the surf zone off Camp Lejeune. (Photo: Greg E. Mathieson)*

Corsairs, Cobras, and Phantoms

Corsairs, Cobras, AND Phantoms

Lieutenant Colonel Ronald J. Brown, USMCR (Ret)

In 1911, twenty-seven-year-old Marine First Lieutenant Alfred A. Cunningham invested almost one-fifth of his monthly pay to rent a clamorous civilian-owned "aero-machine" and tried to fly it around the Philadelphia Navy Yard. Although "Noisy Nan" never got off the ground, Cunningham's enthusiasm won him orders to the new Navy flight school. The day Cunningham reported to Annapolis for flight training, 22 May 1912, is now celebrated as the birthday of the "Flying Leathernecks," and he is considered the "father of Marine aviation."

Since that time, flying Marines have proved themselves in combat during World War I, the Banana Wars in Latin America, World War II, Korea, Viet Nam, Grenada, and the Persian Gulf. The machines they fly progressed from barely airworthy stick-and-canvas contraptions that made every flight a death-defying adventure to the sophisticated high-performance jets and helicopters of today. Marines pioneered the use of aircraft for dive bombing, air transport, medical evacuation, close air support for ground troops, rotary wing operations, and short takeoffs/vertical landings.

Cunningham became the first Marine pilot—and the fifth naval aviator—after logging less than three hours in the air at Wright Field, Massachusetts, in August 1912. But he almost missed his rightful place in history when he was grounded because his skittish fiancée refused to marry a flier. It was not until 1915 that Cunningham was retroactively designated Marine Aviator Number 1.

While Cunningham was grounded, First Lieutenant Bernard L. Smith of Richmond, Virginia, became the first Marine to command an aviation unit. His aviation section of the Advance Base Force—two

Marine fledgling flyers and instructors relax in front of a Curtiss JN-4 "Jenny" trainer at Miami, Florida. The Marines took over the Curtiss Flying School (including all aircraft) in 1918 and assembled the First Marine Aviation Force there. (Photo: USMC)

Facing page: *1st Lt Alfred A. Cunningham swings the "pusher" prop of an "aero-machine" nicknamed "Noisy Nan" at the Philadelphia Navy Yard in 1911. Cunningham became the first Marine aviator in 1912 and was the driving force of Marine aviation during World War I. (Photo: USMC)*

Previous spread: *With its bent wings, down-turned tail, and drooping nose, the tandem-seat twin-jet McDonnell Douglas F-4 "Phantom II" was once described as being "so ugly that it was beautiful." For almost three decades "Phantom" variants served the Marines well as fighter-bomber, interceptor, and reconnaissance aircraft. (Photo: Carl "Tank" Shireman)*

planes (a Curtiss E-1 "Owl" amphibian and a Curtiss C-3 floatplane), two officers, and seven enlisted men—went to the Caribbean to support fleet maneuvers in January 1914. This was the first Marine aviation deployment.

The most daring act of those early days of naval aviation occurred when Marine Captain Francis T. "Cocky" Evans became the first man to loop a seaplane. He performed this dangerous maneuver twice in an ungainly Burgess N-9 floatplane and discovered how to recover from potentially fatal spins—knowledge that saved many lives.

When the United States entered World War I in April 1917, Marine aviation consisted of fifty men (seven officers and forty-three enlisted men) and seven aircraft (two landplanes, two seaplanes, two kite-balloons, and one training plane); they occupied a single hangar at the Philadelphia Navy Yard. Six months later there were two squadrons, one for seaplanes and one for landplanes. The landplane detachment soon moved to Miami where four squadrons under stocky Captain Roy S. Geiger manned the first Marine-only flying field. The pilots trained in Curtiss Jennies, but would fly British-designed De Havillands (DH-4s) in combat.

In April 1917, Capt Cunningham was back flying after recovering from injuries suffered while trying to catapult a seaplane from an underway warship. Demonstrating a unique mix of vision and practicality, he went to France, observed combat operations, selected airfield sites, and formulated a mission for Marine aviation. Returning home he oversaw a fifty-fold expansion of Marine aviation, procured training aircraft and civilian instructors, and recruited prospective fliers.

The Marines who made up the first American aviation unit sent overseas went with Capt Evans, who took a dozen seaplanes and 145

Above: A Curtiss JN-4HG in pristine condition is displayed in the Marine Corps Air-Ground Museum at Quantico, Virginia. "Jennies" continued to give good service until the late 1920s. (Photo: Eric Long)

Below: Maj Alfred Cunningham, commanding the First Marine Aviation Force, stands in front of a DeHavilland DH-4 bomber in France in October 1918. (Photo: USMC)

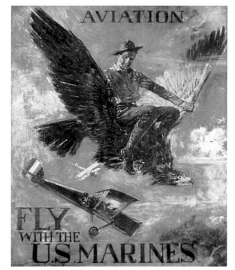

men to the Azores. They searched in vain for German submarines from January 1918 until the Armistice.

The commandant's recommendation that Marine planes support the Marine brigade in France was scuttled because both the Army and Navy opposed an independent Marine Corps air arm.

Capt Cunningham was finally able to get his Marines posted to the Day Wing of the Navy's Northern Bombing Group. The resourceful Cunningham finagled airdrome space near Calais, called in favors to get his men to France, and arranged for some of them to fly with the Royal Air Force while waiting for American-built DH-4s to arrive. When the first mass-produced American aircraft proved unsatisfactory, Cunningham was able to swap Liberty engines for British airframes, and three of the four Marine squadrons saw action.

The 1st Marine Aviation Force, commanded by Maj Cunningham, entered combat only one month before the Armistice. Most assignments were deep interdiction bombing; others were observation and supply runs. In the Marines' brief exposure to aerial combat, they flew fifty-seven missions, dropped more than twenty-seven thousand pounds of bombs, and accounted for four confirmed and eight probable aerial victories. They suffered forty-seven casualties, including four killed in action and sixteen influenza deaths.

The most spectacular single action occurred on 14 October 1918, when a plane manned by Second Lieutenant Ralph Talbot and Corporal Robert G. Robinson took on a dozen German fighters and brought down two. Talbot and Robinson became the first Marine aviators awarded Medals of Honor. Robinson became a gunnery sergeant and survived the war, but Talbot was killed before he received his medal.

Top left: *During World War I and the early 1920s some Marines trained in the single-seat rotary-engined Thomas Morse S4 "Scout." This restored "Tommy" is in the Quantico museum. (Photo: Eric Long)*

Top right: *The World War I recruiting effort was so successful that Marine aviation expanded from only seven planes and fifty men in 1916 to more than a hundred planes and over six thousand Marines by Armistice Day 1918. (Marine Corps Art Collection)*

Above: *Maj Edward H. Brainard in front of his Wasp-powered F6C-4 Curtiss "Hawk" at Quantico. "Chief" Brainard was the officer-in-charge of Marine Aviation from 1925 to 1929. (Photo: USMC)*

The period after World War I brought reduction, reorganization, and refurbishment. Shoestring budgets hampered naval aviation during America's return to "normalcy." By 1920, the number of Marine pilots had fallen from almost four hundred to less than fifty. The Marines flew war surplus aircraft until a few new aircraft, notably Curtiss fighters, joined the weary DH-4s in the late 1920s. Marine pilots showcased their

Above: *On the first all-Marine bombing mission of World War I, DeHavilland DH-4 bombers from Capt Robert S. Lytle's Marine Squadron 9 swoop low over a vital railway junction at Thielt in German-occupied Belgium on 14 October 1918. (Artist: James Butcher, Marine Corps Art Collection)*

Right: *1st Lt Christian F. Schilt with the Vought O2U-1 "Corsair" in which he delivered seven tons of supplies and evacuated eighteen badly wounded Marines from the besieged Marine garrison at Quilali, Nicaragua, in January 1928. Schilt received the Medal of Honor for this action. (Photo: USMC)*

skills in air races, air shows, and a series of well-publicized maneuvers. At that time, flying continued to be a dangerous profession that claimed the lives of many Marines. After being told the pilot casualty rate was one in four, one brash prospective flier replied: "Sign me up for five years. I can't be 125 percent dead."

Marine aviation was the only American flying service that saw combat between 1918 and 1941. United States interventions in Latin America, collectively called "the Banana Wars," allowed the Marines to develop advanced aviation tactics and techniques under combat conditions. Among their innovations were dive bombing, aerial resupply, medical evacuation, and the use of air panels for ground-to-air communications. Major Ross E. "Rusty" Rowell's air group played an important role in the pacification of Nicaragua. Two-seat bombers and scout planes kept Sandanista rebels off balance while tri-motor transports supplied U.S. forward bases. In a spectacular episode in 1928, First Lieutenant Christian F. Schilt, a daring flier who earlier shattered world speed records, made ten trips into the besieged garrison at Quilali in a Vought O2U—the original "Corsair"—biplane, brought in supplies, and flew out wounded.

Major Thomas C. Turner replaced Cunningham as chief of Marine aviation in 1920. While on detached duty with the Army Signal Corps during World War I, Turner had earned his wings and then commanded an Army aviation unit. A strict disciplinarian and a demanding leader, he was an excellent flier who left a permanent stamp of professionalism on Marine aviation. In 1931, during his second tour as director, Col Turner walked into a spinning propeller and was killed. He became the first Marine flier to reach flag rank when he was promoted to brigadier general—posthumously.

Maj Geiger, who had commanded a squadron in France, succeeded

Top: *Arguably the best-known American aircraft of their day, single-seat single-engine Curtiss "Hawks" flew with the Army, Navy, and Marines. The first Hawks entered Marine service in 1927 and were first-line Marine fighters until the early 1930s. (Photo: USMC)*

Above: *Six Marine Boeing F4B-4s fly in echelon over San Diego in 1934. These fast and highly maneuverable fighter planes often appeared at air races and air shows. To make them even more useful, some mounted underwing bomb racks while others carried belly-mounted auxiliary fuel tanks. (Photo: USMC)*

This F4B-3 fighter bears on its tail the distinctive "Red Devil" squadron insignia of San Diego's "Fighting 10." Various models of this aircraft were the main Marine fighter aircraft from 1932 until the eve of World War II. (Photo: USMC)

Turner. Col Rowell, an outspoken aviation proponent and a popular public speaker, took over in 1935. The main tactical aircraft of the 1930s continued to be biplanes; the Vought O3U (also called "Corsair") scout, the Boeing F4B fighter, and the Great Lakes BG-1 and Curtiss O2C ("Helldiver") dive bombers. When the Fleet Marine Force was formed in 1933, Marine aircraft groups (MAGs) were assigned to each of the east- and west-coast expeditionary forces. Overseas detachments served in the Caribbean, Nicaragua, China, and Guam.

That the primary mission of Marine air was to support the landing force was finally recognized in a mission statement issued by the Navy General Board in 1939:

> *Marine aviation is to be equipped, organized, and trained primarily for the support of the Fleet Marine Force in landing operations and in support of troop activities in the field; and secondarily as replacement squadrons for carrier-based naval aviation.*

By the time World War II broke out in Europe, monoplanes had replaced biplanes; and the Marine Corps procured Brewster F2A "Buffalo" and Grumman F4F "Wildcat" fighters, Vought SB2U "Vindicator" bombers, and Douglas SBD "Dauntless" dive bombers. Col Geiger, one of several Marine observers sent to England and North Africa, reported that successful ground and naval operations demanded effective close air support. By the time the United States entered the war, the east- and west-coast air groups had expanded into the 1st and 2d Marine Aircraft Wings (MAWs); the 1st MAW serving with the Atlantic Fleet and the 2d MAW with the Pacific Fleet.

Left: *Hopelessly outnumbered Grumman F4F-3 "Wildcats" of VMF-211 duel with Japanese raiders over Wake Island in December 1941. After all twelve of the squadron's "Wildcats" had been knocked out of action, the surviving pilots fought on as infantry. One of their number, Capt Henry T. Elrod, received a posthumous Medal of Honor. ("Cat and Mouse Over Wake Island," Marc Stewart, Stewart Studios, Sargent, Georgia)*

Below: *A Douglas Dauntless takes off on a bombing mission at Guadalcanal on 22 October 1942 as smoke roils up from the jungle. The two-man, low-wing SBD was the finest Marine dive bomber of World War II and was successfully used against both ground targets and enemy shipping. This particular aircraft was flown by TSgt John Fogerty who was killed in action that day. ("Fogerty's Fate," painting by Col Albert M. "Mike" Leahy, Marine Corps Art Collection)*

Top: *A Marine F4U-1D "Corsair" brings down a Japanese G4M2 "Betty" bomber. The distinctive inverted gull-wings made the Corsair one of the most easily recognized World War II aircraft. The powerful Corsair was one of the few American planes that could outmaneuver the nimble Japanese "Zero." (Artist: Marc Stewart, Stewart Studios, Sargent, Georgia)*

Above: *"Corsair 369," an F4U-4, is on display at the Marine Air-Ground Museum. The "Dash Four" was an improved model Corsair that featured a more powerful engine, large wing, a bubble canopy, and a four-blade propeller. Capt Jesse G. Folmar brought down a MIG-15 jet while flying a "Dash Four" in Korea. (Photo: Eric Long)*

The first months of war were tough ones for the United States. Colonel Claude A. "Sheriff" Larkin acknowledged that his MAG-21—like all U.S. forces at Pearl Harbor—was caught "flat footed" on 7 December 1941. The Japanese destroyed or badly damaged forty-seven of forty-eight Marine aircraft at Ewa airfield, four miles west of Pearl Harbor. Farther west, at Wake Island in the Central Pacific, the pilots of Marine Fighting Squadron 211 (VMF-211) flew their Wildcats against overwhelming numbers of enemy planes; they sank two ships, damaged several more, and shot down seven Japanese planes. When all the Marine planes were destroyed, the American aviators fought on as riflemen until Wake Island fell.

Midway Atoll in June 1942 was the scene of the last American defensive stand in the Pacific. The Midway Marines lost most of their aircraft and three squadron commanders; but after the great naval and air victory known as the Battle of Midway, the United States went on the offensive.

On Guadalcanal, where the Marines landed in August, Henderson Field (named for a Marine aviator killed at Midway) brought together many of the Corps' best fliers. Chisel-featured Captain John Smith's Wildcat fighters and suave Major Richard C. Mangrum's Dauntless dive bombers arrived at Guadalcanal; and Roy Geiger, now a brigadier general, commanded the joint-service "Cactus Air Force."

The year that followed is remembered as "the time of the aces" because more than thirty Marines achieved five or more "kills." Marine fighters, always outnumbered, shot Japanese raiders out of the sky, while dive bombers sank Japanese ships and hit enemy positions. Two avid hunters, Captains Marion E. Carl and Joseph J. Foss, put their stalking skills to use in the skies of the South Pacific. Carl became the first Marine ace in September, and in October Foss got the first of his twenty-six kills. He eventually recorded the Marines' second highest total of aerial victories before recurring malaria ended his Marine flying days. After the war, Foss formed the South Dakota Air National Guard, served two terms as governor, and later became commissioner of the American Football League and president of the National Rifle Association.

When Guadalcanal was secured in early 1943, the formidable Japanese base at Rabaul became the next American target. Now, what is arguably the best recognized Marine airplane of all time—the gull-winged Vought F4U "Corsair"—made its appearance. First Lieutenant Kenneth A. Walsh, an ebullient veteran of seven years of enlisted flying service with encyclopedic technical knowledge, became the first Corsair ace—on his way to twenty-one victories. First Lieutenant Robert M. Hanson knocked down twenty-five Japanese before he was lost during a strafing run.

The most famous Corsair flier, Gregory R. "Pappy" Boyington, was a two-fisted whiskey drinking Marine who left the Corps temporarily in 1941 to join the Flying Tigers in China where he claimed the first six of his twenty-eight kills. Back in the Corps in 1943, Maj Boyington was given a squadron of replacement pilots who had neither specific aircraft nor an assigned ground crew. They shot down fifty-seven enemy planes in the next thirty days and became famous as the "Black Sheep" Squadron (VMF-214). One of the squadron's young guns, First Lieutenant

Bottom left: *Maj Gregory R. "Pappy" Boyington signals three victories to the "Black Sheep" of VMF-214 while his ground crew checks his F4U-1 for battle damage. There is no officially sanctioned "Aces List," but Boyington's combined total of twenty-eight aerial victories—six claimed as a Flying Tiger in China and twenty-two as a Marine in the Pacific—make him the highest scoring Marine pilot of all time. ("Pappy Got Three!," Col Charles Waterhouse, USMCR (Ret), Marine Corps Art Collection)*

Top right: *A Marine maintenance crew works the "night shift" to ready an F4U-1 "Corsair" for battle. These highly skilled "wing wipers" labored in anonymity. Their hard work has always been, and will continue to be, essential to the success of the Flying Leathernecks. ("Night Shift," Kerr Eby, Navy Art Collection)*

Lower right: *At the outbreak of World War II, the Marine Corps had just begun to receive the Grumman F4F "Wildcat." Out-classed by Japanese fighters in speed and maneuverability but reliable and very sturdy, the Wildcats gave the Marines good service, particularly in the first crucial months at Guadalcanal. (Photo: USMC)*

Above: *Marine Capt Herbert H. "Trigger" Long, flying an F4U-1 "Corsair," splashes a Mitsubishi G4M1 "Betty" near New Georgia in the South Pacific on 7 July 1943. Long finished the war as a double ace with ten confirmed victories. (Artist: Marc Stewart, Stewart Studios, Sargent, Georgia)*

Above: *A VMF-323 "Corsair" salvos eight high-velocity aerial rockets in support of the "Mud Marines" on Okinawa in 1945. Marine close air support became progressively more effective as the Marines moved across the Pacific. Strafing, dive bombing, and napalm were delivered with deadly efficiency because they were directed on target by Marine pilots serving with Marine ground units. (Photo: 1st Lt David Douglas Duncan, USMCR)*

John F. Bolt, Jr., destroyed six "meatballs"—slang for the Red Sun painted on the Japanese aircraft. Pappy Boyington was shot down over Rabaul and captured on 3 January 1944. His mental and physical toughness as a prisoner-of-war became as much a part of his legend within the Corps as his flying skill. Boyington is generally recognized as the Marines' top ace.

The most respected aviator in the Corps, however, was MajGen Roy Geiger, widely known for his icy "two-hundred-yard stare" and omnipresent cigar. In May 1943, he left the 1st MAW to become director of aviation for the second time. He returned to the South Pacific in the fall to take over the I Marine Amphibious Corps, which moved to the Central Pacific as III Amphibious Corps.

After his flying days were over, he went on to a distinguished career as a ground commander. On Okinawa in 1945, LtGen Geiger became the only Marine officer to lead a field army in combat. He was the commanding general of Fleet Marine Force Pacific at the end of the war and eventually became the first Marine aviator to achieve four-star rank, albeit posthumously.

Marine aviation strength during World War II peaked at five wings which included 31 groups, 145 squadrons, and 112,626 Marines. Among the new tactical aircraft in 1944 were Grumman F6FN "Hellcat" night fighters and naval versions of the North American B-25 "Mitchell" medium bomber designated the PBJ. Because of the shortage of aircraft carriers, land-based Marine air was used to neutralize by-passed enemy bases in the Central Pacific. As an ever increasing number of escort carriers became available, it was decided Marine planes would be placed on board. MajGen Rowell, the Marine air commander in the Pacific, opposed this plan so vociferously that he was replaced by Major General Francis P. Mulcahy. Marine fighter and composite squadrons (usually made up of Corsair fighters and Avenger torpedo bombers) began flying off carriers. In February 1945, six such squadrons were present when the Marines fought on Iwo Jima.

The techniques of close air support were sharpened in the Western Pacific. Colonel Clayton C. Jerome and Lieutenant Colonel Keith B. McCutcheon pushed hard to make close air support of ground troops a primary mission. Under their tutelage Marine dive bombers and fighters supported U.S. Army units in the Philippines. Fighting on Peleliu was so close that Corsairs dropped napalm on Bloody Nose Ridge before they could retract their flaps or wheels. Marine air at Okinawa in 1945 included carrier-based air combat patrols that held Japanese suicide planes at bay and land-based squadrons that attacked enemy ground troops with rockets, bombs, and napalm. Close air support so effectively dislodged dug-in enemy on Okinawa that aviation planners placed more and more emphasis on that mission for the upcoming invasion of Japan. Okinawa, however, turned out to be the Marines' last major World War II battle.

After the war, Marine Corps aviation was cut to two skeleton wings and barely avoided being absorbed by the new U.S. Air Force. Roy Geiger, now the "old man of Marine Corps aviation," made two crucial contributions just before his death in 1947. First, his blunt testimony before Congress helped stave off unification of the services. And second, he initiated a reappraisal of amphibious doctrine that led to the formulation of "vertical envelopment."

A "Corsair" flight of "Death Rattlers" from VMF-323 patrols the sky over Okinawa April–May 1945. The "Death Rattlers" accounted for more than a hundred enemy planes and seven of its pilots became "aces" during only seven weeks of fighting. (Photo: Sgt Beall, USMC)

A pair of HRS helicopters prepare to deliver sling-loaded multiple rocket launchers to the main line of resistance in Korea. The HRS could carry six men or 1,420 pounds of cargo. (Photo: Sgt Leon F. McClellan, USMC)

The modern era began in 1948 when Marines gained jet planes and helicopters. Keith McCutcheon—who was taciturn except when the situation demanded words, at which time he could demonstrate his brilliance in both speech and writing—was an advocate for, and a pioneer in, the use of both jets and choppers. The McDonnell FH-1 "Phantom" was the first jet fighter used by the Marines. Lanky and laconic Marion Carl, now a lieutenant colonel, commanded the first jet squadron (VMF-122) and formed the first jet aerobatics team, the "Marine Phantoms." The first Marine helicopter squadron, HMX-1, was formed at Quantico where Piasecki HRP "Flying Bananas" and Sikorsky HO3Ss became the first helicopters put into operational use.

In the summer of 1950, the United States desperately needed reinforcements to stem the Communist North Korean invasion of the South, and the timely arrival of the 1st Provisional Marine Brigade helped save the day. MAG-33 Corsairs flew from carriers and helped stabilize the Pusan Perimeter. The 1st Marine Division, supported by the 1st Marine Aircraft Wing, landed at Inchon in September and caught the bulk of the North Korean Army south of the 38th parallel. The Marines next landed at Wonsan on the east coast and drove northward to the Chosin Reservoir

in North Korea. Chinese Communist forces unexpectedly poured over the Manchurian border and reversed the course of the fighting. As the outnumbered Marines fought their way south from the frozen Chosin, Marine F6FNs and Grumman F7FN "Tigercats" prowled the night sky; "Corsairs" and F9F "Panther" jets cleared the way during the day, and helicopters and transport planes supplied the column and evacuated wounded. Several Chinese divisions were destroyed, but the U.N. forces had been pushed south of the 38th parallel for the second time in six months.

At this juncture, the Air Force's "single air management" doctrine broke up the Marine air-ground team. The USAF's Fifth Air Force took control of land-based 1st MAW aircraft for the remainder of the Korean conflict. Despite Marine objections, the new joint air campaign plan emphasized deep interdiction strikes rather than close air support. Each commander of the 1st Marine Division thereafter filed formal complaints about the quantity, quality, and timeliness of air support, but no significant change in air control was made.

Helicopters proved to be versatile and effective in Korea. Bell HTLs and Sikorsky HO3Ss were successfully used as battle taxis, airborne scouts, and aerial ambulances while Sikorsky HRS transports lifted combat troops and supplies to the forward edge of the battlefield. The beating rotor blades of Col McCutcheon's "whirlybird" squadron (HMR-161) soon became a familiar sound at the front.

Major General Christian Schilt, the hero of Quilali (twenty-three years earlier) and now commander of the 1st MAW, thrilled the troops by doing nightly stunts with his Tigercat and celebrated the Marine Corps Birthday in 1951 with a low-level combat strike behind enemy lines. World War II ace Major John "Handsome Jack" Bolt became the only Marine jet ace by bagging six aircraft while flying on exchange duty with the U.S. Air Force. Major John H. Glenn, Jr., a Marine aviator adept at both close air support

A Bell HTL-4 "Bubble Top" helicopter loads wounded Marines on board in Korea. Originally designed as a light observation helicopter, the "Bubble Top" soon became a general-purpose utility aircraft, conducting observation, liaison, and medical evacuation missions. (Photo: PFC C. L. Chance, USMC)

Overleaf: A 2d Marine Aircraft Wing "Seahorse" helicopter unloads an infantry squad in a field problem at Camp Lejeune, North Carolina, in 1957. The single-main rotor medium-lift Sikorsky Seahorse utility helicopter had a crew of three and could carry twelve passengers in combat gear. First labeled "HUS," its designation was changed to "UH-34" in 1962. (Photo: Sgt R. Kotula, USMC)

Top left: *A CH-46D medium assault transport helicopter lifts off the USS* Boxer *in the Viet Nam War in 1968. These venerable Vertol "Sea Knights" have been the mainstay of the Marine helicopter fleet for more than thirty years. (Artist: Col Edward M. Condra III, USMC, Marine Corps Art Collection)*

Top right: *A Bell UH-1E light utility helicopter on a training mission. The UH-1E was officially named "Iroquois," but is universally called "Huey." The Huey was the first turbine-powered helicopter assigned to Marine squadrons. (Photo: Bell Helicopter Textron Incorporated)*

Below: *A Chance-Vought F-8 "Crusader" from VMFA(AW)-312 pulls out after making an air strike in Viet Nam during 1966. The Crusader, a superb fighter, was affectionately called the "MIG Master," but it was poorly configured for ground attack missions. Because of this shortcoming, F-8s were phased out of the Marine Corps by the late 1960s. (Photo: Cpl J. Morales, USMC)*

and dogfighting, received the nickname "Magnet" because of his propensity for drawing flak while flying low and slow during bombing runs. Assigned to USAF exchange duty, Glenn knocked down three enemy aircraft while flying an F-86 "Saber" jet bearing the title "Mig Mad Marine." Later, Glenn would be the first American to orbit the earth and, after his astronaut days, was elected to the U.S. Senate. Second Lieutenant Frank E. Petersen, Jr., of Topeka, Kansas, flew sixty-four missions; he would later become the first black Marine general officer. Among the many Marine Reserve aviators serving in the combat zone were television personality Ed McMahon and professional baseball players Ted Williams and Jerry Coleman.

The Korean conflict came to an inconclusive end in 1953. Marine aviation was not pared to the bone in the wake of that war as it had been after the World Wars. Resources were sufficient to restructure and re-equip the Marine fliers to support the Corps' expanding role as America's force-in-readiness. During the decade following Korea, delta-winged Douglas F4D "Skyray" interceptors, compact Douglas A-4 "Skyhawk" attack jets, and sleek Chance-Vought F-8 "Crusader" fighters bearing Marine markings responded to international crises in Lebanon, Asia, and Cuba.

Helicopters moved into the mainstream of Marine aviation. "Vertical envelopment," whereby Marines came ashore in helicopters, was refined. Assault equipment was designed to be helilifted, the number of helicopters dramatically increased, and the Navy ordered a dozen LPH helicopter assault ships. A pair of Sikorsky helicopters, the HUS (later UH-34) "Seahorse" and the HR2S heavy hauler, represented quantum leaps in helicopter performance and made vertical envelopment practical. Specially configured "white top" Marine helicopters began transporting the president of the United States—a high-profile mission that continues to the present day. Marine helicopters lifted American citizens out of harm's way and brought combat troops ashore during the Dominican Republic intervention. Between 1962 and 1965 about half of the Marine helicopter squadrons rotated through South Viet Nam during Operation Shufly and carried South Vietnamese troops into battle against Viet Cong insurgents.

The American buildup in Viet Nam, beginning in 1965, turned into a ten-year fighting assignment. The 1st MAW became the air combat element

of III Marine Amphibious Force and, eventually, the largest single Marine aviation unit to that time. Its peak strength of six aircraft groups comprised 26 squadrons flying 242 fixed-wing airplanes and 186 helicopters. Marine F-4 "Phantom IIs" and A-4 "Skyhawks" flew close air support; A-6 "Intruders" made deep interdiction bombing runs; KC-130 "Hercules" conducted aerial refueling and supplied forward bases; and OV-10 "Broncos" provided aerial observation. Helicopters conducted combat assault, resupply, medical evacuation, liaison, transport, and observation missions. Eventually, Bell UH-1 "Hueys" and Boeing-Vertol CH-46 "Sea Knights" replaced the venerable Seahorses, Sikorsky CH-53 "Sea Stallions" became the heavy lifters, and Bell AH-1 "Cobra" gunships were introduced.

In 1968 the 1st MAW was subordinated to the Seventh Air Force, but this change had less effect on the quality of air support than the parallel shift in control had had in Korea. American withdrawals from Viet Nam began in 1969, and most Marine air units were out by 1971. The North Vietnamese "Easter Offensive" the next spring brought Marine squadrons hurrying back to Viet Nam.

Marine air took part in the "Linebacker" bombings of North Viet Nam, and Marine helicopters assisted mine-sweeping operations at Haiphong harbor. In 1973, MAG-12 was the last American aviation unit to leave Viet Nam. Two years later, ship-borne Marine helicopters conducted large-scale non-combatant evacuations Eagle Pull (Phnom Penh) and Frequent Wind

A McDonnell-Douglas F-4B "Phantom II" kicks up a dust storm on the runway at Chu Lai, Viet Nam. The Marines used F-4s primarily for close air support of ground troops, but one USMC Phantom downed a North Vietnamese "MIG-21." (Photo: SSgt C. M. Hoar, USMC)

Bottom left: A Douglas A-4 "Skyhawk" gets ready to launch from Chu Lai. Skyhawks were lightweight single-jet attack aircraft whose compact size, simple design, excellent maneuverability, and good payload made them excellent close air support aircraft. (Artist: Col Peter "Mike" Gish, USMCR, Marine Corps Art Collection)

Bottom right: A North American OV-10 "Bronco" defoliates one of South Viet Nam's many "ambush alleys" in 1969. Defoliation became a controversial issue, but the agile Bronco was well suited for these missions. The OV-10 was specifically developed for counter-insurgency warfare in the early 1960s. (Photo: USMC)

Top left: *Marine Lockheed KC-130s fly in formation. These long-serving and versatile "Hercules" are used by Marines for aerial refueling and cargo transport. (Photo: Lockheed Aircraft Corporation)*

Top right: *A Bell UH-1N "Huey Twin" light utility helicopter makes a "fastrope" insertion of a reconnaissance team during a training exercise at Camp Lejeune. Huey Twins are improved dual-turbine versions of Viet Nam-era UH-1Es. Their primary missions are command and control, medical evacuation, and assault support. (Photo: Bell Helicopter Textron)*

Right: *A North American OV-10 "Bronco" light utility aircraft waits on an airstrip south of Da Nang to be called into action. The twin-engine tandem-seat Bronco was used as a forward air controller platform for the most part, but was sometimes pressed into use for close air support, liaison, and light cargo delivery. (Photo: Cpl Alvin K. Mack, USMC)*

(Saigon), finally bringing America's longest armed conflict to an end.

Two aviation Marines received Medals of Honor for actions in Viet Nam. Captain Stephen W. Pless made a daring rescue of ground troops while flying a UH-1E armed helicopter, and Private First Class Raymond M. Clausen leapt from a hovering Sea Knight into a minefield to lift out several wounded men. Marine Captains Doyle D. Baker and Larry Richard each scored kills while on exchange duty with the Air Force. Major Lee T. Lasseter and Captain John D. Cummings won the only all-Marine aerial victory of the war.

BGen McCutcheon took over the 1st MAW in 1965 and later, after being promoted to lieutenant general and serving as deputy chief of staff for air at headquarters, returned to Viet Nam to command III MAF in 1971. He was slated to become assistant commandant and the first Marine aviator to hold four-star rank on active duty but succumbed to cancer.

Another influential aviator of the period was Thomas H. Miller, Jr., a self-assured test pilot, veteran of three wars, and holder of a world speed record. He test-piloted Skyhawks, Phantoms, and Harriers for the Marine Corps. LtGen Miller served as deputy chief of staff for aviation and retired in 1979. General Earl E. Anderson was the first Marine aviator to wear four stars on active duty when he was named assistant commandant as the Viet Nam era came to an end.

During the two decades after Viet Nam, the Marines improved existing airframes and gained two new jets: the superb multi-purpose Grumman F/A-18 "Hornet" and the radical short takeoff/vertical landing McDonnell Douglas AV-8 "Harrier" jump jet. Marine fliers participated in four combat actions during the 1980s: Marine helicopter crews flew in a hostage rescue mission that ended in flames at Desert One in 1980; Marine helicopters flying off USS *Guam* helped rescue Americans threatened by a Communist coup in Grenada in 1983; carrier-borne Marine Hornets attacked Libya in 1986; and Marine Cobra gunships took down armed oil platforms that served as Iranian terrorist bases in the Persian Gulf in 1989.

After Saddam Hussein's Iraqi forces overran Kuwait in 1990, Marine AH-1W "Super Cobras" were the first "tank busting" helicopters to arrive in the Persian Gulf. Major General Royal N. Moore, Jr.'s 3d Marine Aircraft Wing deployed to Southwest Asia in August and within six months became a "super wing" mustering more than sixteen thousand personnel, 222 fixed-wing aircraft, and 186 helicopters. Among the Marine forces afloat were also two aircraft groups, including a twenty-plane Harrier squadron on board USS *Nassau*. The 3d MAW was under the operational control of a Joint Forces Air Component Commander, the newest term for single air management. By then joint operations were so familiar that this was accepted without protest.

During Operation Desert Shield, Marine jets protected Saudi borders and airspace. Marine helicopters conducted a daring night non-combatant evacuation in Somalia, supported the sea quarantine of Iraq, participated in several high-profile training exercises, and formed an experimental maneuver element called "Task Force Cunningham."

The Bell AH-1W "Super Cobra" with its chin-mounted 20mm can also deliver with good effect antitank missiles and ground-attack rockets. "Whiskeys," as "W" model Cobras are also known, provided close-in fire support in low-visibility conditions during the Persian Gulf War. (Photo: Bell Helicopter Textron Incorporated)

McDonnell Douglas AV-8B "Harrier IIs," the world's premier vertical/short takeoff and landing aircraft, fly in tight formation. The Harrier replaced the A-4 "Skyhawk" in meeting the Marine Corps' need for a close-in light attack airplane. (Photo: McDonnell Douglas Corporation)

Middle left: *A Sikorsky CH-53E "Super Stallion" lifts a HUMVEE at 29 Palms, CA. Super Stallions provide the Marines rotary-wing heavy-lift capability. They were used to good effect during humanitarian Operation Provide Comfort when CH-53Es flew more than 500 miles over the rugged Zagros Mountains each day to resupply the base at Silopi, Turkey. This was necessary because there were no fixed-wing air strips available in the forward area. (Photo: Rick Mullen)*

Middle right: *The McDonnell Douglas F/A-18 "Hornet" has proved itself as a high-performance, multi-role (fighter, attack, and fast forward air controller) aircraft in Libya, the Persian Gulf, and Bosnia. This reliable performer is expected to continue to serve the Marines well into the twenty-first century. (Photo: McDonnell Douglas Corporation)*

Bottom: *A CH-46E, an enhanced model of the "Sea Knight" on a training mission. The Sea Knights are still the standard USMC medium-lift assault helicopter after more than thirty years of service. Current pilots are known to say, "If a Sea Knight was good enough for my father to fly, it's good enough for me." (Photo: Carl "Tank" Shireman)*

During Operation Desert Storm, Marine air shaped and isolated the battlefield, then provided close air support in Kuwait, and launched the first Harrier strikes from an amphibious assault ship. Harriers and Hornets destroyed Iraqi convoys along the "Highway of Death." Marine Cobras crushed Iraqi tank attacks, and helicopters played a major role in a successful amphibious deception. Colonel Manfred A. "Fokker" Rietsch commanded the largest aircraft group in Marine history (MAG-70) and personally flew more missions than any other coalition pilot in the Persian Gulf. Rietsch bluffed six Iraqi fighters back home during a tense aerial

incident in November 1990 and then logged sixty-six combat missions in thirty-one days during Desert Storm.

The 1990s saw the Marines place great emphasis on military operations other than war. Marine helicopters provided most of the lift for humanitarian relief operations Fiery Vigil (Philippines), Provide Comfort (northern Iraq), Sea Angel (Bangladesh), and Restore Hope (Somalia). Marine KC-130s delivered relief supplies to Rwanda. Marine helicopters conducted non-combatant evacuations of American embassies in West Africa on three occasions and lifted civilians safely out of Albania. Marine F/A-18D Hornets and EA-6B Prowlers, operating from Aviano, Italy, patrolled the skies over the former Yugoslavia as part of a multi-national force. The most widely reported aviation incident there was the Marine helicopter rescue of a USAF pilot shot down in Bosnia.

Modern Marine aviation is powerful and versatile. Over the years, Marine air has become the most focused air support force in the world. Its squadrons, groups, and wings are vital components in Marine air-ground task forces, and yet, individual units can be smoothly integrated into joint task forces for combat or humanitarian operations. As the twenty-first century approaches, Marine air is a superb combined arms weapon, and today's Flying Leathernecks command a world-wide reputation for skill and élan that is second to none.

Top left: A flight of A-6A "Intruders" from VMA(AW)-224 on a training mission. The A-6 Intruder, a two-seat, all-weather, low-level deep interdiction strike aircraft with a reputation for uncanny accuracy, was the longest-serving tactical aircraft in Marine Corps history, from before Viet Nam until after the Persian Gulf. (Photo: Grumman Corporation)

Top right: A twin-seat twin-engine EA-6A "Prowler" electronic jammer on a training mission in the 1960s. The newer four-seat EA-6B Prowler variants are still in active service, and are frequently used for joint exercises and joint operations, including current service in the troubled skies over Bosnia. (Photo: Grumman Corporation)

Left: The revolutionary Bell-Boeing MV-22 "Osprey," here shown with its rotating wing-tip engine nacelles in the vertical position, will replace the Marine Corps' aging "Sea Knight" medium helicopters. The Osprey—a brand-new high-speed, tilt-rotor, vertical takeoff and landing, medium-lift transport aircraft—takes a three-person crew and can carry either twenty-four combat troops or more than five tons of cargo. (Photo: USMC)

THE
President's

Own

THE
President's
Own

Colonel John R. Bourgeois, USMC (Ret)
Twenty-Fifth Director, U.S. Marine Band

"The President's Own," the United States Marine Band, on the South Front of the White House. (Photo: MGySgt Andy Linden, USMC)

Marine music dates back to the colonial period in Philadelphia, where in 1775 recruiters along with fifers and drummers "drummed up" the first enlistees for the Continental Marines. The drums, emblazoned with a coiled rattlesnake and the motto "Don't Tread on Me," caught the eye of Benjamin Franklin; and later the design was used on the first American battle flag.

From 1775 to 1783 these drummers and fifers served afloat and participated in the naval engagements of the Revolution. They also served ashore with the army at the battles of Trenton, Princeton and Penobscot Bay.

The end of the Revolution in 1783 marked, for a time, the end of everything military in our country. From then until 1797 the only Marine musics were those serving on the few vessels that some of the states maintained. When the United States Navy was born in 1797 with the launching of three frigates, Marine fifers and drummers served on them.

The United States Marine Band, known as "The President's Own," traces its origins to 11 July 1798, when President John Adams signed an Act of Congress that created a corps of Marines and authorized "a drum major, a fife major, and thirty-two drums and fifes."

Some of the thirty-two drummers and fifers of the new Marine Corps created by President Adams were sent out on recruiting duty; and some fell in battle on board American warships in the French naval war from 1798 to 1801.

In 1798 Marine Corps Major Commandant William Burrows assessed every officer in the Corps ten dollars (a second lieutenant then

Above: *Under the approving eye of MajComdt William Ward Burrows, a recruiting party, with fifers and drummers, prepares to move out from the grounds of Independence Hall to beat the streets of Philadelphia for recruits. (Artist: LtCol Donna J. Neary, USMCR, Marine Corps Art Collection)*

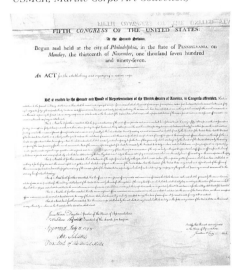

Above: *An Act of Congress, signed by President John Adams on 11 July 1798, created the United States Marine Corps, as such, and authorized musicians for that corps. These musicians would become the Marine Band. (National Archives)*

Previous spread: *Drumsticks, belt, belt buckle, red coat, and gold plated buttons—details of a Marine bandsman's uniform and the tools of his trade. (Photo: Greg E. Mathieson)*

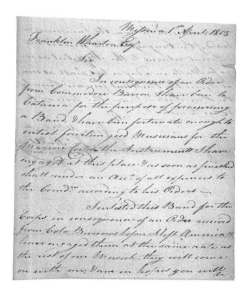

earned twenty-five dollars a month) for a music fund, mostly to acquire
instruments other than the authorized fifes and drums. The musicians so
equipped were the ancestors of today's Marine Band.

Two years later, the national capital moved from Philadelphia to
Washington and the Corps moved with it. Lieutenant Colonel Commandant
Burrows showed his regard for his "musics" by taking them with him
personally. The Marines arrived in the middle of July 1800 and on the
31st pitched their tents on a "beautiful hill overlooking the Potomac"—
the site today adjoins the State Department near Georgetown.

The first documented concert by the Marine Band in Washington
City was held on 21 August 1800 under the direction of Drum Major
William Farr. There is no record of what instruments were played by
the band on this date, but on 31 August Commandant Burrows wrote
Lieutenant Edward Hall in New York to "procure and send with all
convenient dispatch the articles hereafter mentioned—

> *2 French horns, 2 C Clarinets, 1 Bassoon, 1 Bass Drum,*
> *2 feet & long and 2 feet in diameter.*
> *Let some reeds be sent for the Clarinets and Bassoon.*
> *You must endeavor to have them selected by a judge of*
> *musical instruments."*

By December the band's inventory consisted of two oboes, two
clarinets, two French horns, a bassoon and a drum. For several months,
efforts to secure a bass drum were unsuccessful.

After playing for dances of the Washington Assembly at Stelle's
Hotel late in 1800, the band made its official debut when President
Adams held a reception at the President's Mansion—not yet known as
the White House—on New Year's Day 1801.

The Marine Band performs at the ground-breaking for the Chesapeake and Ohio Canal outside Washington on 4 July 1828. The band played Hail to the Chief *upon the arrival of President John Quincy Adams and a tradition was born. (Artist: LtCol Donna J. Neary, Marine Corps Art Collection)*

On 4 March 1801 at the first presidential inauguration held in Washington, the Marines, along with their band, riflemen and artillery, paraded at ten o'clock in the morning in front of President-elect Thomas Jefferson's lodgings at McMunn and Conrad's hotel. The Marine Band played *Jefferson's March* and other airs. The inauguration took place at noon. Since then, the Marine Band has played at every presidential inaugural.

Lieutenant Colonel Franklin Wharton, who succeeded Lt Col Burrows as commandant in 1804, was amazed to receive on 28 February 1805 a letter from Captain John Hall on board the *Congress* at Palermo, Italy. It stated that he had enlisted a "Band of Music" for the Corps and had supplied them with instruments at the Corps' expense.

A month later, Capt Hall again wrote Commandant Wharton from Messina, that, under the orders of Commodore Barron, he had visited Catania "for the purpose of procuring a band;" that he had "been fortunate enough to enlist fourteen good musicians." He noted that he had secured instruments at Messina, and that he had enlisted this band in accordance with orders he had received from Commandant Burrows prior to his departure. Capt Hall hoped Commandant Wharton would be "pleased with them."

Commandant Wharton was anything but pleased to have a second "band of music" on his hands. The last we hear of Captain Hall's "band of Italians" was on 31 July 1806 when Commandant Wharton ordered that the "Italian Band" was to live in "quarters within the garrison" and be "under the same regulations as the old band is and has been."

The Italian musicians were assimilated into the original Marine Band and became an integral part of the organization. Francisco Pulizzi,

The 1805 muster roll of the "Italian Band" recruited by the enterprising Capt John Hall. The Italians were incorporated into the Marine Band, and for the rest of the century the band would be dominated by Italian musicians. (National Archives)

age 40, and Venerando Pulizzi , age 12, were among those Hall enlisted at Catania. Later both served in the positions of fife major and drum major. Venerando served twice as leader of the band; briefly in 1816 and then from 1818 to 1827. He left the band and was promoted to Sergeant Major of the Marine Corps in 1832 and served at Headquarters until 1852.

During Thomas Jefferson's two administrations, the Marine Band played both the official and social music in the city of Washington, and it was through the patronage and interest of Jefferson that the band came to be known as "The President's Own."

The band played for James Madison when he became president on 4 March 1809, and that evening at Long's Hotel played for the first Inaugural Ball ever held in America. Under the direction of Drum Major Charles Ashworth, the band struck up *Jefferson's March* at the appearance of the former chief executive and *Madison's March* on the arrival of President and "Sweet Dolly" Madison.

During the War of 1812 with Great Britain, the Marine bandsmen helped maintain morale in the capital with their patriotic airs and martial strains. Some fought at the battle of Bladensburg, while others assisted in saving the Corps' early records when in 1814 the British burned most of Washington.

The most elaborate event of those days was the return visit of Marquis de Lafayette to the United States in 1824-25. He arrived on 12 October 1824 and was greeted with the largest parade ever held in Washington. Two days later, President Monroe hosted a state dinner in his honor. Music for both occasions was furnished by the Marine Band.

Lafayette's birthday on 6 September 1825 gave President John Quincy Adams the opportunity to rise and propose the first toast at the White House: "The Twenty-Second Day of February [Washington's birthday] and the Sixth of September." As the guests stood for the toast, Venerando Pulizzi led the Marine Band in playing *The Marseillaise*. Lafayette responded with a toast to "The Fourth of July, the birthday of liberty in both hemispheres."

At the ground breaking of the Chesapeake and Ohio Canal on 4 July 1828, Marine Band leader John Cuvillier saluted the entrance of President John Quincy Adams with *Hail to the Chief*. This was the first use of this music to announce the arrival of a president. *The National Intelligencer* reported the event and added "airs from the Marine Band lightened the toil."

Marine Band appearances grew routine with succeeding presidents. The band performed for President Andrew Jackson on 4 March 1829 in the first inaugural ceremonies to be held on the Capitol steps. And later that day the band played Jackson's favorite air, *Auld Lang Syne*, in the presence of a 1,400-pound "Mammoth Cheese," outdoing the 750-pound "Great Cheese" presented to Thomas Jefferson in 1802.

Under the direction of Raphael Triay, the band played for the inauguration of the former governor of the Indiana Territory, William Henry Harrison, on 4 March 1841. The ceremonies were held in brutally cold weather, and as a result President Harrison became ill from exposure and expired a month to the day of his inauguration. On 7 April the Marine Band led the late president's funeral cortege through the streets of the capital.

On 7 January 1845 President John Tyler directed that the Marine Band, then under the leadership of Joseph Lucchesi, play public concerts

---

MARINE BAND MUSICIANS: *Musicians of "The President's Own" Marine Band are selected through audition procedures similar to those of a major symphony orchestra. Candidates perform behind a screen to ensure anonymity, while the audition committee, composed of the band's principal players, section leaders, and directors, listen out of sight. The committee makes its selection based on musical ability and a subsequent personal interview.*

There are no academic degree requirements to become a member of the Marine Band, but most current members are graduates of some of the nation's best music schools and many hold advanced degrees in music.

The musician who is selected and successfully completes the physical examination enlists in the Marine Corps under a four-year contract "for duty with the U.S. Marine Band only." The chosen man or woman is guaranteed exclusive assignment to "The President's Own." Upon enlistment, each new Marine Band member is immediately appointed to the rank of staff sergeant

Marine Band clarinetist takes a "Dixieland" solo ride. (Photo: MGySgt Andy Linden, USMC)

(E-6) and reports directly to duty in Washington. More than 90 percent of those recruited become career Marines who serve in the band for twenty years or more.

As is the case of all members of the military, band personnel are subject to the Uniform Code of Military Justice, and the band members must be capable of passing and maintaining a White House security clearance. Training in military subjects, customs, traditions, and drill is required under the guidance of the drum major of the Marine Band, who as the senior enlisted Marine also serves as the band sergeant major.

The Marine Band consists of the usual number of woodwind, brass and percussion instrumentalists who are the nucleus of any "band." But to fulfill the requirements of the White House, a complement of strings - violin, viola, cello, bass - is also part of the band's contingent. They contribute the flexibility to perform as a strolling string ensemble, a string quartet, and, with the addition of the winds and brass, a chamber orchestra. Additionally, the band has pianists, harpists, guitarists, combo players, and one vocalist-concert moderator.

The directorate of the band consists of one director and two assistant directors, each of whom traditionally is chosen from within the ranks of the band by the director and recommended to the commandant and the president.

—JRB

From the halls of Montezuma
To the shores of Tripoli,

We fight our country's battles
In the air, on land, and sea.

First to fight for right
and freedom,
And to keep our honor clean,

We are proud to claim the title
Of United States Marines.

Our flag's unfurl'd to every breeze
From dawn to setting sun;

We have fought in every
clime and place
Where we could take a gun.

In the snow of far-off
northern lands
And in sunny tropic scenes,

You will find us always
on the job—
The United States Marines.

Here's health to you and
to our Corps
Which we are proud to serve;

In many a strife we've
fought for life
And never lost our nerve.

If the Army and the Navy
Ever gaze on Heaven's scenes,

They will find the streets
are guarded
By United States Marines.

on the grounds of the Capitol on Saturday afternoons. That became a tradition that continues to this day.

During the administration of President James K. Polk, the strength of the Marine Corps was doubled; and the band under the direction of Antonio Pons was increased to fifty-five drummers and fifers.

The Marine Band played for the laying of the cornerstone of the Washington Monument on 4 July 1848. Earlier that day, a wagon hauling the 24,500-pound stone of Maryland marble broke through the bridge over the city canal on the way to the site. Civilian workers at the Navy Yard volunteered to spend their lunch hour rescuing the stone, and the band urged them on with spirited melodies.

Francis Scala became the director of the band in the administration of President James Buchanan. His Secretary of the Navy Isaac Toucey wrote Marine Colonel Commandant John Harris on 23 April 1860:

> *Be pleased to direct the Marine Band to perform, until further orders, at the President's grounds every Wednesday afternoon and at the Capitol grounds every Saturday afternoon from 5 o'clock until sun-set, commencing on Wednesday next the 25th instant.*

During the Civil War, President Lincoln insisted that the band continue its outdoor concerts on the White House grounds. Secretary of the Navy Gideon Welles' diary of 6 June 1862 gives a first hand account of official and social life in the capital during the war years; he wrote:

> *Spoke to the President regarding weekly performances of the Marine Band. It has been customary for them to play in the public grounds of the Mansion once a week in summer, for many years. Last year it was intermitted, because Mrs. Lincoln objected in consequence of the death of her son. There was grumbling and discontent, and there will be more if the public are denied the privilege for private reasons.*

THE MARINES' HYMN: *When Marine Lieutenant Presley O'Bannon and his troops captured Derne, Tripoli, during the war with the Barbary Pirates in 1805, the American flag was hoisted for the first time over a fortress of the Old World. To mark the event, the Colors of the Marine Corps were inscribed with the words: "To the Shores of Tripoli."*

Following the war with Mexico and the capture of Mexico City in 1847, Chapultepec Castle and the National Palace, known as the "Halls of Montezuma," the words on the Colors were changed to read: "From the Shores of Tripoli to the Halls of the Montezumas." These two historical references give us the origin of the opening words to The Marines' Hymn. But the musical origins of the hymn have been a matter of dispute through the years.

Marine Colonel Albert S. McLemore and Walter F. Smith, assistant director of the Marine Band during John Philip Sousa's directorship, attempted to trace the tune of The Marines' Hymn *to its source. Col McLemore wrote, "Major Wallach, USMC, says that in 1878, when he was in Paris, France, the air to which the* Marines' Hymn *is now sung was a very popular one; that two Frenchmen, whose reputation in that day approximated the later reputation of Montgomery and Stone, sang a song to that tune. The opera ran hundreds of nights, and was enthusiastically acclaimed."*

The name of the opera and a part of the chorus was secured from Maj Wallach and forwarded to Mr Smith, who replied: "Major Wallach is to be congratulated upon a wonderfully accurate memory, for the air of the Marine Hymn *is certainly to be found in the opera,* Genevieve de Brabant ... *The melody is not in the exact form of the Marines' Hymn, but it is undoubtedly the air from which it was taken. I am informed however by one of the members of the band, who has a Spanish wife, that the air was one familiar to her childhood and it may, therefore be a Spanish folk song."*

The melody from Jacques Offenbach's comic opera Genevieve de Brabant *appears in a duet sung by two gendarmes. However, this opera was first heard in 1859 in two acts without the duet. As a result of the opera's popularity it was expanded to three acts in 1867, and then to five acts in 1875. Both of these later versions contain the duet. It is quite reasonable to accept Maj Wallach's report as correct. But one could conjecture that Offenbach, a prolific writer of musical satire, might just as easily have based his music to this duet on a pre-existing melody; and even perhaps on a Spanish folk song.*

The words and the air of The Marines' Hymn *have been sung and played in every corner of the globe, and it is recognized today as the most popular and revered of our service songs.*

—JRB

The public will not sympathize in sorrows which are obtrusive and assigned as a reason for depriving them of enjoyments to which they have become accustomed, and it is a mistake. The President said Mrs. Lincoln would not consent, certainly not until after the 4th of July. I stated the case pretty frankly, although the subject is delicate, and suggested that the Band could play in Lafayette Square. The President told me to do what I thought best.

Marine Band concerts continued, but in Lafayette Square across from the White House.

On 19 November 1863, the band, still under the direction of Francis Scala, accompanied Lincoln to Gettysburg for the dedication of the National Cemetery when he delivered his immortal Gettysburg Address. The train manifest roster of band personnel on that day includes the name Antonio Sousa, trombonist, the father of John Philip Sousa.

While Lincoln had no formal musical education, he had a deep love for popular music. He especially enjoyed ballads and political songs honoring Jackson and Adams. However, in 1860, while attending a minstrel

Facing page: A Civil War drum with an 1859 kepi on top. A First Manassas bugle on a post–Civil War drum, a field music shoulder knot, and a white dress helmet from 1888–1904. (Marine Corps Museum. Photo: Eric Long)

Above: *A somewhat portly John Philip Sousa immediately after his appointment in 1880 as leader of the Marine Band. He would hold that post until 1892. (Courtesy of MGySgt Michael Ressler, USMC)*

Above right: *The 1868 enlistment papers of John Philip Sousa. His father, Antonio Sousa, himself a member of the Marine Band, thought his obstreperous 13-year-old son needed Marine Corps discipline and signed him up as a "music boy." (Marine Band Library)*

show in Chicago, he had heard *Dixie* for the first time, and it immediately became his favorite song. On 9 April 1865, after the surrender of Robert E. Lee, the Marine Band and a great, exuberant crowd assembled on the White House lawn and called repeatedly for the president. He appeared on the balcony and addressed the crowd, ending his remarks by commanding the band to play *Dixie* because, he said, "now it belongs to the nation." This jubilation turned to somber mourning eleven days later and the band led the funeral cortege of the assassinated president.

During the Civil War years, the influence of military music on the young Washingtonian, John Philip Sousa, was so compelling that later he wrote in his autobiography, *Marching Along*: "I loved all of them (the bands) good and bad alike." When he was tempted to run away and join a circus band, the plot was discovered by his father, Antonio, who brought his thirteen-year-old son to Marine Commandant Jacob Zeilin. And on Tuesday, 9 June 1868, John Philip Sousa was enlisted as a boy or apprentice in the Marine Band for the "tentative period of seven years, five months, and twenty-seven days."

After two enlistments lasting nearly seven years, followed by a brief period as a conductor of theater orchestras and then as a member of the violin section of Jacques Offenbach's American Centennial tour orchestra, John Philip Sousa was re-enlisted as the seventeenth leader of the Marine Band on 1 October 1880.

Sousa led the Marine Band from 1880 to 1892 and during those years he elevated it to a prominence it had not known before. He proudly wrote, "the Marine Band is the national band...as great among bands as America is among nations." It was under Sousa's leadership that the band participated in the dedication of the Statue of Liberty in New York harbor on 4 July 1886.

Sousa was followed by Francesco Fanciulli, who led the band at the dedication of Grant's Tomb in New York City on 25 April 1897. Fanciulli was an accomplished musician, but he was blanketed by the shadow of Sousa. During a street parade in the capital on 1 June 1897, he made an unwise decision not to play a requested Sousa march. As a result he was charged with insubordination and ordered by Lieutenant Herbert L. Draper to return to the barracks and place himself under "house arrest." The incident caused a fury in the Washington press, which referred to Fanciulli as the "Prisoner of 15th Street," and the news filtered into the White House.

President Grover Cleveland had an engagement the next day to deliver a major speech in Philadelphia. Calling the secretary of the Navy and the commandant of the Marine Corps together, the president prevailed upon them to release Fanciulli from custody so the band could accompany him to Philadelphia.

When Fanciulli and the band returned to Washington, a board of inquiry convened to investigate the allegations against him. The board found Fanciulli guilty of "failure to obey a lawful order, use of disrespectful language toward an officer, and conduct being prejudice to the conduct of good order and discipline." The recommended sentence was dishonorable

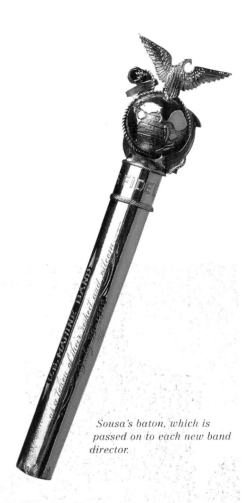

Sousa's baton, which is passed on to each new band director.

The Marine Band, in its earliest known photograph, attributed to Matthew Brady and taken in 1864, stands on the parade ground at the Marine Barracks, Washington, with the Commandant's House in the background. Legend has it that the little boy with the toy tin horn is John Philip Sousa, standing by his father, Antonio Sousa, a trombonist. (Library of Congress)

"The March King"

John Philip Sousa made the U.S. Marine Band the nation's premier military band—and world famous. He directed "The President's Own" from 1880 to 1892 and during those years wrote most of the music that earned him the title of "The March King." Two of the most famous of his early marches are The Washington Post (1889), written for the newspaper of that name, and Semper Fidelis (1888), dedicated "to the officers and men of the United States Marines."

A musical genius and son of a member of the Marine Band, Sousa began his career as a violinist and conductor. His musical output included fifteen operettas, numerous vocal works and, what he is remembered for best, 136 marches.

"He was truly an American phenomenon," states Paul Bierley, his biographer, "and his expressed mission in life was to raise the level of his country's music appreciation and improve its image abroad."

In the Marine Band's nearly twelve years under Sousa, it rose to be comparable to those of long tradition in Europe, and its director attained dignity and fame. And at the same time, it is doubtful that Sousa would have ever have been known as "The March King" without the opportunities gained from the Marine Corps. He applied the disciplines he learned there to his civilian band that he directed for the next thirty nine years.

After his long service with the Marine Band, John Philip Sousa formed his own "Sousa Band" in 1892. It became immensely popular both in the United States and throughout the world. His tours earned him wealth and fame and the distinction of being one of the most recognizable figures of his day.

When America entered World War I, Sousa enlisted on 31 May 1917 and was given the rank of lieutenant in the U.S. Naval Reserve. He was the first Navy musician to be a commissioned officer. He joked about his age (sixty two) and was the oldest man known to have entered the Navy until that time. At his own insistence, his salary was set at one dollar a month.

Although he twice declined promotions, he was promoted to lieutenant commander when he was released from duty in January 1919.

He returned to directing the Sousa Band for another dozen years, and eight weeks after its final tour in 1931, Sousa celebrated his seventy fifth birthday.

The last two weeks of his life were like a grand finale—as eventful as he could have wished. On George Washington's two hundredth birthday, 22 February 1932, he conducted the combined bands of the Army, Navy and Marine Corps in front of the Capitol. The concert's highlight was the playing of the George Washington Bicentennial, a march he had written for the occasion. Five days later, he participated in his

John Philip Sousa. Portrait by Col John J. Capolino, USMC

final concert, conducting the orchestra of the Marine Band in his march Hands Across the Sea. *This took place in Washington at the annual dinner of the Military Order of the Carabao, an organization of officers who had served in the Philippine Islands. General Douglas MacArthur, chief of staff of the U.S. Army, presided as the Grand Paramount Carabao.*

Sousa died on Sunday, 6 March 1932, in Reading, Pennsylvania, following a rehearsal with the Ringgold Band. The concluding number of the rehearsal and the last composition ever played under his baton was his own immortal Stars and Stripes Forever.

Sousa's body lay in state in the Marine Band Auditorium, and the service on 10 March was aired by the Columbia Broadcasting System. Eight white horses drew the caisson to his final resting place in Congressional Cemetery where so many well known Americans are buried, seven blocks southeast of the Marine Barracks.

As the procession began, the Marine Bands played Semper Fidelis *in dirge time. The thousands who lined the streets to pay their last respects heard, between cadences, two of Sousa's dirges:* In Memoriam *and* The Honored Dead. *Following a brief graveside ceremony, a Navy firing squad gave a salute and* Taps *was sounded by former Sousa Band cornetist Del Staigers.*

Since then, many memorials have been created for "The March King." A U.S. postage stamp bears his likeness; a World War II Liberty ship was named for him; there is the ever-present "sousaphone," and perhaps most meaningful of all his honors is his election to the Hall of Fame for Great Americans.

—JRB

Top: John Philip Sousa stands on the podium in front of the U.S. Marine Band in about 1891.

discharge from the Marine Corps. The transcript of the proceedings of the board was forwarded to Acting Secretary of the Navy Theodore Roosevelt. After much deliberation, Roosevelt decided that the sentence was too severe and ordered the findings of the board to be set aside. Fanciulli resumed his post, but on 27 October 1897, Marine Corps Headquarters announced that Fanciulli would not be re-enlisted.

The term "Marine Band" had long been used as a technical description for a type of mouth organ or harmonica. At the end of the nineteenth-century the Hohner Harmonica Company sought to capitalize on the growing prominence of "The President's Own" and released a new harmonica with a picture of the U.S. Marine Band on the front of the instrument's case. This product-identity campaign ultimately proved to be very successful. To this day Marine Band harmonicas are thought to refer to the Marine Band in Washington, though Hohner and the band have no affiliation with one another.

One of the most brilliant social events held at the White House was the wedding of Alice Roosevelt, daughter of President Theodore Roosevelt, to Nicholas Longworth on 17 February 1906. More than a thousand guests were in attendance as Alice, on the arm of her illustrious father, proceeded to the altar to the strains of *The Wedding March* from Wagner's *Lohengrin* performed by the Marine Band under the direction of

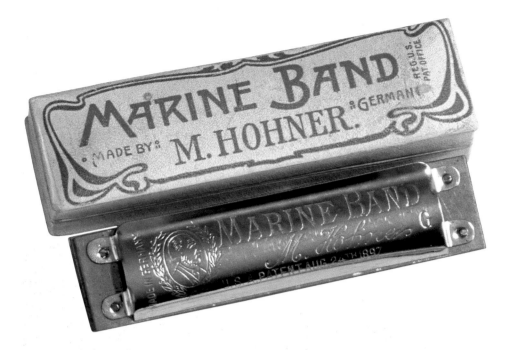

William H. Santelmann. Santelmann was to become the "Archibald Henderson" of the band with a tenure of twenty nine years as director—from 13 March 1898 to 1 May 1927. He was the first director in the band's history to become a commissioned officer, retiring in the grade of captain.

Captain Taylor Branson, who followed Santelmann as director, pioneered weekly radio broadcasts of the band's concerts, and they became the longest sustained programs in that medium. On 21 August 1932, Branson conducted the band at the Canadian Exposition in Ottawa—the first time that the Marine Band performed outside the United States.

During World War II, on 20 May 1943, President Franklin D. Roosevelt hosted a special concert on the White House lawn for Great Britain's prime minister, Winston Churchill. In attendance were the prime minister of Canada, Lord Halifax, several American generals, and twenty five British officers of similar rank. The band was under the direction of Lieutenant Colonel William F. Santelmann (son of William H.). Despite a steady rain, Roosevelt and Churchill stayed for the entire performance and at its conclusion sang with the band *The Battle Hymn of the Republic*.

Winston Churchill addressed the Massachusetts Institute of Technology's Mid-Century Convocation in Boston on 1 April 1949. As he was about to leave the speakers' dais, Churchill turned to the audience and declared that he would like to "ask one favor." He requested that Lieutenant Colonel Santelmann and the band "play one more number—*The Marines' Hymn*." And to the delight of the audience and the band, Churchill sang the words to every verse.

When the band played the background music for the signing of the North Atlantic Treaty on 4 April 1949, LtCol Santelmann conducted a varied program that included selections from Gershwin's Porgy and Bess. The following morning *The Washington Post* reported: "NATO treaty signed, Marine Band says *It Ain't Necessarily So!*"

The band became a fixture at Blair House while the White House was being renovated during the administration of President Harry S Truman. Warrant Officer Albert F. Schoepper, assistant director, led string ensemble performances there, with President Truman often joining in at the piano. While Truman may not have been a fan of the "public relations" efforts of the Marine Corps itself, he wrote the band's leader: "Let

Albert F. Schoepper, shown here as a lieutenant colonel, was the first leader of the band to achieve the rank of colonel. Himself an accomplished violinist, he served as director from 1955 to 1972. (Marine Band Library)

Marine Band recording made by RCA Victor for the benefit of the Kennedy Center for the Performing Arts in 1963. Some of the earliest "Victrola" records, made at the turn of the century, featured the Marine Band. (Photo: MGySgt Andy Linden, USMC)

me just say that the U.S. Marine Band is not only a most attractive ceremonial institution but musically eloquent and highly professional as well. Through the years it has been a source of comfort and pleasure to the occupant of the White House."

On 10 November 1954, the Marine Corps' birthday, during the administration of President Dwight D. Eisenhower, the band participated in the dedication ceremonies of Felix de Weldon's heroic representation of the flag-raising on Iwo Jima at the Marine Corps War Memorial.

Following the retirement of LtCol Santelmann, Schoepper, with a promotion to captain, inherited the directorship of the band on 1 May 1955. He served in the position of director for almost seventeen years and became the first director to achieve the rank of colonel.

While attending an evening parade at Marine Barracks, Eighth and "Eye" Streets, on 12 July 1962, President John F. Kennedy told the audience that he had just discovered that one illustrious title was no longer his—namely that of Commander-in Chief. He explained that the commandant could order Marines to deploy anywhere in the world without consulting him; the Marine bandsmen were the only troops that were solely his. The Kennedy wit became evident when he went on to say, "The Marine Band is the only force that cannot be transferred from the Washington area without my express permission. Let it be hereby announced that we, the Marine Band and I, intend to hold the White House against all odds!"

At the request of Mrs Kennedy, the Marine Band led the funeral
procession of the assassinated president on November 25, 1963.

Throughout the years of service to the White House, many inci-
dents have added to the band's lore. None could be more illustrative of a
communications gap than that between President Lyndon B. Johnson
and the leader of the Marine dance band, Captain Dale L. Harpham.

President Johnson had pre-determined that during his press reception of 1965 he was going to dance with all of the ladies present. Unfortunately, he had not informed the dance band leader of his intentions.
While the band was playing a medley of Broadway show tunes, the president glided by, and over the shoulder of his dance partner he gruffly
whispered to Captain Harpham, the band leader: "Faster !" Harpham
increased the tempo of the music. Several times more the president
passed by and said: "*Faster*!" and the last time: "Damn it, I said *faster*!"
With each pass the tempo of the music increased until the long-legged
president was galloping around the room. In exasperation Johnson
retired from the dance floor and nothing more was heard from him.

The next day an aide phoned Harpham at the band office and
asked: "Captain, what in the world did you do last night that so infuriat-

ed the President of the United States?" Harpham related his version of the story and the aide said he would get back to him shortly. Five minutes later the aide called again and relayed, "Captain, when the President says *faster*, he means *shorter*." It was the president's intention to dance a few moments with one lady, stop, change partners, go to the next, and in so doing the press would have reported that "last night the president danced with every lady in the room."

The Marine Band performed during the dedication of a memorial on 27 October 1967 on Theodore Roosevelt Island in the Potomac River near Georgetown. The ceremony was attended by President Johnson and the daughter of Theodore Roosevelt, Alice Roosevelt Longworth, for whose wedding the band had performed sixty-one years earlier.

When President Richard M. Nixon was the first president to visit Yugoslavia on 1 October 1970, he brought with him to Belgrade a 13-piece orchestra from the Marine Band to provide music at a reception and a "return" dinner for Yugoslavian Premier Josip Broz, known as "Tito." This marked the first time that members of the band played outside the United States for a State function. At the end of the evening,

LtCol Dale I. Harpham, director from 1972 to 1974, conducts for President Richard M. Nixon, who said of the band, "I have never failed to be proud of this splendid musical organization." When Nixon visited the Soviet Union in 1974, he took a five-piece string ensemble with him. (Photo: The New York Times)

Below (top to bottom) : *Following in the footsteps of SSgt Ruth Johnson, the first woman member of the band, a female clarinet player waits for performance time, and a flautist performs on the porch of the White House, during the 1998 Easter Egg Roll at the White House. (Photos: Greg E. Mathieson)*

Nixon visited with each of the musicians and thanked them for their performance on that historic occasion.

During the directorship of Dale Harpham, who was by then a lieutenant colonel, Staff Sergeant Ruth Johnson, a French horn player, was the first woman to win an audition and become a member of the Marine Band on 16 May 1973. Since that time, women have become an integral part of the organization.

Musicians from the band traveled out of the country again when in July 1974 a five-piece string ensemble accompanied President Nixon to the Soviet Union. The group performed traditional chamber music during a dinner hosted by the president in Moscow. On that occasion Nixon said of the band:

> *During my years of service as Vice President and President, I have never failed to be proud of this splendid musical organization. Foreign visitors have often remarked to me that they felt it was the finest organization of its kind in the world. Thomas Jefferson is remembered for the Declaration of Independence and his other contributions. One of his least known and most delightful legacies is the President's Own Band.*

During the Bicentennial observances of 1976 in the administration of President Gerald R. Ford, the Marine Band, now led by Lieutenant Colonel Jack T. Kline, performed for festivities throughout the country.

The celebration culminated with the State visit of Queen Elizabeth II of Great Britain in July. For this occasion a larger than usual number of guests was invited and Marine ensembles were deployed throughout the White House—a full concert band on the South lawn, harp and flute in the Diplomatic Entrance, a chamber orchestra in the Grand Foyer, a show band accompanying the singing duo of "Captain and Tenille" in the East Room, and a seven-piece combo playing dance music in the State Dining Room.

The Public Broadcasting System reported the event "live" and cameras were everywhere. At one point the crowd parted to allow President Ford to escort the Queen into the dining room, where he asked her to dance to the Marine combo playing a Rodgers and Hart medley. It was not until several weeks later that a review of the PBS tapes revealed that the Rodgers and Hart tune the combo was playing was *That's Why the Lady Is a Tramp*. The medley was immediately removed from the dance folder.

During the presidency of Jimmy Carter, on 31 May 1979, I became the twenty-fifth director of the Marine Band and served in that position for more than seventeen years. It was also during the Carter administration that the press repeatedly reported that the president had eliminated the playing of his traditional honors, *Hail to the Chief*. Although President Carter did not require ceremonial music at all public events when he was away from the White House, *Hail to the Chief* was still performed there by the Marine Band whenever presidential honors were appropriate.

President Carter had an avid interest in music and often took time

President and Mrs Jimmy Carter and guests enjoy the Marine Orchestra after a state dinner for President and Mrs Jose Lopez Portillo of Mexico on 14 February 1977. President Carter was particularly fond of Broadway show music and a little ill at ease with Hail to the Chief. *(Jimmy Carter Library)*

Top: *The Marine Band orchestra, with LtCol John R. Bourgeois conducting, greets President Ronald Reagan and the First Lady at a White House evening function. (Ronald Reagan Library)*

Above: *Baritone MGySgt Michael Ryan sings* America the Beautiful *at Ronald Reagan's first inaugural, 20 January 1981. (Photo: MGySgt Andy Linden, USMC)*

from his busy schedule to listen to the band's music. The musicians performed for a variety of events ranging from an outdoor performance of Rodgers and Hammerstein's *Carousel* with soloists from the Metropolitan Opera and Richard Rodgers in attendance, to a South Lawn performance with composer-pianist Marvin Hamlisch. Following that performance President Carter told the audience, "...the only problem is that Mr. Hamlisch wants to take my Marine Band back with him. He can't have them!"

When Ronald Reagan was inaugurated as president on 20 January 1981, for the first time the ceremonies were held on the west-front of the Capitol. It was a memorable occasion, and not only because of the change of venue. At precisely the same time that baritone Master Gunnery Sergeant Michael Ryan and the Marine Band were performing *America the Beautiful* during the inaugural program, the American hostages were released from Iran. The news flashed over television screens around the world just as a bright sun broke through the clouds and illuminated the ceremony.

The Marine Band gave its first overseas concert performance in Rotterdam, Netherlands on 26 November 1985 in celebration of the 320th birthday of The Royal Netherlands Marines. In attendance were H.R.H. Princess Margriet, Royal Netherlands Marine Commandant Rudolphe, and U.S. Marine Commandant Paul X. Kelley.

The 100th birthday of the Statue of Liberty was celebrated on 4-6 July 1986 in New York City. The festivities included the Parade of Tall Ships, reviewed by President Reagan aboard the USS *Iowa* while the Marine Band played musical selections from each country participating in the event. On the evening of the Fourth a mammoth fireworks display was choreographed to music played by the band from the deck of the aircraft carrier USS *John F. Kennedy*. The celebration culminated with a joint concert of the New York Philharmonic Orchestra and the Marine Band for a live audience of a million people in Central Park and was televised around the world to millions more.

On 11-14 November 1986 the band traveled to Dublin and U.S. Ambassador Margaret Heckler arranged for a gala performance at Dublin's National Concert Hall. The concert, at which the Marine Band performed a program of Irish and American music, was attended by the president of Ireland, Patrick Hillary, the lord mayor of Dublin, and the commandant of the Marine Corps, Boston-Irishman General P. X. Kelley.

The Marine Band was the featured concert band of the 11th International Band Music Festival in Hamar, Norway from 29 June through 5 July 1989. In addition to concerts in Hamar and the rural countryside, the band played for the U.S. ambassador and the American community at the U.S. Embassy in Oslo on Independence Day.

During the last week of the Reagan presidency, the orchestra of the Marine Band was present at the White House for the president's farewell to his staff. After his remarks, he came over to say farewell to the band and I told him how proud we were to have been his band. Since I had heard of his proficiency on the harmonica, I gave him a personalized Marine Band harmonica and said that now he would always have his own Marine Band to play *Hail to the Chief* whenever he wished. He took the instrument in his hands and looked at it quizzically. My first thought was that maybe my information was wrong and that perhaps he didn't play. To my relief he put the harmonica to his lips and drew three notes. "Ah," I said to myself, "*The Marines' Hymn*"; but when he continued, I realized he was playing the *Red River Valley*. How

Col Bourgeois presents President Reagan with a Marine Band harmonica during the president's last days in office. The president immediately demonstrated that he could play it. (Ronald Reagan Library)

poignant, I thought, as he played the western folk song that laments "From this valley they say you are going."

In the administration of George Bush, the Marine Band made an 18-day concert tour of the Soviet Union in February 1990 as part of an historic U.S.-Soviet Armed Forces Band Exchange. The band performed in the cities of Moscow, Kiev, L'vov, Minsk, and Leningrad. As the Russians are fond of exchanging souvenirs, we brought Marine Band harmonicas inscribed in Cyrillic as gifts from the musicians to commemorate the visit.

The first concert of the tour occurred at the same time as the convening of the Plenum of the Communist Party, and the huge Bolshoi Military Theater was filled to capacity with visiting musicians from the far reaches of the Soviet Union. Our concert concluded with a joint effort of our Marine Band and the massed bands of the Soviet Armed Forces performing Tchaikovsky's *1812 Overture*. The senior music director of all the Soviet bands, Major General Nikolai Mikhailov, was the conductor.

When played in the non-Soviet world, the final measures of the *1812 Overture* conclude with *The Tsar's Hymn*. However, at this perfor-

The Marine Band performs in the L'vov Opera House during its historic eighteen-day tour in 1990 of what was still the Soviet Union. (Photo: MGySgt Andy Linden, USMC)

254

mance—as with all performances in the Soviet Union since the October Revolution of 1917—the Soviets replaced this hymn with a tune by Glinka which fit well into the musical structure. Their performance parts already had a pasted-over insert, and we were given copies of the insert to cover the offensive passage in our music.

The tour ended in Leningrad, the home of the October Revolution. Again, at the conclusion of the concert, the Marine Band was joined by massed Soviet Army and Navy Bands for a performance of the *1812 Overture*. This time I was asked to conduct, and it was further requested that the overture be performed "the way you do it." I advised them that we performed the original Tchaikovsky version which included *The Tsar's Hymn*. The officials insisted again: "Play it the way you do it." So I instructed all of the musicians to peel back the pasted-over inserts from their music and, that evening, *The Tsar's Hymn* was heard in Leningrad for the first time since the 1917 revolution. The audience roared its approval. And later they cried unrestrainedly when, as an encore, we played the old *Hymn to the City*. (The hymn dates back to when the city was called St. Petersburg, and it remained a symbol of identity and

Below: *A Marine Band percussionist performs at the 1998 Easter Egg Roll as a curious child watches from behind a window. (Photo: Greg E. Mathieson)*

Above: *Members of the Marine band walk past the portico of the White House in preparation for their performance at the 1998 Easter Egg Roll. (Photo: Greg E. Mathieson)*

strength to the people, especially during the siege of Leningrad by the Nazis in World War II.)

The Marine Band played its first concerts in England at the Royal Albert Hall in London on 15-22 February 1992. As part of the Mountbatten Festival of Music, the U.S. Marine Band and the massed bands of Her Majesty's Royal Marines performed a joint concert in the presence of Royal Marine Commandant, Lieutenant General Sir Henry Beverly, and the U.S. Marine Commandant, General Carl E. Mundy, Jr.

The 250th birthday of Thomas Jefferson was celebrated on 13 April 1993, at the Jefferson Memorial, which the band had dedicated on 13 April 1943. President William Jefferson Clinton gave the birthday address honoring his mentor and namesake. Later the president wrote me: ". . . the Marine Band's precision and discipline, which prompted a proud Jefferson to refer to it as The President's Own, serve as a standard for aspiring musicians throughout the nation."

There were many occasions during the Clinton presidency when I had the opportunity to speak with the president about music, and I was always surprised by the depth of his knowledge. Perhaps my most memorable event with this musical president was conducting him in a satirical saxophone solo performance during the annual Gridiron Club dinner. The Gridiron Club, which Sousa led as its first music director, is a Washington institution that presents a dinner each spring during which the government's leaders are satirized in skits.

That evening, former president George Bush was seated to the left of the Gridiron Club president at the head table. When the Marine Band marched into the room, Bush leaned to his right and said to the Gridiron president, "You know, the thing I miss most about my former job is the Marine Band." Unaware of this comment, President Clinton, seated on the Gridiron president's right, leaned over and said "You know, the thing I enjoy most about this job is the Marine Band."

During the band's 198th birthday commemoration on 11 July 1996 at the Daughters of the American Revolution's Constitution Hall, I was relieved of command by Lieutenant Colonel Timothy W. Foley, who became the 26th Director of the Marine Band.

On 20 January 1997, LtCol Foley led the Marine Band in its traditional place of honor at President Clinton's second inaugural. One of the highlights of the musical program was the performance by the great American soprano Jesse Norman, accompanied by the Marine Band.

At the traditional "surprise" New Year's serenade on I January 1998, the commandant, General Charles C. Krulak, saluted the band as it entered its bicentennial year. Late in the month the American conductor and director of the National Symphony, Leonard Slatkin, conducted the band at Constitution Hall in a program of contemporary American wind music.

By the end of the twentieth century, the Marine Band had come a long way from the original thirty-two drums and fifes. Today, with 143 musicians and 5 officers, the band still proudly continues its unique mission "to provide music for the President of the United States and the Commandant of the Marine Corps."

LtCol Timothy W. Foley, twenty-sixth director of the Marine Band, stands above at attention, and, below, is shown in action.

Facing page: *Members of the Marine Band perform at the White House during the 1998 Easter Egg Roll. (Photo: Greg E. Mathieson)*

THE
Comman

dants

THE
Commandants
Thirty-One Men Who Have Led the Corps

Brigadier General Edwin H. Simmons, USMC(Ret)

Director Emeritus, Marine Corps History and Museums

Samuel Nicholas received on 28 November 1775 the first naval commission issued by the Continental Congress, signed with a flourish by the president of the Congress, John Hancock. (Original in the Marine Corps Museum, Washington, D.C.)

No Marine Corps traditions are more deeply rooted than those that surround its commandants. Since 1775 the Corps has had thirty-one of them—allowing for the fact that the first never bore the title during his lifetime. None of the other services has a leader with a title as old and as continuous as "commandant." "Chief of staff," which designates the uniformed heads of the Army and Air Force, and "chief of naval operations," which does the same for the Navy, are of twentieth-century origin. "Commandant" goes back to the beginning of the nineteenth century. Here are summaries of where the Corps finds its leaders and what kind of careers in the Corps bring its commandants to the fore.

Previous spread: *The Commandant's House, rear or garden view, as seen from across the parade ground. The ship's bell in the right foreground tolls the hours and half-hours in best naval fashion. Ship's bells are similarly used at many other Marine Corps posts and stations. (Photo: Eric Long)*

Samuel Nicholas

FIRST COMMANDANT

28 November 1775 – 25 August 1781

The clerk of the Continental Congress had no blank commissions specifically for Marines. When Samuel Nicholas was commissioned on 28 November 1775, a blank printed for officers of the Continental Navy, none of whom had yet been commissioned, was used with pen changes and signed by John Hancock, president of the Congress. So Nicholas became a "Captain of Marines" and his was the first naval commission.

Nicholas was the thirty-one-year-old only son of a Philadelphia blacksmith, and his qualifications were slim. His maritime experience seems to have consisted of sailing as a super-cargo in merchant ships for Robert Morris, the leading financier of the Revolution, and enjoying an active sporting life on the Schuykill and Delaware rivers. Morris's patronage probably got Nicholas his Marine commission. Although early congressional intentions to field two battalions of Marines soon faded, Nicholas did well in the raid on New Providence in the Bahamas, in raising Marine guards for the new frigates being built in the Delaware, and in Washington's victory at Princeton.

For the remainder of the war he acted chiefly as a confidential agent for his patron, Robert Morris, as that worthy juggled the precarious finances of the fledgling republic. Nicholas had a final adventure in 1781 when he, with his few remaining Marines, escorted an ox cart laden with a million silver crowns, a loan from Louis XVI of France, the 350 miles from Newport, Rhode Island, to Philadelphia, much of it through Tory country.

Although Nicholas never bore the title of commandant, Marines with considerable justification regard him as their first.

SAMUEL NICHOLAS. *Portrait by LtCol Donna J. Neary, USMCR.*

William Ward Burrows

SECOND COMMANDANT

12 July 1798 – 6 March 1804

President John Adams, on 12 July 1798, the day after he signed the act that created the United States Marine Corps, named William Ward Burrows, earlier of Charleston, South Carolina, but now of Philadelphia,

WILLIAM WARD BURROWS. *Portrait by Col John J. Capolino, USMC.*

as major commandant. The handsome forty-year-old Burrows was a vehement and articulate Federalist, the party of Adams and Hamilton, and his credentials were more political than military.

In the summer of 1800 the Federal government moved from Philadelphia to the new District of Columbia. Burrows took his Marines, such as were not at sea, to Washington, encamped them near the site of the present-day Washington Monument, and found a house for himself in Georgetown. In the fall, Thomas Jefferson defeated John Adams in the presidential election. The Marine Band played for Jefferson's inauguration on 4 March 1801.

The day before the Federalist Congress went out of office, it appropriated $20,000 for the building of a Marine barracks. At the end of the month, Jefferson and Burrows rode out on horseback to pick a site; Jefferson, a superb horseman, undoubtedly was riding "Wildair," his favorite saddle horse.

The grid of the city, as laid out by the Frenchman, Major Pierre L'Enfant, made a pretty map, but on the ground it consisted of a few scattered houses along rutted, muddy roads. The new president and Burrows, now a lieutenant colonel, picked a double city block in southeast Washington, bounded by G and I streets and 8th and 9th streets, because "it lay near the Navy Yard and was within easy marching distance of the Capitol."

Money for building came in dribbles, and the barracks and the Commandant's House at 801 G Street were not yet completed when Burrows resigned for reasons of health in 1804. He died less than a year later at age forty-five.

Franklin Wharton

THIRD COMMANDANT
7 March 1804 – 1 September 1818

Franklin Wharton, a member of a very prominent Philadelphia family, was commissioned a captain in the Marines in 1798 and succeeded William Burrows. Wharton had been Marine detachment commander in the frigate *United States* during the quasi-war with France. He pressed for the completion of the Commandant's House and moved into the house with his large family in 1806.

As lieutenant colonel commandant, Wharton performed competently, following the precedents of good training and firm discipline set by his good friend Burrows. But, unfortunately, he failed to take the field with the Marines from the Washington barracks when they marched out to meet the British at Bladensburg in August 1814. When President James Madison's government fled the city, Wharton and his paymaster commandeered a wagon and took the Marines' pay chest to Frederick, Maryland.

After Bladensburg, the British commander, Major General Robert Ross, accompanied by Rear Admiral George Cockburn, whose speciality was putting the torch to American towns, raided Washington. The British burned or wrecked most public buildings—including the Presi-

FRANKLIN WHARTON. *Portrait by Louis H. Gebhardt.*

THE COMMANDANT'S HOUSE: *A notice in the Washington newspaper* National Intelligencer *on 3 April 1801 offered "a premium of 100 dollars" for "the best plan of barracks for the Marines, sufficient to hold 500 men, with their officers, and a house for the Commandant." George Hadfield, an English architect recently arrived (and younger brother of Maria Cosway, President Jefferson's good friend in Paris), won the competition.*

The barracks would be laid out as a quadrangle, much like a typical European caserne, with the buildings backing to the streets and enclosing a parade ground. The north or G Street side was reserved for the Commandant's House. To give the new capital city presence and dignity, the young government encouraged the building of stately houses. The house Hadfield designed was essentially a transitional red-brick Georgian, not yet flat-fronted as most of the Federal town houses would be later.

That June, Jefferson ordered $4,000 be paid for "square No. 927 in Washington for the purpose of erecting thereon Barracks for the Marine Corps." When construction began, Marines provided much of the labor.

It is certainly possible that Jefferson added his own touches to the house's design. A twentieth-century architectural historian said, "Considering its plan, and general appearance, it was a most daring composition in its day and showed, as Thornton had in the Octagon House sometime earlier, the Federal desire to escape the monotonous confinement of Georgian geometry."

The original house had on the first floor a vestibule leading to a main hall, the dining room to the left, a small parlor to the right, and beyond the main hall two large drawing rooms. Cooking was done in the basement, as it would be for many years. The second floor had four bedrooms and there was an attic with dormered windows. A square cupola topped the pyramidal roof. Clay was dug in a nearby pit and burned into a soft brick so that the walls had to be especially thick.

—EHS

The Commandant's House, greatly changed from 1806, as it stands in 1998 at 801 G Street, Southeast. (Photo: Eric Long)

dent's Mansion, not yet called the White House—but exempted the Commandant's House and Marine Barracks. Marines spin many tales as to why the house and barracks were spared. We do know that Ross and Cockburn spent the night in the Commandant's House. Survival of the house supports the Marines' claim that the Commandant's House is Washington's oldest public building in continuous use for its original purpose.

Wharton's caution in saving the pay chest did not impress his officers. They never forgave him for what they saw as cowardice. Three years later, in 1817, he was tried by an Army general court-martial, instigated by his affronted officers, for neglect of duty and conduct unbecoming an officer and a gentleman. He was acquitted and, even though the new president, James Monroe, urged him to resign, held on stubbornly as commandant until he died in office a year later, at age fifty-one.

Anthony Gale

FOURTH COMMANDANT

3 March 1819 – 8 October 1820

For six months after Franklin Wharton's death, Major Archibald Henderson acted as commandant; then Major Anthony Gale, as the senior officer, took charge. Gale had been born in Ireland and was thirty-seven when he became lieutenant colonel commandant. In an era when hot tempers were fashionable, his was particularly flaming. As a young lieutenant serving in the *Ganges*, he had been struck by a Navy junior officer. He had "called his man out" and shot him, an action that was applauded by his commandant, William Burrows.

Gale's tenure as commandant was brief. He soon fell afoul of the secretary of the Navy, and there was a court-martial. Among the specifications was one of "being intoxicated in common dram shops and other places of low repute." Gale pleaded not guilty by reason of temporary insanity. He was found guilty and sentenced to dismissal from the service.

Archibald Henderson

FIFTH COMMANDANT

17 October 1820 – 6 January 1859

A week after Anthony Gale's dismissal, Major Archibald Henderson became the lieutenant colonel commandant. The new resident would occupy the Commandant's House for more than thirty-eight years—by far the longest tenure of any commandant.

Henderson had been born in 1783 near the present-day Marine Corps base at Quantico in the now-lost town of Colchester, Virginia. He had been commissioned in 1806, and in September 1813 became the captain commanding the Marine detachment in the *Constitution*, leading the Marines in the capture of His Majesty's frigate *Cyane* and the sloop-of-war *Levant* in February 1815—after the Treaty of Ghent had

ARCHIBALD HENDERSON. *Portrait by Reuben LeGrand Johnston.*

already been signed. Ships at sea did not know they were at peace until weeks and months after the treaty was signed. Henderson was breveted (given an honorary rank without the pay) as a major for his bravery.

The Peace Establishment Act of 1817 authorized 50 officers and 942 enlisted Marines, but funding seldom allowed more than half this strength. The act also gave the commandant a staff of an adjutant and inspector, quartermaster, and paymaster—a structure that would survive until World War II. Henderson decreed that all newly commissioned officers come to Marine Barracks, Washington, for instruction. Out of this came The Basic School of today.

President Andrew Jackson, perhaps forgetting the good service the Marines had rendered him at New Orleans, in 1829 recommended to the Congress "that the Marine Corps be merged in the artillery or infantry, as the best mode of curing the many defects in its organization." Henderson deftly played the game of Washington politics, and in 1834 Congress passed a favorable "Act for the Better Organization of the Marine Corps." It provided that the president could direct the Marines to perform such duties as his judgment dictated, including service with the Army. It also said that the Marine Corps, afloat or ashore, was part of the Navy Department, but separate from the Navy itself.

On President Jackson's orders in May 1836, Henderson led into the field a two-battalion regiment against the Creeks and Seminoles in Georgia and Florida. Henderson's regiment was brigaded with the

LtColComdt Henderson Takes a Wife

On 16 October 1823, Archibald Henderson, the fifth commandant, married Anne Maria Casenove, the sixteen-year-old daughter of a prominent Alexandria, Virginia, merchant. Too busy for a honeymoon, Henderson gave his bride an alfresco reception and supper at the Commandant's House. All of the officers stationed at the Marine Barracks and the cream of Washington's fledgling society attended. Henderson is standing to the left of the bride. All went well until the close of the evening when the new Mrs. Henderson noted tables being set up in the drawing rooms. Asking the butler what they were for, she was told that the gentlemen would be playing cards after supper. She is reported to have said, "No cards will ever be played in my house!" And this prohibition apparently remained in effect for the thirty-six years she lived in the house. Six children were born to the Hendersons during that time. (Painting by Col Charles Waterhouse, USMCR (Ret), Marine Corps Art Collection)

Army's 4th Infantry Regiment, some artillery, and an assortment of friendly Creeks and Georgia volunteers. With Henderson in command, the brigade pushed a band of Seminoles to the Hatchee-Lustee River northeast of Tampa, fought them on 27 January 1837 in a battle that was more noise than killing, and persuaded their chiefs to move to a reservation. Henderson's reward was a brevet promotion to brigadier general.

During these years Henderson extensively modified the Commandant's House—where he both lived and kept his office. In 1840 he added a two-story extension to the east side of the building and a year later, a one-story west wing as servants' quarters. He also gave the house its first bathroom.

He would like to have taken the field once again during the Mexican War. This did not happen, but he served as commandant during that war, which much enhanced the Corps' reputation by demonstrating its usefulness in sea-going expeditions. Archibald Henderson, after thirty-eight years as commandant, died in office on 6 January 1859, and so was spared the paroxysm of the Civil War.

John Harris

SIXTH COMMANDANT
7 January 1859 – 12 May 1864

John Harris, the new colonel commandant, born in Pennsylvania in 1790, had entered the Corps during the War of 1812 and already had forty-five years of service. He had commanded a detachment of "horse Marines" in the Seminole Wars; and after the battle at the Hatchee-Lustee River, he had carried back to Washington the treaty Archibald Henderson had reached with the Indian chiefs. In the Mexican War he took a battalion to Mexico but arrived after hostilities had ceased. Altogether, his service had been solid and satisfactory but uneventful.

When the Civil War came, Harris's sympathies seemed to be with the South. Nearly half of the Corps' officers resigned to take commissions under the Confederacy, and Harris let them go, giving at least one of them a letter of recommendation. During the war his service, again, was dutiful but uninspired. Marines gave good service on board ship and in minor landing operations, but Harris made little effort to expand the Corps or to exploit its amphibious potential. In the mind of Secretary of the Navy Gideon Welles, his performance left much to be desired. When Harris died on 12 May 1864, Welles wrote in his diary, "His death gives embarrassment as to a successor."

The officers of the Corps most probably would have chosen hard-drinking but hard-fighting Lieutenant Colonel John Reynolds to succeed Harris. At First Bull Run Reynolds had shown himself a better troop handler than most of the Union officers, and he had done well as a battalion commander on the Atlantic coast, including the bloodless capture of Saint Augustine, Florida. But in May 1862, Harris brought Reynolds up on charges of drunkenness and contempt, and Reynolds countered with charges against Harris. An exasperated Gideon Welles gave both Marine

JOHN HARRIS. *Portrait by Louis H. Gebhardt.*

officers letters of reproof. When it came time, Welles made Major Jacob Zeilin commandant and retired all officers senior to him, thus getting rid of the troublesome Reynolds.

Jacob Zeilin

SEVENTH COMMANDANT
10 June 1864 – 31 October 1876

Jacob Zeilin had been born in Philadelphia in 1806, commissioned in the Marine Corps in 1831, and was a seasoned sea-going officer by the time of the Mexican War. He and his detachment of Marines on board the new forty-eight-gun frigate *Congress* outdid themselves in the Pacific coast landings at Santa Barbara and San Pedro, the capture of Los Angeles, and the rescue of Kearny's Army of the West at San Bernardo Ranch. By the war's close he was the fleet Marine officer of the Pacific Fleet. When Commodore Perry sailed to Japan in 1852, Zeilin went with him. His Marines, with their colorful uniforms and their precision drill, dazzled the Japanese.

Zeilin commanded a company in Reynolds's battalion at Bull Run and was critically wounded in the fighting around Henry House Hill. In August 1863, perhaps not fully recovered, he was sent with a battalion to join operations against Charleston, South Carolina. He fell sick, turned the battalion over to Reynolds, and was sent to the sinecure of barracks commander at Portsmouth, New Hampshire. There he received word from Secretary of the Navy Welles on 10 June 1864 that he was the colonel commandant.

As a reflection of the Corps' lackluster performance in the Civil War, the House of Representatives in 1866 again considered abolishing

JACOB ZEILIN. *Portrait by Reuben LeGrand Johnston.*

267

the Marine Corps or transferring its functions to the Army. But after listening to a long line of witnesses, the Committee on Naval Affairs finally in February 1867 reported: "No good reason appears either for abolishing it, the Marine Corps, or transferring it to the Army; on the contrary, the Committee recommends that its organization as a separate Corps be preserved and strengthened." For Zeilin there was a promotion to brigadier general.

The Corps' existence was again challenged in 1874, and once more, the Corps, with friends in Congress, survived. Zeilin stayed on as commandant until after the nation's Centennial celebration on 4 July 1876 and then, not waiting to die in office as had his predecessor, retired on 31 October.

Charles Grymes McCawley

EIGHTH COMMANDANT

1 November 1876 – 29 January 1891

Jacob Zeilin's successor, Charles McCawley, was yet another Philadelphian. Born in 1827, he was twenty when commissioned—in time to be sent to Mexico and win a brevet promotion to first lieutenant in the storming of Chapultepec and entry into Mexico City.

He added to his laurels in the Civil War, taking part in the capture of Port Royal, South Carolina—the eventual site of the recruit depot at Parris Island—and in operations in and around Charleston. In the summer of 1863, as a captain, he took over the battalion that had been commanded by Zeilin and Reynolds. On 8 September McCawley tried a night assault against Fort Sumter. Everything went wrong; the Marines were beaten off with forty-four casualties, but McCawley received a brevet promotion to major.

He became colonel commandant—the grade of brigadier general that Zeilin held had been a one-time honor—the day following Zeilin's retirement. He was a master at administration and methodically set about establishing higher enlistment standards, better training, and better officer selection (from 1882 on the Corps would get a quota of graduates from the Naval Academy). To the bemusement of his clerks he introduced the typewriter and the telephone. He started a clothing factory in Philadelphia which provided high-quality uniforms at low cost to the Corps until the factory was consolidated out of existence by Secretary of Defense Robert S. McNamara in the 1960s. McCawley followed Zeilin's precedent of retiring (at age sixty-four) rather than waiting to die in office.

Charles Heywood

NINTH COMMANDANT

30 June 1891 – 2 October 1903

Although the succession was obvious, five months passed after Charles McCawley's retirement before Charles Heywood became colonel commandant. Heywood was born in Maine in 1839 and was made in much

the same fighting mold as McCawley. He was commissioned in 1858 and had both navy yard and shipboard duty before the Civil War.

In 1861 he did his part in the captures of forts Clark and Hatteras that commanded Hatteras Inlet. In the fight between the *Cumberland* and *Virginia* (better known to history as the *Merrimac*), he commanded the gun division that fired the last gun before the *Cumberland* went down. This won him the brevet rank of major.

As fleet Marine officer with the West Gulf Squadron, he was with Admiral David Farragut in the *Hartford* at Mobile Bay. This gained him another brevet promotion—to lieutenant colonel. In 1885, while serving at the Brooklyn Navy Yard, he organized in twenty-four hours a battalion for service in Panama, took it there, and opened up the railroad across the Isthmus.

One of Heywood's first actions as colonel commandant was to execute plans McCawley had made for the remodeling of the Commandant's House. In 1891 the original Georgian-Federal design became staidly late-Victorian. The old roof was removed and the present mansard roof installed. A one-story porch (today's solarium), overlooking the back garden and parade ground, was added.

The Spanish-American War saw the Marine Corps double and then triple in size under Heywood's leadership. For his good services he was promoted to brigadier general, and in 1903, he retired at age sixty-four, as the law now required.

George Frank Elliott

TENTH COMMANDANT

3 October 1903 – 30 November 1910

GEORGE FRANK ELLIOTT. *Portrait by Bjorn Egeli.*

The next commandant, George Elliott, was another fighter. Almost immediately after becoming the brigadier general commandant, he left Washington to lead the Marine brigade that was building up in Panama—the last time a commandant would take the field.

Born in Utah, Alabama, in 1846, Heywood "bilged out" of West Point and took a consolatory commission in the Marine Corps in 1870. As a junior officer, he did his tours of sea and shore duty punctuated by the expedition to Panama in 1885 and the march through war-torn Korea to install the legation guard in Seoul in 1894. In the Spanish-American War he fought effectively at Guantanamo, and in the Philippine Insurrection, at Novaleta.

In this period, to the consternation of the Marines, a faction of Navy officers argued for the elimination of Marine detachments from the battleships and cruisers of the fleet. (The Navy faction favored the expeditionary uses of Marines but believed their sea duty, with modern sailors no longer mutinous, obsolete.) President Theodore Roosevelt, who thought Marines more decorative than useful, ordered their removal.

Elliott successfully maneuvered in Congress to get his Marines back on the ships. He soft-pedaled their duties as policemen and emphasized their usefulness both in manning secondary gun batteries and in stiffening landing parties. Elliott was promoted to major general. Until the middle of World War II "Major General Commandant" was the sonorous title that sergeants major liked to roll off the tongue, particularly when asked by a young lieutenant to interpret some arcane provision of the *Marine Corps Manual.*

WILLIAM PHILLIPS BIDDLE. *Portrait by Richard Norris Brooke*

William Phillips Biddle

ELEVENTH COMMANDANT
3 February 1911 – 2 February 1914

The choice of William Biddle as commandant was not popular with the Corps, which would have preferred Littleton W. T. "Tony" Waller, hero of a dozen Marine expeditions. But the Samar affair, in which Waller had summarily had eleven Filipinos shot for treachery, made him politically unacceptable.

Biddle was a Philadelphian, member of a family at least as prominent as the Whartons. His service record was steadfast. Commissioned in 1875, he had a long string of assignments at sea and was in Admiral Dewey's flagship *Olympia* at the Battle of Manila Bay. He commanded a battalion on the march to Peking in 1900 and again in the Panama intervention of 1903. In 1906 he led the 1st Brigade in the Philippines and later, a brigade in Panama. His time as commandant was uneventful. Fairly or unfairly, the aura of unpopularity stuck to him, and after three years in the post, he asked for early retirement in 1914.

George Barnett

TWELFTH COMMANDANT
25 February 1914 – 30 June 1920

Secretary of the Navy Josephus Daniels would have preferred John A. Lejeune as William Biddle's successor, but Lejeune was too junior to make the jump. With some reservations, Daniels nominated George Barnett; and over the next six years, these reservations grew into an open breach.

Barnett had come from Wisconsin and graduated from the Naval Academy in 1881. Under the agreement negotiated between the secretary of the Navy and Charles McCawley, he chose a commission in the Marine Corps after two years at sea as a passed midshipman.

During the Spanish-American War he served in the *New Orleans* and was with her when she shelled the Spanish forts at Santiago, Cuba. He briefly commanded a battalion in Panama in 1902 and later took it to the Philippines. He led a battalion into Cuba in 1906, and two years later went to China to command the legation guard at Peking. On his return he was assigned as commanding officer of the Marine barracks at the Philadelphia Navy Yard and from there sallied forth on three more brief interventions in Cuba. In 1913 he was given command of the 1st Advance Base Brigade.

MajGen Barnett, with the help of such as Col Lejeune, did a good job of readying the Corps for war under the military service expansions

COMMANDANTS' PORTRAITS: *Major General Commandant George Barnett began the formal collection of commandants' portraits in 1916. He apparently waited until Secretary of the Navy Josephus Daniels was out of town and then sought approval to make the collection from the assistant secretary of the Navy, the young Franklin D. Roosevelt. As acting secretary, FDR delighted in taking charge in Daniels's absence. Roosevelt wrote the comptroller of the Treasury on 16 October 1916: "The Commandant of the Marine Corps is desirous of procuring, for historical purposes, in oil, [portraits] of as many of the Commandants of the Marine Corps since its reorganization in 1798 as may be obtainable, probably eight or nine in all, such portraits to be preserved at the Headquarters of the Corps."*

Then, perhaps with his tongue in his cheek, Roosevelt asked for a decision on whether the expenditure could be made from the appropriation "Maintenance, Quartermaster's Department," under any of several subheads such as "office furniture" or "expenses arising at home or abroad but impossible to anticipate or classify." He added a postscript in his own handwriting: "I believe that it is the duty of the government to encourage in every way possible the collection and preservation of every kind of historical material."

In less than a week the comptroller came back with a finding that such paintings fell within the category of "furniture." Three weeks later the quartermaster general, Charles G. McCawley, son of the former commandant, reported that a contract was in place with artist Richard N. Brooke for paintings of as many former commandants as desired at $225 each. Although portraits of nineteenth-century commandants were reconstructed, a portrait of Anthony Gale is missing because no image of that miscreant has ever been found. For his own portrait, Barnett went to a slightly more expensive artist, Louis H. Gebhardt, who charged the Corps $235. Each subsequent commandant has chosen his own artist.

The tradition, not written but strictly observed, is that the original portraits hang only in the Commandant's House. Their presence accentuates the character of the house although commandants' wives have been heard to decry giving wall space to "all those bearded gentlemen."

—EHS

authorized by the 1916 Defense Act (up to fifteen thousand for the Marines). When war with Germany was at last declared in April 1917, the politically astute Barnett was determined to have a Marine regiment in the first convoy to sail for France and to make good the Corps' recruiting slogan, "First to Fight." The secretary of the Army told him that there was no space for Marines in the first convoy, so Barnett organized space in Navy transports and tartly replied, "Please give yourself no further trouble in this matter, as transportation for the Marines has been arranged."

In his sometimes strained partnership with Navy Secretary Josephus Daniels, Barnett supervised the expansion of the Corps from fifteen thousand to seventy-six thousand, developed a major new base at Quantico, Virginia, and sent two large brigades to France. Still, the Marines continued to police the Caribbean and the Mexican border with smaller brigades and regiments, man the legation guard in Peking, and provide Marine detachments to the Navy's battleships and cruisers.

Barnett had been appointed to a four-year term, which was by then the law, and his term was extended for two years because of the war. In 1920 he fully expected another term, but relations with Daniels were now badly frayed, and Daniels wanted to move war hero Lejeune into the commandancy. Barnett refused to retire, so Daniels sent him to San Francisco as the first commanding general of the Department of the Pacific, a sinecure created for the purpose.

GEORGE BARNETT. *Portrait by Louis H. Gebhardt.*

John Archer Lejeune

Thirteenth Commandant

1 July 1920 – 4 March 1929

John Archer Lejeune. *Portrait by Samuel Curtis Baker.*

Navy Secretary Josephus Daniels's choice for commandant, John A. Lejeune, had come home from Germany in August 1919 and marched at the head of his U.S. 2d Infantry Division in its victory parade in New York City. Assigned to command at Quantico, he served there until appointed commandant.

Born in Louisiana in 1867 into a family impoverished by the Civil War (in which his father served as a Confederate captain), Lejeune graduated from tuition-free Louisiana State University. Then, still dirt poor, he accepted an appointment to the Naval Academy from which he graduated in 1888. The obligatory two years of sea duty as a naval cadet convinced him that he wanted his commission to be in the Marine Corps. He served in the *Cincinnati* during the Spanish-American War, took a battalion into Panama in 1903, and bobbed in and out of Cuba and the Philippines for the next ten years. In April 1914 he commanded the 1st Advance Base Brigade in the Veracruz intervention.

On returning from Mexico, Lejeune became the principal assistant to the commandant, George Barnett. He did well with the Congress and attracted Daniels's attention. He planned most of the Marines' mobilization for the coming war. Early in World War I Barnett sent him to take charge of the burgeoning new camp at Quantico. In June 1918, as a brigadier general, Lejeune went to France while the mopping up at Belleau Wood was still going on. He carried to General Pershing an offer from Barnett to form a Marine division. Pershing turned down the offer but, impressed by Lejeune, placed him briefly in command of a National Guard brigade and then of the 4th Marine Brigade before giving him command of the U.S. 2d Infantry Division, which included the Marine brigade. Lejeune showed his mettle (and got along with both French and American generals) at St. Mihiel, Blanc Mont, and the Meuse-Argonne, and continued to command the division until it returned home.

Not since Archibald Henderson had the Marine Corps had such a strong commandant. He gave the Corps nine years of forward-looking leadership. Intensely proud of the Marines' service with the Army in France, he nevertheless regarded that use as an aberration to be avoided in the future. He foresaw a war with Japan and put his planners to work considering an amphibious role for the Marine Corps in a war reaching across the Pacific.

He moved the 1st Advance Base Force headquarters from Philadelphia to Quantico. The School of Application for new lieutenants became The Basic School at Philadelphia, and company-grade and field-grade schools were organized at Quantico.

A master at public relations, Lejeune fielded varsity-quality baseball and football teams at the major Marine Corps bases, staged Civil War reenactments to entertain the Congress and the public, and was the main impetus in the organization of the Marine Corps League as a counterpart to the Navy League. A second four-year term followed the first. At the end of it, Lejeune was reluctant to retire and stayed in place yet another year. On retirement in 1929 he became superintendent of the Virginia Military Institute.

Wendell Cushing Neville

FOURTEENTH COMMANDANT
5 March 1929 – 8 July 1930

WENDELL CUSHING NEVILLE. *Portrait by Sidney E. Dickinson.*

To no one's surprise, John A. Lejeune's successor was his old friend and *compañero*, Wendell C. Neville. "Buck" Neville had commanded a regiment in Lejeune's brigade at Veracruz and in France led the Marine brigade in the 2d Infantry Division throughout Lejeune's command of the division.

Neville was born in Portsmouth, Virginia, and graduated from the Naval Academy in the class of 1890. Following two years of sea duty as a passed midshipman, he, like Barnett and Lejeune before him, elected to take his commission in the Marines. At the outbreak of the Spanish-American War, he was assigned to Lieutenant Colonel Robert W. Huntington's hurriedly assembled battalion. He came out of the action at Guantanamo with a brevet promotion to captain and the new Brevet Medal—ranking with the Medal of Honor, which was not yet authorized for officers. For his performance as a regimental commander, under Lejeune, at Veracruz in 1914, he did receive the Medal of Honor, which was now authorized for officers and was at that time rather freely given. In the beginning of 1917 he was in Peking as the commander of the legation guard.

On America's entry in World War I, Neville requested (some say demanded) a transfer to France, and, arriving there in the fall of 1917, took command of the 5th Marines. After Belleau Wood he moved up to lead the Marine brigade.

When he was named commandant more than a decade later, the always robust "Buck" Neville was in failing health. He died after only sixteen months in office. His official portrait was unfinished; in order to complete it, another officer who was approximately Neville's size was assigned to pose wearing his uniform and medals.

Ben Hebard Fuller

FIFTEENTH COMMANDANT
9 July 1930 – 28 February 1934

BEN HEBARD FULLER. *Portrait by Bjorn Egeli.*

Ben H. "Uncle Ben" Fuller, Michigan-born, followed the path of Barnett, Lejeune, and Neville into the Corps: four years at the Naval Academy, two years at sea, and then a Marine Corps commission. He was one of the six new second lieutenants who in 1891 made up the first class of the School of Application. He served at sea in the Spanish-American War, fought at Novaleta in the Philippines, and in 1900 commanded a company of artillery in the battle for Tientsin and the march to Peking. World War I found him sidelined as commanding general of the 2d Provisional Brigade in Santo Domingo. Later he moved across the border to command the 1st Brigade in Haiti. Lejeune made him his assistant commandant in

1928, and he continued as such (often serving as acting commandant) during Neville's brief tenure.

Fuller's commandancy was largely shaped by the Great Depression and retrenchment. Franklin D. Roosevelt, who as assistant secretary of the Navy had admired greatly the Marines' performance in the Caribbean, now as president, ordered them home from Nicaragua in 1933 and from Haiti in 1934, under his "Good Neighbor" policy.

John Henry Russell, Jr

1 March 1934 – 30 November 1936

JOHN HENRY RUSSELL, JR. *Portrait by Bjorn Egeli.*

John Russell's time as major general commandant was a brief but very important two years and eight months in the Marine Corps' development as an amphibious force. A much stronger personality than his predecessor, Ben Fuller, he had become the assistant to the commandant in February 1933—and virtual commandant when Fuller absented himself on a five-month-long inspection trip.

Born at Mare Island, California, the son of an eventual admiral, Russell came into the Marine Corps by the now-familiar pathway of Naval Academy and sea service. He received his Marine commission in 1894 and served in the *Massachusetts* in the Spanish-American War. This new battleship bombarded the Spanish fortifications at Santiago, Cuba, but, by returning to the newly seized advance base at Guantanamo to coal, missed the great victory over the Spanish fleet. Subsequently, Russell had more sea duty and served ashore at stateside navy yards and abroad in Guam, Honolulu, and Peking. He commanded a battalion at Veracruz in 1914, but the command of a regiment in Santo Domingo kept him out of the fighting in World War I. In 1922, with the rank of brigadier general, he became high commissioner of Haiti and served there for nine years.

While assistant commandant, Russell was the main driving force in the conversion of the East and West Coast Expeditionary Forces into the Fleet Marine Forces, Atlantic and Pacific.

Withdrawal of the Marines from Nicaragua and Haiti made it possible to bring home the 1st Marine Brigade to Quantico and the 2d Marine Brigade to San Diego. Landing exercises, up to brigade size, were held with the Atlantic and Pacific fleets; and the British amphibious performance at Gallipoli in 1915, good and bad, became the focal point for study and analysis at Quantico.

During Russell's brief residence in the Commandant's House, he extended the east wing, giving the exterior its present balanced appearance.

Thomas Holcomb

1 December 1936 – 3 December 1943

John Russell, while commandant, supplanted the old seniority system for officer promotions with selection boards, a reform long overdue. President Franklin D. Roosevelt, who approved the reform, dug deep for

Russell's replacement and chose Brigadier General Thomas Holcomb, a good friend and a distinguished battalion commander in World War I.

Holcomb had come into the Corps by direct appointment from civilian life in 1900 (as had Smedley Butler two years earlier). He was the first commandant since William Biddle not to attend the Naval Academy. Holcomb's service followed the usual pattern of alternating sea and garrison duty, including two lengthy tours with the legation guard in Peking during which he mastered the Chinese language. He qualified for the Marine Corps Rifle Team in 1901, and nearly every year thereafter when his posting permitted it. His friendship with Franklin Roosevelt, himself an ardent marksman, dated to those shooting days before World War I. In the summer of 1917 Holcomb formed the 2d Battalion, 6th Marines, took it overseas and led it at Belleau Wood and Soissons. Wartime service brought him a string of French and American decorations including the Navy Cross.

After the war he commanded the Marine Barracks at Guantanamo, attended the Army's Command and General Staff School at Fort Leavenworth (finishing as a Distinguished Graduate), served in operations and training at Headquarters, and in 1927 returned to China for a three-year tour as commander of the legation guard. He headed Quantico's Marine Corps Schools when he was selected to be commandant.

Roosevelt reappointed Holcomb for a second four-year term in 1940. He oversaw the expansion of the Corps from seventeen thousand in 1939 to more than three hundred thousand in 1943. In the frantic first few months after 7 December 1941, he successfully resisted the notion of President Roosevelt, abetted by Winston Churchill, that the Corps be divided up into commando units or used in an early invasion of North Africa.

Holcomb resisted the entry of blacks and women into the Marine Corps but lost both of these battles. A story, substantiated by several persons present, holds that when, at a dinner party in the Commandant's House, Holcomb announced that a decision had been made that day to admit women into the Corps, the portrait of Archibald Henderson fell off the dining room wall. On 1 January 1944 he was raised to full general and shortly thereafter sent to South Africa as minister, serving for four years before retiring to a Maryland farm.

THOMAS HOLCOMB. *Portrait by McClelland Barclay.*

Alexander Archer Vandegrift

EIGHTEENTH COMMANDANT

1 January 1944 – 31 December 1947

Alexander Archer "Archie" Vandegrift returned in triumph from the South Pacific at the end of 1943, wearing the pale blue ribbon of the Medal of Honor for his staunch defense of Guadalcanal, and became the lieutenant general commandant.

Born in Charlottesville, Virginia, and after attending the University of Virginia (he was always the quintessential Virginian), he had been commissioned in the Marine Corps in 1909. He was present at the assault of Coyopete in Nicaragua and in the landing at Veracruz (nursery for so many

ALEXANDER ARCHER VANDEGRIFT. *Portrait by Bjorn Egeli.*

Marine Corps leaders) and chased "bandits" in Haiti throughout World War I. After a second tour in Haiti, he went with the 3d Brigade to China in 1927. A second tour in China followed, culminating as commanding officer of the legation guard. On his return home in 1937, he served the commandant, Thomas Holcomb, as military secretary and assistant until November 1941 when he was given command of the new 1st Marine Division.

Vandegrift led the division ashore at Guadalcanal on 7 August 1942, and by December, when he turned over the island to the Army, there no longer was any doubt as to the outcome. Promoted to lieutenant general, he was given command of the 1st Marine Amphibious Corps which he headed through the landing phase of the Bougainville operation.

Ordered home to be commandant, Vandegrift supervised the expansion of the Marine Corps to an ultimate wartime strength of 485,000 and six divisions. And after the war he led the Corps in a narrowly successful rear-guard action in the "unification" battle fought on Washington's Capitol Hill. "Tri-elementalists" wished to package U.S. forces neatly into land, sea, and air components and they saw no need for a Marine Corps that had all three. While the Navy was busy defending naval aviation against the demands of what would become the separate Air Force, the Marine Corps bore the brunt of the battle against the Army which had never admitted much reason for a Marine Corps.

Many Marines felt that Gen Vandegrift's finest hour came not at Guadalcanal but on 6 May 1946 when in testimony before the Senate Naval Affairs Committee he said:

> *Sentiment is not a valid consideration in determining questions of national security. We have pride in ourselves and in our past, but we do not rest our case on any presumed ground of gratitude owing us from the nation. The bended knee is not a tradition of our Corps. If the Marine as a fighting man has not made a case for himself after 170 years of service, he must go. But I think you will agree with me that he has earned the right to depart with dignity and honor, not by subjugation to the status of uselessness and servility planned for him by the War Department.*

The debate culminated with the National Security Act of 1947, which clarified and reaffirmed the Marine Corps' place as a military service within the Department of the Navy. The Fleet Marine Forces, ground and air, were given statutory standing, and the Corps was given the clear mission to seize and defend advanced naval bases, as well as to conduct land operations incident to naval campaigns, and primary responsibility for the development of amphibious warfare doctrine, tactics, techniques, and equipment.

Although military experts pontificated that the atomic bomb made amphibious assaults obsolete, the Marines studied the most vulnerable stage of an amphibious operation: the ship-to-shore movement during which troops were slowly ferried ashore in landing craft. They examined large-scale use of transport submarines and giant seaplanes and discarded them as unrealistic. Use of helicopters—then still frail and uncertain—showed more promise.

Vandegrift was to retire on 31 December 1947, and President Harry Truman had to choose as his successor from between two closely matched contenders, Clifton B. Cates and Lemuel C. Shepherd. Both had emerged from World War I as heroes. Both had commanded regiments and divisions in World War II. Truman summoned them together to the Oval Office. Opining that as a military man himself he had always favored seniority, he turned to Gen Shepherd and said, "General Cates is senior to you and he is older than you are. I'm going to make him commandant this year, and I trust that I'll be able to have you follow him four years from now."

Clifton Bledsoe Cates

NINETEENTH COMMANDANT
1 January 1948 – 31 December 1951

CLIFTON BLEDSOE CATES. *Portrait by Bjorn Egeli.*

Clifton B. Cates came from Tiptonville, Tennessee. He attended the Missouri Military Academy and already had a law degree from the University of Tennessee when he came into the Marine Corps as a reserve second lieutenant two months after the United States entered World War I. In France he fought in all the Marine brigade's battles—Belleau Wood, Soissons, St. Mihiel, Blanc Mont, and the Meuse-Argonne—as a member and often acting company commander of the 96th Company, 6th Marines. He was repeatedly wounded and gassed and was left with permanently weakened lungs, aggravated no doubt by cigarettes, which, in later years, he smoked in a long filter holder that suited his debonair manner. His World War I medals included the Navy Cross, a twice-awarded Army Distinguished Service Cross, two Silver Star Medals, and, from the French, the Legion of Honor and the Croix de Guerre with gilt star and two palms. Along the way he picked up the nickname "Lucky."

On his return to the States in the late summer of 1919, Cates became the aide-de-camp to Gen Barnett and accompanied him to the Department of the Pacific. Highlights of Cates's post–World War I career included service at sea in the battleship *California* and a three-year tour with the 4th Marines in Shanghai. After attending the Army's Industrial College and fulfilling other domestic assignments, he had a second tour in China in 1937, this time as a battalion commander in the 6th Marines during the Japanese invasion of China. He stayed on in Shanghai with his old regiment, the 4th Marines, and returned home in 1940. Serving as the director of The Basic School when World War II came, he received command of the 1st Marines and landed with it at Guadalcanal. In March 1943 he took charge of the Marine Corps Schools at Quantico, and after a year was assigned to command the 4th Marine Division, which he led through the battles on Saipan, Tinian, and Iwo Jima. He was again serving at Quantico when he was elevated to the commandancy.

Cates sought and found an appropriate role for the Marine Corps in the Korean War. In this he was in an unlikely partnership with General of the Army Douglas MacArthur. At the time, the Marine Corps still had no direct voice in the Joint Chiefs of Staff but was dependent upon the chief of naval operations (who often had his own Navy fish to fry) for representation.

Using powers of persuasion and Pentagon-style diplomacy, Cates saw to it that the 1st Provisional Marine Brigade was formed and dispatched to Korea to shore up the faltering Pusan perimeter, and that MacArthur had his 1st Marine Division (and accompanying aircraft wing) in time for the Inchon assault landing. Later, during the epic Chosin Reservoir campaign, he backed the obstinate resistance of the 1st Marine Division commanding general against the demands of the Army corps commander.

Just before the Inchon landing, Cates had to deal with an angry commander-in-chief. President Harry Truman, enraged by a congressman's request that the Marines be given a voice on the Joint Chiefs of Staff, fired off a reply that said in part, "For your information the Marine Corps is the Navy's police force and as long as I am President that is what it will remain. They have a propaganda machine that is almost equal to Stalin's. . . . The Chief of Naval Operations is the Chief of Staff of the Navy of which the Marines are a part."

This outburst got into the newspapers, and Truman was assailed from all sides. He faced up to it with a note of apology to Cates and a personal appearance before a Marine Corps League banquet. Cates accepted the apology with Southern good manners, but left the picture of Truman in his office turned to the wall.

On completing his tour as commandant, Cates took the unusual step of reverting from four-star to three-star rank and taking command, once again, of the Marine Corps Schools at Quantico.

Lemuel Cornick Shepherd, Jr

TWENTIETH COMMANDANT

1 January 1952 – 31 December 1955

President Truman made good his promise of four years earlier and nominated Lemuel C. Shepherd, Jr, to be the next commandant. Shepherd came to the job from Hawaii where he was the commanding general of Fleet Marine Force, Pacific, and very much involved in the conduct of the Korean War. He had the confidence of Gen MacArthur, and most Marines (and some others) thought he should have had command of the landing force at Inchon. Command had gone to a less-qualified Army general junior to him, but Shepherd remained unruffled and went along as an "observer." When disaster threatened at the Chosin Reservoir, he again rode to the sound of the guns and oversaw the evacuation of the Marines from Hungnam.

Lemuel Shepherd had been a bright light since Belleau Wood. In a career remarkably parallel to that of Cates, he came into the Corps in 1917 as a graduate of the Virginia Military Institute and went to France with the 55th Company of the 5th Marines in the first convoy to sail. He was three times wounded (twice seriously) but had a proclivity for

LEMUEL CORNICK SHEPHERD, JR. *Portrait by Bjorn Egeli.*

returning to the battlefield, healed or not. He received a Navy Cross, a Distinguished Service Cross, and the Croix de Guerre.

In 1920 he was chosen as aide-de-camp to the commandant, then John Lejeune, whose favorite exercise was riding. Shepherd was also a horseman and they rode together on mornings in Rock Creek Park. After a tour of sea duty in the battleship *Idaho*, he was given command of the Sea School in his home town of Norfolk, Virginia. He, like Cates, went to China in 1927, serving in Tientsin and Shanghai, where he admired British swank. Assigned to Haiti, he played polo and served with the Garde d'Haiti. He then attended the Naval War College at Newport and afterwards commanded the 2d Battalion, 5th Marines at Quantico, where it was testing amphibious doctrines and techniques.

Four months after war was declared with Japan, Shepherd had orders to form the 9th Marines as part of a new 3d Marine Division. On promotion to brigadier general, he moved to assistant command of the 1st Marine Division, served with it at Cape Gloucester, and then was given command of the 1st Provisional Marine Brigade formed for the liberation of Guam. When the brigade expanded into the 6th Marine Division, Shepherd received his second star and led the division brilliantly on Okinawa, and then took it to Tsingtao, China, for occupation duty. With his love of ceremony, he arranged a dramatic surrender of ten thousand Japanese at the Tsingtao race track.

He left China in the fall of 1946 to become the assistant to the

Gen Lemuel Shepherd, a combat hero in both World War I and World War II, is shown here visiting the front lines in Korea in September 1952 while he was commandant. Ahead of him, with the broad grin, is Col Walter F. Layer, then commander of the 1st Marines. (Photo: SSgt E. J. Scullin, USMC)

commandant, Gen Vandegrift, and chief of staff of Headquarters, Marine Corps. Duty as commanding general, Marine Corps Schools, Quantico, followed; and just before the outbreak of the Korean War, he received his third star and command of Fleet Marine Force, Pacific.

Inchon and Chosin added fresh luster to Marine battle honors and public esteem and helped make possible legislation favorable to the Corps. Two Marine veterans, Senator Paul H. Douglas of Illinois and Congressman Mike Mansfield of Montana, sponsored a bill in January 1951 which emerged, after much acrimonious debate, as Public Law 416, 82d Congress. It provided for three active Marine divisions and three air wings, and co-equal status for the commandant on the Joint Chiefs of Staff when matters of direct concern to the Corps were considered.

Much of the pageantry at Marine Barracks, Washington, and at the Marine Corps War Memorial at Arlington (as well as existence of the monument itself) is attributable to Shepherd's interest. More substantively, he reorganized the antiquated structure of Headquarters, Marine Corps, into a general staff and special staff, paralleling the staff organization of field units. Gen Shepherd retired at the end of 1955 but was recalled to active duty to serve as chairman of the Inter-American Defense Board, a position involving much travel and ceremony and one he enjoyed immensely.

Randolph McCall Pate

TWENTY-FIRST COMMANDANT

1 January 1956 – 31 December 1959

Randolph McC. Pate, President Eisenhower's choice as commandant on Gen Shepherd's recommendation, was born at Port Royal, South Carolina, but was a Virginian by lineage. After brief enlisted service in the Army in World War I, he graduated from the Virginia Military Institute in 1921.

Although most of his World War II service was on staff duty—he gained a reputation as a logistician—Pate commanded the 1st Marine Division during the latter part of the Korean War. His time as commandant was shaken by the Ribbon Creek tragedy in which six recruits drowned at Parris Island.

During the hearings that led to the Defense Reorganization Act of 1958, espoused by President Eisenhower, the Marine Corps mustered its defenses against what it considered encroachments upon service prerogatives. But the Marine defense lacked the fire of previous Capitol Hill campaigns. The act moved the defense establishment closer to the blueprint originally drafted by General of the Army George C. Marshall at the close of World War II. The powers of the secretary of Defense, the chairman of the JCS, the Joint Staff, and the unified commanders increased at the expense of the secretaries of the military departments and the service chiefs, including the commandant.

Pate gained a reputation for being languid, detached, and too fond of travel and for absenting himself from Washington—somewhat unfairly as it turned out. He was not a well man and died within a year and a half of his retirement.

RANDOLPH McCALL PATE. *Portrait by Albert K. Murray.*

David Monroe Shoup

TWENTY-SECOND COMMANDANT

1 January 1960 – 3 December 1963

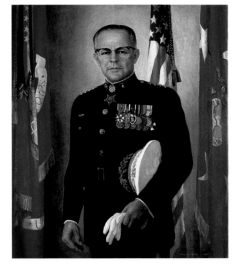

DAVID MONROE SHOUP. *Portrait by Frances Norris Streit.*

As chief of staff of the Army, General Dwight D. Eisenhower proposed that the Marine Corps be limited to units no larger than a regiment; and as president, he was greatly annoyed by what he considered to be a cabal of senior Marine officers seeking to block his reorganization of the defense establishment. So when it came time to replace Gen Pate, he reached down deep into the seniority list, past the lieutenant generals, and settled on an independent-minded, outspoken major general known to be a loner.

David Shoup, Eisenhower's maverick choice, was born on a farm in Battle Ground, Indiana, and in 1926 was commissioned in the Marine Corps from Army ROTC at DePauw University. His was The Basic School class that left Philadelphia early to join the 1927 expedition to China. Later he served at Quantico and San Diego and in 1929 had sea duty in the battleship *Maryland* (which would later be the flagship for Tarawa). In the Depression years he served variously at the recruit depot in San Diego, at the Puget Sound Navy Yard, and on detached duty with the Civilian Conservation Corps. He went to China again in 1934, first to the 4th Marines in Shanghai and then to the legation guard in Peking. He sailed with the 6th Marines to Iceland in 1941, getting in due time command of the 2d Battalion. On returning to San Diego, he moved to the staff of the 2d Marine Division and sailed for New Zealand in September 1942. He missed out on Guadalcanal except for a brief period as an observer.

President John F. Kennedy, standing on the steps to the back porch of the Commandant's House, receives honors immediately before proceeding to the evening parade. Saluting, to his left, is Gen Shoup and to his rear his naval aide, Capt Tazewell T. Shepard. (Photo: Cpl L. T. Warner, USMC)

Shoup was a principal planner for the assault of Tarawa, and just before the landing on 20 November 1943 received command of the 2d Marines. As the senior officer ashore the first dubious day, he took charge under fire of the fragmented battalions and held on grimly to the narrow band of beachhead, and for this received the Medal of Honor.

After the war he commanded The Basic School, became the Corps' fiscal director, was promoted to major general and as inspector general conducted a thorough probe of the Ribbon Creek recruit drownings in 1956. He commanded in succession the 1st Marine Division at Camp Pendleton and the 3d Marine Division on Okinawa (at which time he formed opinions about the futility of any involvement in Viet Nam) and was serving as commanding general of the recruit depot at Parris Island when Eisenhower selected him. A general exodus of lieutenant generals followed his nomination, and in the interregnum he served briefly as a lieutenant general and chief of staff at Headquarters.

Brusque in manner, his language frequently reflecting the barnyard, he thought the Corps had grown too effete and he set about to tighten its fibers. Although a favorite of President John F. Kennedy, he was skeptical of the actions designed to unseat Fidel Castro in Cuba and openly opposed sending American ground forces to war in Viet Nam. After his retirement he became even more vocal in his criticisms of President Lyndon Johnson's handling of the Viet Nam War.

Wallace Martin Greene, Jr

TWENTY-THIRD COMMANDANT
1 January 1964 – 31 December 1967

David Shoup was succeeded by his good friend and loyal chief of staff, Wallace M. Greene, Jr, a flinty Vermonter and the first Naval Academy graduate (Class of 1930) to become commandant since Russell. Greene's early assignments included going to sea in the battleship *Tennessee* and garrison duty on Guam. From there he went in 1937 to Shanghai and the 4th Marines, and for two years he watched the Chinese war with Japan and learned much that was to be of value later. In the fall of 1941, while serving with the 1st Marine Division, he was sent to Britain as an observer of commando training. On his return he went with the 3d Brigade to Samoa, then joined the V Amphibious Corps. There he won a high reputation as an operations officer in the invasion of the Marshalls and later, with the 2d Marine Division, on Saipan and Tinian. After the war there were more years of staff duty at Headquarters and in the field.

While serving as assistant division commander of the 2d Marine Division in 1956, he was transferred abruptly to Parris Island to straighten out, in partnership with Shoup, the aftermath of the Ribbon Creek incident. He moved from there in the summer of 1957 to Camp Lejeune as commanding general of the base. After six months at Lejeune he went to Headquarters, Marine Corps, where with a promotion to major general he became deputy chief of staff for plans. On 1 January 1960, as Shoup's choice, Greene was promoted to lieutenant general and made the commandant's chief of staff.

WALLACE MARTIN GREENE, JR. *Portrait by Everett Raymond Kinstler.*

Unlike Shoup, Greene believed the Viet Nam War could be won if the proper courses of action were followed—principally taking the war to North Viet Nam by blockading and mining Hai Phong (long before it was partially done), blowing up the dams and dikes along the Red River, and even an Inchon-like amphibious assault reaching to Hanoi. Much of his time as commandant was spent in frustration over the wavering policies of President Lyndon Johnson and Secretary of Defense Robert McNamara.

General Wallace M. Greene, Jr., then commandant of the Marine Corps, meets with General William C. Westmoreland, then commander, U.S. Military Assistance Command, Vietnam, in Da Nang on 11 August 1967. (Photo: USMC)

Leonard Fielding Chapman, Jr

TWENTY-FOURTH COMMANDANT
1 January 1968 – 3 December 1971

Wallace Greene's successor came as something of a surprise. Most Marines thought the race lay between Lewis W. Walt, hero of three wars and then the assistant commandant, and Victor H. Krulak, the brainy commanding general of Fleet Marine Force, Pacific. Faced with that apparently difficult choice, President Johnson picked a dark horse: Leonard Chapman, a career artillery officer then serving as chief of staff and with a reputation for cool efficiency.

Chapman had entered the Marine Corps by way of Army ROTC at the University of Florida. Commissioned in the summer of 1935, he had gone to Fort Sill for his artillery training. He served at sea in the cruiser *Astoria* during the early years of World War II, including the battles of

LEONARD FIELDING CHAPMAN, JR. *Portrait by Albert K. Murray.*

J. De Masse
72
COMMANDANTS H
FRONT ENTRA

the Coral Sea and Midway. He finished out the war with the 11th Marines, an artillery regiment, at Peleliu and Okinawa. After the war and more command and staff assignments, he made a particular mark as commanding officer of Marine Barracks, Washington, where, under the eye of Gen Pate, he brought the evening parades up to an even higher polish.

Soon after Chapman took over as commandant in 1968, the Tet offensive boiled across South Viet Nam. The battle for Hue was fought and the siege of Khe Sanh lingered on. The American public grew increasingly disenchanted with the war. Chapman's overriding goal in his last years as commandant was to get the Marines out of Viet Nam in the best possible condition. His much repeated watchword was: "Don't leave anything behind worth more than five dollars."

Facing page: *The Commandant's House faces G Street in Southeast Washington. This sketch was done by MSgt John DeGrasse, 1972. (Marine Corps Art Collection)*

Robert Everton Cushman, Jr

TWENTY-FIFTH COMMANDANT
1 January 1972 – 30 June 1975

The next commandant, Robert E. Cushman, Jr, was also something of a dark horse. Originally from Michigan, a Naval Academy graduate, class of 1935, and a member of the same Basic School class as Chapman, Cushman had been an exceptional battalion commander at Bougainville and Guam, and in Viet Nam had succeeded LtGen Lewis Walt as commanding general of the III Marine Amphibious Force. Afterwards he became deputy director of the Central Intelligence Agency and was considered sidelined by most of the members of the Corps who made guesses on who the next commandant would be. What those observers had forgotten or underestimated was that Cushman had been Vice President Richard Nixon's military assistant and had done much of the planning for Nixon's celebrated ground-breaking visit to Moscow. Nixon

ROBERT EVERTON CUSHMAN, JR. *Portrait by Albert K. Murray.*

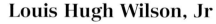

Members of the Silent Drill Platoon demonstrate their skills on the Marine Barracks parade ground with the Commandant's House in the background. (Photo: MSgt R. W. Savatt, Jr., USMC)

remembered, and Cushman was his personal choice for commandant.

Plagued by problems, including a charge that he was manipulating the selection of his successor, and possibly following the example of President Nixon who had already left the White House, Cushman elected to retire six months earlier than the expiration of his four-year term.

The Cushmans undertook an energetic refurbishment of the Commandant's House, including a fund-raising effort for embellishments that could not be made with government funding. The interior of the house was given a new look from top to bottom; it pleased most interested parties, but bothered some traditionalists. The Corps' "alumni," particularly the retired senior officers, have a possessive pride in the house comparable to the nation's pride in the White House.

Louis Hugh Wilson, Jr

TWENTY-SIXTH COMMANDANT
1 July 1975 – 30 June 1979

The search for Cushman's successor was politically charged and carefully done. Louis H. Wilson, Jr, considered to be in lofty exile as commanding general, Fleet Marine Force, Pacific, was the final choice—one that was applauded by most of the Corps. Wilson—like Neville, Vandegrift, and Shoup before him—wore the Medal of Honor. His was for extreme bravery in the fight for Fonte Hill during the reoccupation of Guam, where he served as a company commander in Cushman's battalion.

Born in Brandon, Mississippi, and educated at Millsaps College, Lou Wilson had come into the Marine Corps because the United States was approaching entry into World War II. He enrolled in the officer candidates program in May 1941 and gained his commission. Two years later he went to war with the 9th Marines. Seriously wounded in the

LOUIS HUGH WILSON, JR. *Portrait by Albert K. Murray.*

battle for Guam, he subsequently served at Marine Barracks, Washington, and, as a colonel, commanded The Basic School at Quantico and deployed with the 1st Marine Division to Okinawa and later to Viet Nam. Service, in the grade of brigadier general, as legislative assistant to Gen Chapman sharpened his already considerable political skills. These, when he became commandant, facilitated his gaining full membership on the Joint Chiefs of Staff. His other big achievements were to focus Marine Corps combined arms training at Twenty-nine Palms, California, and to speed the repair of the damage done to the Corps by Viet Nam. Tall and with a commanding presence, his Deep South charm and manner cloaked an iron will.

The Wilsons' time in the Commandant's House was marked by particularly gracious entertaining and skillful use of evening parades and garden parties. One house guest was Prince Phillip of Britain. With no apparent effort, the Wilsons attracted significant contributions to the fund created by the Cushmans for the improvement of the House.

Robert Hilliard Barrow

TWENTY-SEVENTH COMMANDANT
1 July 1979 – 30 June 1983

The selection of Robert H. Barrow to be the next commandant surprised no one. Loū Wilson and Barrow were longtime associates; their southern backgrounds were similar. When Wilson became commandant, he brought Barrow to Washington to be his principal assistant on manpower matters. This was the area that needed the most urgent attention after Viet Nam. Barrow served first as deputy chief of staff for manpower, and then—after a brief tour as commanding general, Fleet Marine Force, Atlantic—as assistant commandant.

Born in Baton Rouge, Louisiana, Barrow, as a child, had returned

ROBERT HILLIARD BARROW. *Portrait by Peter Egeli.*

with his family to "Roseale" in St. Francisville, long a Barrow plantation and now impoverished, and to a Mark Twain–style boyhood along the Mississippi. He attended nearby Louisiana State University—as had John Lejeune long before him. Early in World War II, impatient to get into the fighting, Barrow left the university to enlist in the Marine Corps and, after a brief spell as a drill instructor, was commissioned.

Barrow was a hero in three wars: a guerrilla leader deep in central China in World War II; commander of Company A, 1st Battalion, 1st Marines, at Seoul and the Chosin Reservoir in Korea; and commander, 9th Marines, in high-mobility operations in Viet Nam. He held both the Navy Cross and the Army's Distinguished Service Cross. A tall, commanding figure like Wilson, Barrow's persona and style of leadership as he moved up in grade were increasingly formal, dignified, and patrician. A masterful speaker, he could captivate an audience with the cadences of old-fashioned oratory.

Barrow continued the manpower and training reforms begun by Wilson. His credo was "quality"—most especially in the recruiting process. He determined that a high school diploma was the best predictor of a recruit's success in becoming a Marine. By personal drive he reduced the incidence of drug abuse in the Corps to the vanishing point. He shepherded the beginnings of "maritime prepositioned shipping," which would prove its worth in the Persian Gulf War. During his commandancy, elegant use continued to be made of the Commandant's House.

Paul Xavier Kelley

TWENTY-EIGHTH COMMANDANT
1 July 1983 – 30 June 1987

Barrow's successor, Paul Xavier "P.X." (as he was always called) Kelley, was an exuberant Boston Irishman who entered the Corps through Naval ROTC at Villanova University and was a front-runner from the time of his commissioning in 1950. His early years of service included such plum assignments as sea duty in the cruiser *Salem*, command of the 2d Force Reconnaissance Company, exchange duty with the Royal Marines, assignment as tactics chief of The Basic School, and command of the Marine Barracks at Newport, Rhode Island.

On his first tour in Viet Nam he was the combat intelligence officer for III Marine Amphibious Force and then commanding officer of the 2d Battalion, 4th Marines. Before his second Viet Nam tour, he served as the Marine Corps representative at Fort Benning, attended the Air War College, and was aide to the assistant commandant, then General Lewis Walt. When he returned to Viet Nam, "P.X." was given command of the 1st Marines, the last Marine regiment to serve in that war.

As a general officer his good assignments continued: command of the Reserve 4th Marine Division, director of the Development Center and then the Education Center at Quantico, deputy chief of staff for Requirements and Programs at Marine Corps Headquarters, and then, most prestigious of all, the first commander of the Rapid Deployment Joint Task Force—which became the U.S. Central Command. When he moved

PAUL XAVIER KELLEY. *Portrait by Everett Raymond Kinstler.*

up to assistant commandant during Robert Barrow's last year, it was obvious to all that he would be the next commandant.

Immensely popular, Kelley had a breezy, outgoing personality that contrasted sharply with that of the more reserved Barrow. His happy time ended, however, when a terrorist's truck bombed the Beirut barracks and killed 241 Americans, 220 of them Marines, and cast a pall over the remainder of his tenure.

Alfred Mason Gray, Jr

TWENTY-NINTH COMMANDANT
1 July 1987 – 30 June 1991

ALFRED MASON GRAY, JR. *Portrait by Peter Egeli.*

Alfred M. Gray, Jr, was cast in a mold different from any of his predecessors. Born in northern New Jersey, he left Lafayette College in 1950 to enlist in the Marine Corps and reached the rank of sergeant before being commissioned a second lieutenant in 1952. His enlisted experience in amphibious reconnaissance plus cross-training as an officer in artillery, communications, and intelligence led to some esoteric assignments, first in Cuba and then in Viet Nam. A long-time bachelor, he was an avid and retentive reader seemingly blessed with total recall.

Gray extended his tour in Viet Nam from the required one year to three, serving conventionally with Marine artillery and less conventionally in electronic intelligence. Even after his return to the United States in 1968, there were further trips to Viet Nam on surveillance and intelligence assignments.

After getting back into the mainstream as a student at Quantico's Command and Staff College, he commanded first a battalion and then a regiment of the 2d Marine Division at Camp Lejeune. He attended the Army War College and then was given command of the 4th Marines in East Asia; in that post, he directed the ground element in the final evacuation of Saigon in 1975. On becoming a general officer, he commanded in rapid succession the 4th Marine Amphibious Brigade, the 2d Marine Division, and Fleet Marine Force, Atlantic.

Al Gray swept into headquarters determined to "clean house" and refurbish the "warrior image" of the Corps. His uniform, whenever circumstances would permit, was camouflaged utilities, even to the point of wearing them for his official portrait. With tremendous energy, he poked and prodded into every corner of the Corps. At Quantico he combined and expanded the resident schools into a Marine Corps University. He changed the names of Marine air-ground task forces from amphibious back to expeditionary to stress their versatility. And he made the deployed Marine Expeditionary Units "special operations capable"—qualifying them for such missions as raids and evacuations.

During Gray's years as commandant, the Persian Gulf saw the largest-scale Marine Corps deployment in history, which gave him great satisfaction and caused him great frustration—satisfaction that the well-equipped and superbly trained I Marine Expeditionary Force performed so splendidly, and frustration that he, as a service chief, had little or no role to play in events in the field.

Carl Epting Mundy, Jr

THIRTIETH COMMANDANT

1 July 1991 – 30 June 1995

Carl E. Mundy, Jr, picked up where Gray left off, affably smoothing some of the feathers ruffled by Gray. The Marines, just returned from the Persian Gulf, were at a peacetime operational peak, but that readiness had to be demonstrated and defended when the administrations of both President George Bush and President Bill Clinton downsized the armed forces and reexamined their roles and missions.

Mundy was the son of a North Carolina small-town—and immensely patriotic—storekeeper and had wanted to be a Marine for as long as he could remember. At Auburn University, unwilling to wait for a commission through the ROTC process, he enlisted in the Marine Corps Reserve and spent two summers in the Platoon Leaders Course at Quantico. Commissioned on graduation from Auburn in 1957, his early service included tours of sea duty in the aircraft carrier *Tarawa* and the cruiser *Little Rock*. In Viet Nam in 1965, he served with the 3d Battalion, 26th Marines, and on the staff of the III Marine Amphibious Force. In the latter assignment he caught the eye of the commanding general, Lewis Walt. When Gen Walt became assistant commandant, he made Mundy his aide-de-camp.

More choice assignments followed: command of the 2d Battalion, 4th Marines, on Okinawa; chief of staff of the 6th Marine Amphibious Brigade (which began his considerable experience with NATO-reinforcing missions); command of the 2d Marines at Camp Lejeune; and, afloat, the regiment's 36th and 38th Marine Amphibious Units.

Promoted to general officer, he alternated between high-level personnel, operations, and training staff positions, and important troop commands beginning with the 4th Marine Amphibious Brigade. He was serving as commander of Fleet Marine Force, Atlantic, and II Marine Expeditionary Force when he was selected for commandant.

As commandant, Mundy successfully held the Marine Corps peacetime strength at 174,000. He won a reaffirmation of the Corps' traditional roles and missions, including an endorsement of the long-held claim of being the nation's "force-in-readiness." He did much to make the Navy and Marines equal players in developing a new "From the Sea . . ." power projection strategy. During his tenure, the Corps achieved acceptance of the elevation of the Fleet Marine Forces, which had been subordinated under the Navy's operating forces, to "component" status and full partnership under the unified commanders.

Charles Chandler Krulak

THIRTY-FIRST COMMANDANT

1 July 1995 –

Charles "Chuck" Krulak, born at Quantico in the wartime year 1942 as the youngest son of the celebrated Marine Lieutenant General Victor H. Krulak, was Gen Mundy's chief lieutenant in defending force structure and articulating naval strategy. He zoomed up from brigadier to lieutenant general after a spectacular success as the 1st Marine Expeditionary Force's forward logistic chief in the Persian Gulf. Driving, energetic, and imaginative, he created almost overnight deep in the desert a huge base—which he named "Al Khanjar" (the Dagger)—to support the Marines' assault of the Saddam Hussein Line.

Chuck Krulak graduated, like his father, from the Naval Academy— his was the class of 1964. Later he went back to the Academy as a company officer. During two tours in Viet Nam, he commanded a rifle platoon and two rifle companies, was twice wounded, and received the Silver Star (an award that in the Marine Corps is given only for gallantry in combat).

On the way up the ladder, he served at the recruit depot at San Diego and commanded the Marine Barracks at North Island, California, and the 3d Battalion, 3d Marines, in Hawaii. At Headquarters in Washington, he had much to do with developing doctrine and procedures for the "maritime prepositioning" of supply ships for Marine expeditionary use. He was on the military staff at the White House when selected for brigadier general in 1988. At Camp Lejeune, he served as assistant division commander of the 2d Marine Division (which included command of the 10th Marine Expeditionary Brigade) and was commanding the 2d Force Service Support Group when he went to the Persian Gulf in 1990. On his return from the Gulf War, he commanded the Marine Corps Combat Development Command at Quantico. He was commanding general of Marine Forces Pacific when selected to be commandant.

On taking office, Gen Krulak had ready a much polished and ambitious plan to prepare the Corps for the changing demands of the approaching new century, primarily by taking advantage of new technology to enhance war-fighting skills. Taking the Marine Corps into the twenty-first century was the central course he set for his commandancy and he pursued his goals with boundless energy.

CHARLES CHANDLER KRULAK. *Portrait by Laurel Stern Boeck.*

The Commandant's House, rear view, and senior officers quarters as seen from across the parade ground in 1998. (Photo: Eric Long)

The Sergeants Major of the Marine Corps

Captain John C. Chapin, USMCR (Ret)

*O*nly one enlisted Marine bears the title of *"Sergeant Major of the Marine Corps," the highest enlisted grade in the Corps. He works in the Office of the Commandant and represents the more than 154,000 active duty enlisted Marines. On his sleeves he wears chevrons with a fourth "rocker" and he*

alone carries within those chevrons the eagle, globe, and anchor.

The rank of sergeant major is an ancient one, going back to the sixteenth century British army. The first sergeant major in the United States Marine Corps was Archibald Summers, appointed in 1801. Today there are some 424 sergeants major on active duty in the Marine Corps in posts and stations all over the world.

The title of sergeant major of the Marine Corps was created in1957 by the commandant, General Randolph McC. Pate.

Gen Pate appointed Wilbur Bestwick, a veteran of battles in Bougainville, Guam, and Korea, as the first man to hold the new rank. Bestwick had been Pate's division sergeant major in Korea and had been serving as sergeant major, Headquarters, Marine Corps. Initially, he had a rather generalized job description that said he "assists the Chief of Staff, the Deputy Chiefs of Staff, and the Secretary of the General Staff in the performance of their duties." Symbolizing his new exalted status, SgtMaj Bestwick was given the "Sword of Office," engraved with the new title. The sword would be regularly passed on to his successors.

Over the next forty years, twelve men followed Bestwick, and today the sergeant major of the Marine Corps is a fixture in the Office of the Commandant. The power and responsibilities of the incumbents have grown exponentially, and their terms in office now coincide with those of the commandants who appoint them.

A meticulous screening process has evolved to winnow the ranks of active duty sergeants major and give a new commandant a short list of five recommended

Above: The Marine Corps' first sergeant major was Archibald Summers, appointed in 1801. Visualization of what he might have looked like is by Marine artist Col Charles Waterhouse, USMCR (Ret).

names. He then makes his personal selection. Pay grade is now "E 9," at the top of the enlisted ranks, and pay has escalated from Bestwick's $320 a month to today's $4,777.

With a series of remarkably capable men leaving their imprint on the billet, the role of the sergeant major of the Marine Corps has developed so that now he has a crucial voice in all policies affecting the enlisted personnel of the Corps, including, of course, the vital issues that involve women Marines. He is sometimes called the "enlisted Marine's general."

His office is in the Pentagon, some fifty feet from that of the commandant; he travels regularly with the commandant (as well as on his own), and he meets regularly with the senior generals at Headquarters. When he telephones, or meets face to face, with a salty old sergeant major with twenty-five or more years of service and he has some comment or advice, the other man listens very carefully. The sergeant major of the Marine Corps' recommendations to the commandant bear great weight.

Who have these twelve men been? In the early days, many came out of humble backgrounds and most never went beyond high school. Now, when the job requires sophisticated testimony before a U.S. Senate committee, knowledge of high tech weapons, complex budget problems, etc., the demands upon the occupant are extraordinarily varied. The "precept" for the selection board for this unique position specifies that the sergeants major recommended must have "proven excellence in war fighting skills, training and operational environments, and administrative capability."

Carrying on this tradition today is Sergeant Major of the Marine Corps Lewis G. Lee, at the time of his selection for this post in June 1995 the most senior sergeant major in the Marine Corps. Now 48 years old, with thirty years of service, he says, "My hardest job, day in and day out, is to maintain the quality of our enlisted personnel. You have to enforce an 'up or out' policy. Fortunately, our incoming quality is as good as ever, even though we have the highest enlistment requirements of any of the Armed Services. Some 97 percent are high school graduates."

Above: Sergeant Major of the Marine Corps Wilbur Bestwick, appointed in 1957, was the first to hold the new rank. (Photo: SSgt Shkymba, USMC)

Below: The tenure of Sergeant Major of the Marine Corps Lewis G. Lee, begun in 1995, coincides with that of the commandant, Gen Charles C. Krulak. In many ways his duties can be compared to those of an ombudsman. (Photo: USMC)

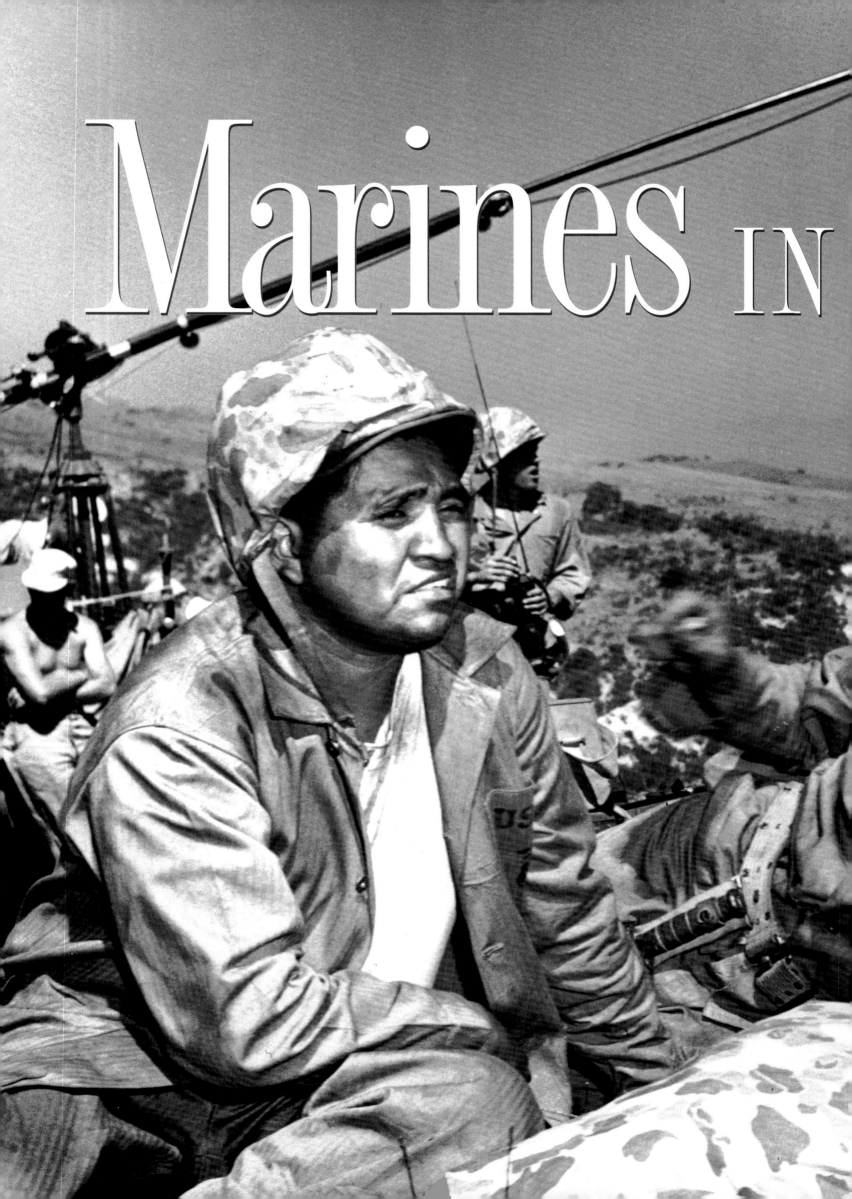

Marines IN

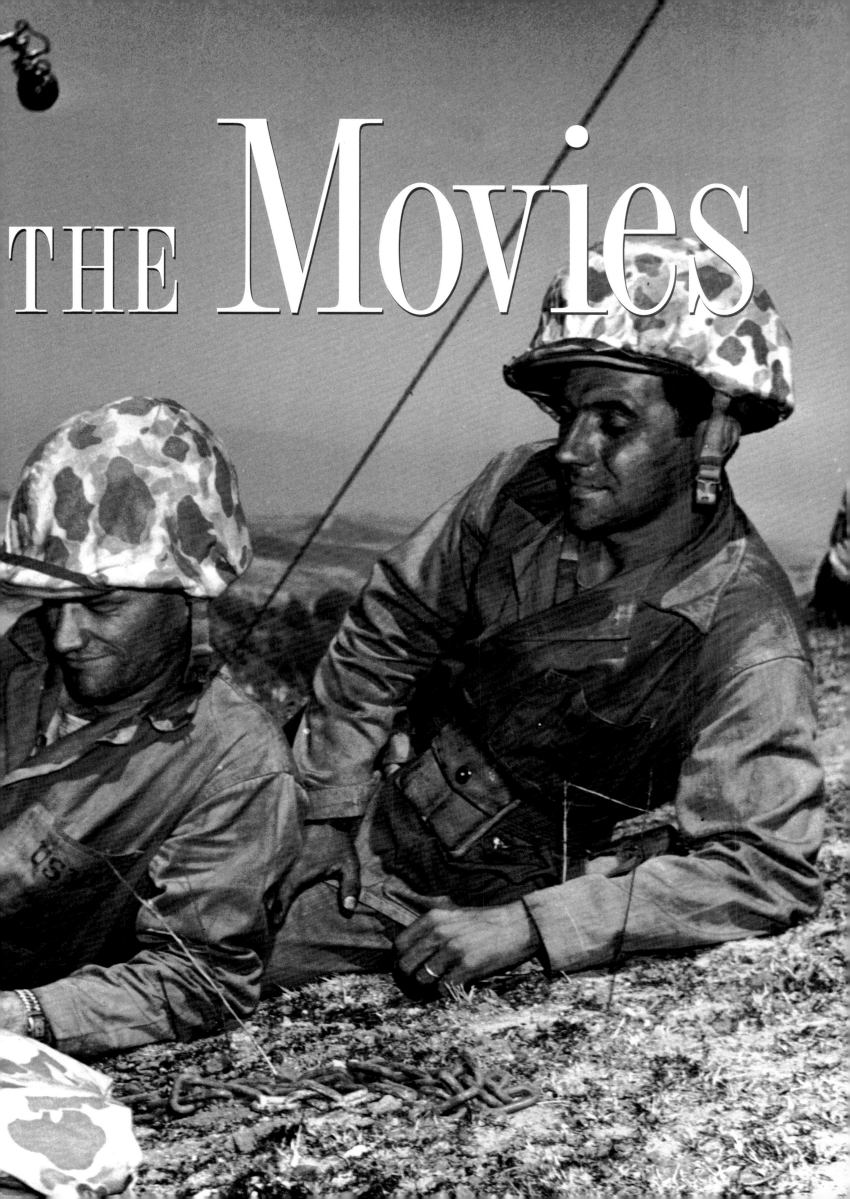

THE Movies

Marines
IN THE
Movies

Lawrence H. Suid, Ph.D.

All illustrations, unless otherwise noted, from the author's collection and the Marine Corps Art Collection.

THE MARINES' GREATEST HOUR

SANDS OF IWO JIMA

JOHN WAYNE

A Republic Picture

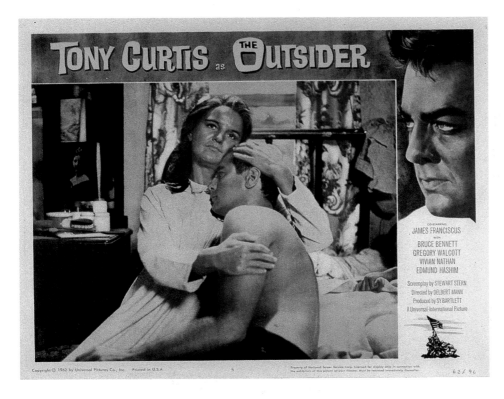

Describing his boyhood reaction to *The Sands of Iwo Jima*, Ron Kovic, a Viet Nam veteran and author of *Born on the Fourth of July*, recalled: "The Marine Corps hymn was playing in the background as we sat glued to our seats, humming the hymn together and watching Sergeant Stryker, played by John Wayne, charge up the hill and get killed just before he reached the top. And then they showed the men raising the flag on Iwo Jima with the Marines' hymn still playing."

Kovic remembered crying. "I loved the song so much, and every time I heard it, I would think of John Wayne and the brave men who raised the flag on Iwo Jima that day. I would think of them and cry. Like Mickey Mantle and the fabulous New York Yankees, John Wayne in *The Sands of Iwo Jima* became one of my heroes."

The impact of *The Sands of Iwo Jima* and the John Wayne military man image had that effect on many young Americans. While filming *The Outsider* (1960), the story of Ira Hayes, one of the flag raisers on Mount Suribachi, director Delbert Mann asked ten newly arrived Marines at Camp Pendleton, California, why they were willing to join the Marines and undergo its tough training. Three recruits told him they did not know, and a couple said their brothers had served in the Marines. The other five told him either: "I seen a movie once" or "I saw a John Wayne movie."

From the first appearance of Marines in movies before World War I to the present day, the Corps has used motion pictures to convey the message that Marines have a special place in the military establishment. Even if early Marine Corps movies had few memorable characters, the films did help create a strong and positive image of the Marines as an elite organization.

Cooperation between the Marine Corps and filmmakers produced movies that reinforced this image, giving the Corps access to a hugely popular medium through which to tell its story. In return for providing

Marines from the Sixth Fleet, playing GIs, recreate the Normandy landing on "Omaha beach" (actually Corsica) during the making of The Longest Day *in June, 1961.*

the Marines access to the screen, Hollywood found colorful stories and assistance that saved many thousands of dollars in production costs.

Over the years, Marines have appeared in combat movies, peacetime stories, and even some esoteric roles:

- A Marine pilot flew one of the planes that shot the original King Kong off the Empire State Building.

- Marines served as extras in the 1936 disaster film *San Francisco* because the director, a Marine reserve officer, needed men who could follow orders precisely during the re-creation of the earthquake.

- Marines, stationed at a communications facility in North Africa, played French Legionnaires in *March or Die* (1977).

Herbert Evans as "Colonel Barron," stands before real Marines at roll call in front of Marine Barracks at Bremerton Navy Yard in Washington state during the filming of Star Spangled Banner *in 1917.*

- Marines, serving afloat in the Mediterranean, played American soldiers in the Normandy landings in the 1962 epic *The Longest Day*.

- Off-duty Marines played Navy aviation cadets in *An Officer and a Gentleman* (1982) even after the Navy had refused to cooperate because of the four-letter words, explicit sex, and the suicide of one of the would-be pilots.

The Star Spangled Banner, which the Edison Company put into production before the United States entered World War I, was the first major film to feature the Marine Corps. It focused on the peacetime Marines and their training, but after the nation's declaration of war against Germany in April 1917, the producers tacked on a postscript to help rally the American people to the Allied cause.

Set at the Marine Barracks in Bremerton, Washington, *The Star Spangled Banner* told the story of a half-American, half-British teenager who considered himself English and disdained the United States and particularly the Marines. In portraying the boy's adjustment to life as the stepson of the commander of the barracks, the film provided the Marines ample opportunity to show off their skills at marching, drilling, training with boats, and ceremonies. When the boy falls down a cliff and is rescued by Marines, he changes his views and symbolically places the Stars and Stripes on his mirror beside the British Union Jack and the French Tricolor.

With the United States preparing its World War I expeditionary forces for deployment, the Edison Company turned to portraying Marines in combat. *The Unbeliever* became the model for all future Marine combat movies, most of which have burnished the Corps' image as an elite organization prepared for any eventuality. Using a "rite of passage" construct which became endemic to Leatherneck films, *The Unbeliever* followed Phil, "a rich, young sophisticate," from his life of leisure in Long Island society to enlistment in the Marines and then into

Having saved her from the German menace, "Phil" (Raymond McKee) bids a fervent adieu to his sweetheart (Marguerite Coutot) before returning to his comrades at the front in The Unbeliever *(1918).*

combat. At the front in Belgium, Phil experiences life in the trenches, gives a good account of himself in battle, learns equality, finds God as a result of his serious wounds, overcomes prejudice, and wins a bride.

The Marines, of course, never fought in Belgium and when the combat scenes were shot in November 1917, the only Leathernecks overseas were still in training. Inaccuracies aside, the battle scenes had the feel of actual combat, thanks to assistance from the Marines at their new base at Quantico, Virginia.

Today, *The Unbeliever* and *The Star Spangled Banner* seem hopelessly stilted. The young man maturing through his experiences in combat has become a cliché at the heart of too many war movies. Nevertheless, the two films mark the beginning of a long and honorable relationship with filmmakers that the Corps has found an invaluable way to inform the nation of the Corps' mission—and to aid in recruiting.

With peace in 1918 came demobilization, and as the isolationist impulse deepened during the 1920s and military appropriations dried up, all the armed services shrank in size. The first postwar film to portray Marines had its origins in an antiwar play written by Lawrence Stallings, a former Marine captain who had lost a leg as a result of wounds received at Belleau Wood. *What Price Glory?* opened as a play in New York in 1924 to "some of the wildest applause" Broadway had ever heard. When director Raoul Walsh transferred the play to the screen, he created sweeping battle scenes that were the progenitor of all future large-scale combat spectaculars. Within this framework, Captain Flagg (Victor McLaglen) and Sergeant Quirt (Edmund Lowe) engage in a boisterous rivalry over Charmaine (Dolores Del Rio) when not engaging the enemy.

In the movie's battle sequences, *What Price Glory?* conveys the horrors of combat and thereby pays lip service to the antiwar sentiments of the play. At one point Flagg orates; "There's something rotten about a world that's got to be wet down every thirty years with the

Above: *Jimmy Cagney as "Capt Flagg" and Dan Dailey as "Sgt Quirt" shout each other down in the John Ford–directed remake of* What Price Glory? *(1952).*

Right: *Victor McLaglen and Edmund Lowe, "Capt Flagg" and "Sgt Quirt," face off for the love of Dolores Del Rio in* What Price Glory? *(1926). The original stage play, bitterly antiwar, was by Marine Capt Lawrence Stallings, severely wounded at Belleau Wood. (Photo: Museum of Modern Art, Film Stills Archives)*

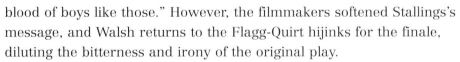

Top left: *Lon Chaney, as the archetypical Marine sergeant, drills a collection of actors and real Marines in a "Central American jungle" found near San Diego, California, for* Tell It to the Marines *(1927).*

Above: Lon Chaney, a consummate actor, contrasts sharply in his taut portrayal of a sergeant with an over-age, over-weight actor playing a corporal.

Left: The Singing Marine *(1937) with Dick Powell (center rear) as the "singing Marine" turned life in the peacetime Marine Corps into a musical comedy. It was not the image the Marine Corps wanted.*

blood of boys like those." However, the filmmakers softened Stallings's message, and Walsh returns to the Flagg-Quirt hijinks for the finale, diluting the bitterness and irony of the original play.

The Marines loved the way they appeared in this "war is romantic and exciting" film. Walsh said that after making *What Price Glory?*, he always enjoyed a good rapport with the Corps; he claimed the Marines "had more recruits after that picture than they'd had since World War I. It showed the boys having fun, getting broads. Young fellers saw it, they said, 'Jesus, the Army [sic] is great.'" Years later, when Walsh was directing *Battle Cry* (1955), a World War II Marine epic, a general came up to him during the filming and told him he had joined the Corps after seeing *What Price Glory?*

Despite the box office success of the film and other World War I re-creations, most Hollywood military movies before Pearl Harbor depicted the peacetime activities of the armed services. The Marines appeared in their fair share of these films including *Tell It To the Marines* (1927); *The Cockeyed World* (1929)—a McLaglen-Lowe sequel set in the South Seas; *Flight* (1929); *Devil Dogs of the Air* (1935); and *The Singing Marine* (1937).

In Frank Capra's Flight *(1929), the first movie about Marine aviation, Ralph Graves shares a romantic moment with Lila Lee before flying off to battle Nicaraguan guerrillas.*

Actor John Payne drills Marines at the recruit depot at San Diego in To the Shores of Tripoli *(1942). In production before World War II began, the film got a hurriedly changed ending after Pearl Harbor.*

In deciding whether to assist on these films, the Corps remained firm on the images and messages it wanted to convey. By providing assistance to *Flight*, the Marines clearly hoped the film would do for the Corps what *Wings* had done for the Army Air Corps two years earlier. Within the framework of a conventional Hollywood romantic comedy buddy movie, director Frank Capra portrayed the peacetime Marines developing close air support techniques and putting them into practice in Nicaragua. The manner in which Marine pilots worked with their comrades on the ground presaged the air-to-ground teamwork that would prove so successful in the Pacific war.

Devil Dogs of the Air told virtually the same story except that it substituted a training exercise for Nicaragua combat. It also contained romance and comedy with Marine fliers Jimmy Cagney and Pat O'Brien cavorting through the air and chasing the same beautiful waitress. More important for the Marines, it featured spectacular flying sequences for which the Corps provided planes, men, and locations. And in a grand, ten-minute documentary-like montage, the Navy's Pacific Fleet supported a Marine assault on a beach south of La Jolla. Navy ships simulated pre-assault bombardment and the USS *Saratoga* launched Navy and Marine planes to support the amphibious landing. The Marine squadrons provided the close air support of landing forces, while Navy units protected the fleet. *Devil Dogs of the Air* remains the only Hollywood film showing Marine planes flying off a carrier and serving as a component of naval aviation.

The screen excitement of this film conveyed the message the Marines sought. One reviewer observed, "Young American men and women, seeing the actual flying, extraordinary courage and skill of American war pilots, will be fired with the ambition to fly and help conquer man's newly acquired realm, the ocean of the air."

Top left: *William Bendix and Robert Preston prepare for a scene in* Wake Island *(1942). It turned out well with very little Marine assistance.*

Right: *The Japanese begin their attack on Wake Island, created for the purpose on the shore of the Salton Sea in California.*

Bottom left: *The 1st Battalion, 24th Marines, stages a remarkably peaceful landing across beaches at San Clemente, California, for* Guadalcanal Diary *(1943).*

By boosting recruiting, these and other peacetime films helped the Marine Corps prepare for the coming war. *To the Shores of Tripoli* with Randolph Scott and John Payne became the first military film released after Pearl Harbor. When the movie appeared in March 1942, the filmmakers updated the ending, as the Edison Company had done with *The Star Spangled Banner*, by adding a message about the need to defeat Japan.

The Marines appeared in the first Hollywood production about the war against Japan. Released in September 1942, *Wake Island* portrayed the Leathernecks' brave, but doomed, struggle to hold the island against an overwhelming Japanese invasion force. The re-creation of the last days of the fight resulted from radio communiques broadcast before the surrender and the imagination of the screen writers. Paramount made *Wake Island* with virtually no help from the service since at that time the Corps had more urgent things to do than assist filmmakers. The studio used its own equipment, miniatures, some stock footage, and special effects to create the battle sequences. Despite these limitations, the film roused the emotions of the nation in a way that few other movies of the period were able to do. One critic noted that the story of Marines fighting to the very end would "surely bring a surge of pride to every patriot's breast."

Once the tide of battle had shifted and the Americans went on the offensive in the war against Japan, the Marines assisted several major stories set in the Pacific including *Guadalcanal Diary* (1943), *Gung Ho!*

Pat O'Brien, who played a Marine in several pictures, peers over the shoulder of a rifleman in Marine Raiders (1944), a fictionalized account of the Makin Island raid early in World War II.

(1943), *Marine Raiders* (1944), and *Pride of the Marines* (1945). Among these films, only *Guadalcanal Diary* duplicated the success of *Wake Island* or became an enduring classic of the magnitude of *What Price Glory?* However, they all provided the American people with a reasonable facsimile of how the Marines contributed to victory in the Pacific.

Not until Hollywood began to refight World War II in the late 1940s and created the classic Marine film did the Corps find its image for all seasons. *The Sands of Iwo Jima* originated when Edmund Grainger, a producer at Republic Pictures, discovered that no studio currently had a Marine story in development. He came up with the title for a film about the Marines after seeing the phrase "Sands of Iwo Jima" in a newspaper. Joe Rosenthal's picture of the flag-raising on Mount Suribachi then provided Grainger with the concept for the movie's climax. He personally wrote a forty-page treatment about a leathery drill sergeant and the men he leads into battle, and he hired Harry Brown to write the screenplay. According to the producer, Brown, who had created the screenplay for *A Walk in the Sun* (1946), did a "brilliant job" of translating the treatment into a shooting script.

The Sands of Iwo Jima followed the odyssey of Sergeant Stryker, a tough, outwardly stoic leader, and the squad he takes into battle. Stryker molds his unit into a first-rate fighting force after the formalistic war film conflicts between the sergeant and his men. While seemingly without feelings, Stryker bears the pain of a wife who has left him because of his commitment to the Marines and of a son he loves from afar. He becomes a father and teacher to his men, who come to respect, if not love him. The film takes the unit through the invasions of Tarawa and Iwo Jima to the successful capture of Mount Suribachi. As the men rest before the final assault to the top, a sniper kills Stryker—without spilt blood, in the cinematic style of the time. Their leader's death inspires Stryker's men to carry on as he had taught them.

General David Shoup, winner of the Medal of Honor at Tarawa and later the commandant of the Marine Corps, observed that most of the battle sequences in the film related to the struggle for Tarawa: "It was sort of a screwed up thing, really. The sands of Iwo Jima really didn't have anything to do with the rest of the film."

To re-create the battles for Tarawa and Iwo Jima, Grainger

Top: *John Wayne, himself never in the armed forces, created the quintessential Marine sergeant in* The Sands of Iwo Jima.

Above: *Marines, using amphibian tractors for the purpose, restage the landing on Iwo Jima for the cameras at Camp Pendleton in* The Sands of Iwo Jima. *The Marine Corps cooperated fully in its making.*

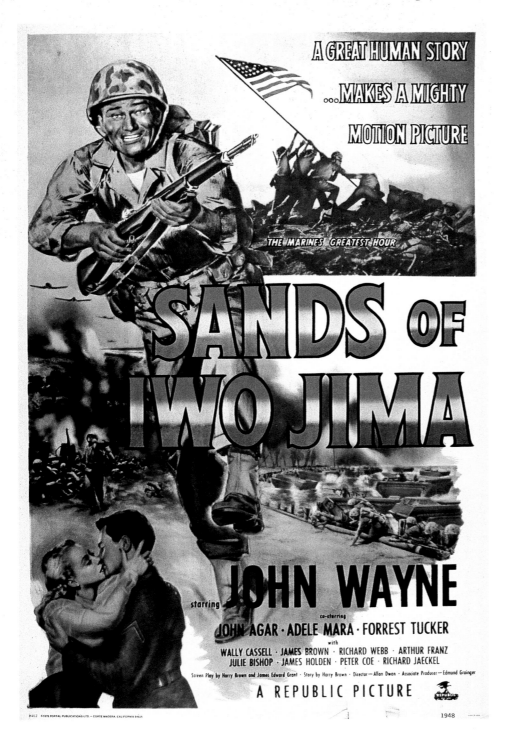

Felix De Weldon, sculptor of the Iwo Jima monument, advises the actors playing the flag-raisers on the proper position to take during the shooting of the climactic scene of The Sands of Iwo Jima.

Facing page, top: *Preparing for a scene in* The Sands of Iwo Jima *at Camp Pendleton, left to right: Capt Leonard Fribourg, the technical advisor; director Allan Dwan; John Wayne; and LtCol Andrew Geer, a Marine Reserve consultant.*

Facing page, bottom: *John Wayne discusses his role as Sgt Stryker with two heroes of Tarawa, then-Col David Shoup, who received the Medal of Honor, and LtCol Henry "Jim" Crowe, who was awarded the Navy Cross.*

received extensive assistance from the Marines. The Marines assigned Captain Leonard Fribourg to serve as technical advisor, and he worked with Grainger and Brown on polishing the script and selecting combat footage to be cut into the staged action. In addition, the technical advisor made arrangements with Camp Pendleton to provide the locations, manpower, and equipment that director Allan Dwan would need during the film company's stay on the base. As a result, the film was an accurate depiction of Marines in combat. It became the classic Marine film, however, not because of its authenticity, but because of John Wayne's portrayal of Sergeant Stryker.

Wayne told Fribourg he wanted to do the role so badly "he could taste it." Seeing the script as "a beautiful personal story [which] made it a different type of war picture," Wayne believed Stryker's relationship to his men "was the story of Mr. Chips put in the military. A man takes eight boys and has to make men out of them. Instead of four years in college, he's given eighteen months before they go into battle."

Fribourg said later that he had no problem getting the cast to go through a modified boot camp: "They wanted to do it, wanted to cooperate. They wanted to wear the uniforms right, the emblems, wanted to know what the stripes meant, wanted to know Marine lingo, and put

Below: *Marines move inland at Camp Pendleton during the filming of* Halls of Montezuma *(1951).*

Bottom right: *Richard Widmark played a Marine officer with a nasty headache in* Halls of Montezuma.

the right words in the right places." For his part, the director never shot a scene without first asking, "Does that look okay?"

The commitment to the film by both the Marines and the studio produced a film that General Shoup found "very, very accurate." *The New York Times* thought *The Sands of Iwo Jima* contained "so much savage realism [and] so much that reflects the true glory of the Marine Corps' contribution to victory in the Pacific that the film has undeniable moments of greatness." The *Times* found Wayne "especially honest and convincing for he manages to dominate a screenplay which is crowded with exciting, sweeping battle scenes. . . . His performance holds the picture together." For the Marines, *The Sands of Iwo Jima* not only helped recruiting and provided an enduring symbol—it led the way for Marine films during the 1950s. *"The Halls of Montezuma"* appeared in late 1950 and also followed a small group of Marines ashore in an attack on a Japanese-held island. In contrast to Wayne's film, however, *The Halls of Montezuma* focused on officers and their problems with command. Richard Widmark, the company leader and a former school teacher, must watch his men die in combat. Throughout the film, he takes pills to fight off the migraine headaches that result from his fears in battle. Karl Malden, the medical corpsman, tries to minister to Widmark's troubled mind, as well as his body, as he drives himself to the limits of endurance.

Despite fine performances by Widmark and Malden, *The Halls of Montezuma* lacked the intensity that set *The Sands of Iwo Jima* apart from the traditional war movie. Still, *The Halls of Montezuma* did come alive in the battle scenes thanks to the full cooperation of the Marines. The Corps' only question about the script involved the drug that Widmark took for his headache. Once satisfied that Widmark was not taking some kind of narcotic, the Corps went all out to ensure the completed movie would be authentic.

To accomplish this, the Marines arranged to have the film company come to Camp Pendleton in May 1950 to shoot a major Marine-Navy amphibious assault exercise. In addition, Lewis Milestone, who a gener-

ation earlier directed the classic *All Quiet on the Western Front* (1930), received use of a company of Marines while he was at Pendleton. With this help, the maneuvers he filmed, and the combat footage he cut into the staged action, Milestone created a story that spotlighted the individual without sacrificing the broader images of men at war.

The film's excitement and the ultimate Marine victory enhanced the service's image, but *The Halls of Montezuma* broke no new ground. Recognizing this and the need to portray other aspects of the Corps, Major General Clayton Jerome, director of Marine aviation, suggested to Edmund Grainger that he make a movie portraying Marine fliers.

Grainger, by then at RKO, initially planned to create a story about Marine fliers in Korea. However, after the Navy withdrew the loan of an aircraft carrier because of the demands of the Korean War, the producer changed the setting to World War II Guadalcanal and told the story of Marine pilots flying close air support against the Japanese. During the filming in early 1951 at Camp Pendleton, the Marines provided Grainger with fighter aircraft from the air base at El Toro, as well as a few airplanes to masquerade as Japanese fighters. This enabled director Nicholas Ray to re-create the Corps' World War II exploits in the air. The scenario itself was a rehash of earlier war stories, and not even John Wayne's presence could give the film any originality. But, *Flying Leathernecks* reminded Americans

Marine F4-U Corsairs from El Toro Marine Air Station fly over "Mount Suribachi" during the filming of Flying Leathernecks *(1951) at Camp Pendleton.*

Above: Retreat, Hell! *(1952), the story of
the epic withdrawal of the Marines from
Chosin Reservoir, was filmed in artificial
snow at Camp Pendleton where even a
frost is a rarity.*

Right: *The brown Southern California hills
at Camp Pendleton, dusted with "snow,"
became a convincing backdrop for the road
back from the Chosin Reservoir in* Retreat,
Hell!

that the Marines had an air arm that had performed with distinction in
World War II. It also suggested that Marine aviation was again supporting
Marines on the ground in Korea.

Marines doing the fighting in Korea received their due recognition
in *Retreat, Hell!*, the story of the Marine withdrawal from the Chosin
Reservoir in December 1950. Made at Camp Pendleton among hills
painted white to simulate snow, the film shows the Marines "advancing
in a different direction" under the most adverse conditions, finally
reaching the sea bloodied but unbowed.

In cooperating on these and subsequent films during the 1950s,
the Marines remained careful of their image that was to be shown on
the screen. Caution in approving scripts occasionally backfired, most
noticeably when the Corps turned down a request for assistance on a
small budget production entitled *Beachhead!* with Tony Curtis once again

a Marine. The script told the story of a four-man patrol seeking information about Japanese defenses on a Pacific island. During the mission, two of the Marines die. The two survivors bring back the needed intelligence. Marine Headquarters liked the portrayal of the men carrying out their jobs heroically. But the Corps did not want to become involved with a film showing Marines suffering 50 percent casualties at a time when it was in the midst of a recruiting campaign designed to create a new image of a more cautious Marine.

The Pentagon's public affairs office, however, liked the script and thought the film should be made. It arranged for the Navy, National Guard, and Coast Guard to provide the minimal assistance the filmmakers needed while shooting in Hawaii. When the producer screened the film in the Pentagon, the Marines "were enthusiastic and loved it," and agreed to help promote the film's opening in 1954.

The Marines then allowed Warner Brothers to film at the recruit depot at San Diego and shoot a training exercise in Puerto Rico during the making of *Battle Cry*, based on Marine veteran Leon Uris's best-selling novel. Some officers thought that Uris, as an enlisted man, had not accurately portrayed officers in his book and found that the film had the same defect. Most Marines, however, felt the movie captured their World War II experiences even better than had *The Sands of Iwo Jima*. Still, John Wayne's Sergeant Stryker remained their role model.

Right: *Marines, some real, some actors, trudge behind the camera truck through Hollywood-made rain in* Battle Cry *(1955). The film was based on a novel by Leon Uris, himself a World War II Marine.*

Below left: *Van Heflin, a former Air Force lieutenant, made a convincing "High Pockets" Huxley, a Marine battalion commander, in* Battle Cry.

Below right: *MajGens John Selden and James Riseley discuss nuances of* Battle Cry *with director Raoul Walsh (left) and actor Van Heflin. Walsh directed many war films including the ground-breaking* What Price Glory?

At about this same time, the Marines were very much aware of the need to counter the bad publicity resulting from the death of six recruits in the Ribbon Creek tragedy. They found the proper vehicle in Jack Webb's *The D.I.*, which was released in 1957. The film did not even hint at the tragedy, but captured as well as any Marine movie, fictional or documentary, the boot camp process by which drill instructors turn recruits into Marines.

By the early 1960s, World War II was fading from memory and all the Marine stories seemed to have been told on movie screens many times over. Possibly reaching for something new, Otto Preminger included in *In Harm's Way* (1965) an assault from the air on some unnamed Pacific island by Marine parachutists—something that never happened. The Corps did not object to such dramatic license.

The Cold War, with its threat of a nuclear holocaust hanging heavily over American lives, changed the public image of the military services, particularly after the Cuban missile crisis. Kirk Douglas, as a Marine colonel, single-handedly foiled a military coup by the chairman of the Joint Chiefs of Staff in *Seven Days in May* (1964). But during the rest of the decade, the Marines appeared only occasionally in Hollywood movies and, when they did, the portrayal did not always suit the Corps.

An exception was *55 Days at Peking* (1963) a re-creation of the 1900 Boxer uprising in China in which Charlton Heston played a brave and gallant major, loosely modeled after real-life Marine Captain John Twiggs ("Handsome Jack") Myers. The Marines under Heston's command, and those in the subsequent *The Wind and the Lion* (1975) set in Tangier, performed in an exemplary manner "to protect American lives and property," the conventional explanation for such interventions.

But sometimes stories with a more recent setting proved too sensitive for the Corps. Marine Headquarters did little to help Cornel Wilde in the making of *Beach Red* (1967) but acknowledged that the story of a Marine assault on a Japanese-held island contained a very positive portrayal of the service. After giving the director/producer/actor access to some old combat footage, the Marines informed Wilde that the Corps could not cooperate further because the film would contain a powerful antiwar statement at a time when American involvement in Viet Nam was escalating.

Not until the United States had been out of Viet Nam several years did American filmmakers turn to that war for images of combat, and in virtually every movie, soldiers or Marines bore the brunt of the wrath over the nation's failure, for the first time, to succeed in battle.

The Boys in Company C (1978), the first Viet Nam movie in which the Corps appeared, seemed on the surface little different from tradi-

Bruce Dern with his long hair was a totally unconvincing Marine captain in Coming Home, *an anti-Viet Nam War picture that co-starred political activist Jane Fonda.*

tional rite of passage Marine films set in any war. However, by portraying the Viet Nam conflict as an absurdity, the filmmakers hoped to show that the war had become an obscenity. In their antiwar zeal to create this message, they made a movie containing the worst things, real and imagined, that occurred in Viet Nam: the Marines used drugs, privates talked back to their officers, discipline collapsed, poor tactics led to slaughter and atrocities. With such portrayals in the script, the film company did not even approach the Marines for assistance.

The initial script for *Coming Home* contained no such egregious scenes of carnage or American incompetence. Instead, a disillusioned Marine officer on R & R in Hong Kong describes to his wife the horrors he has seen in Viet Nam, including his men cutting off the ears of dead Viet Cong soldiers. The wife was to be played by the film's producer, the newly politicized war protester, Jane Fonda. The Corps' office of information stiffly conceded it found the story "interesting and [it] will undoubtedly result in an entertaining and controversial film." However, it felt *Coming Home* would "reflect unfavorably on the image of the Marine Corps" because it portrayed drug use by officers and men and included a description of how Marines mutilated enemy bodies.

Before reaching the screen, the script went through many revisions. Later, some Marine public affairs officers admitted that if they had read the final script they might have been willing to provide some assistance to the filmmakers, particularly if Bruce Dern, playing the Marine officer, had cut his hair. Still, Jon Voight, as a paralyzed Viet Nam veteran and Fonda's love interest, despite his injury, turns on the service and the war when he responds to a Marine recruiter's sales pitch: "The Marine Corps builds body, mind, and spirit."

In the film, Voight says that seeing death in Viet Nam causes a person to grow up quickly. He acknowledges that people seeing men in uniform will "remember all the films and . . . the glory of other wars and think about some vague patriotic feeling and go off and fight this turkey too. . . .I'm telling you, it ain't like it is in the movies, that's all I want to tell you." Instead, he says, he doesn't feel good about having killed for his country: "I'm here to tell you it's a lousy thing, man. I don't see any reason for it."

Although *Coming Home* contained a negative image of Marines, it did cause the Corps to reevaluate its policy on providing assistance to filmmakers. The Marines came to realize Hollywood could make war movies without its help and concluded the Corps would best be served by using its materiel and personnel as leverage to obtain the best possible image of itself, even if it meant only that an actor would sport the proper haircut. As a result, the Marines entered into long and sometimes acrimonious negotiations with filmmakers leading to assistance on *The Great Santini* (1979) and *Rumor of War* (1980), as well as an agreement to cooperate on the first effort to make *Born on the Fourth of July.*

Philip Caputo's *Rumor of War*, released as a TV mini-series, did not benefit the Corps. However, the Marines believed the series would have portrayed the Corps more harshly if they had refused to assist. Similarly, Robert Duvall as the "Great Santini" did not portray an officer with whom most Marines could be comfortable. Even with changes in the script, Duvall remained a spouse and child abuser and much closer to an out-of-control Patton than a heroic Sergeant Stryker. Still,

Robert Duvall receives technical advice during the filming of The Great Santini *(1979) at the Marine Corps Air Station at Beaufort, South Carolina.*

people could empathize with the flawed aviator, and *The Great Santini* helped rehabilitate the Marine Corps' image that the Viet Nam War had savaged.

Paradoxically, the Navy refused to become involved in a naval aviation story because of the language, graphic sex, and the suicide of one of its cadets. Since Marine D.I.s train would-be Navy aviators, the Corps' Los Angeles public relations office read the script of *An Officer and a Gentleman* and agreed to assign an active-duty D.I. to the production. The film's D.I. as portrayed by Louis Gossett ranked with that of Jack Webb and redounded positively on all Marines.

The Corps' relationship with filmmakers sometimes led to embarrassing results, as when it agreed to help re-create the 1950 Marine landing at Inchon. *Inchon* portrayed the most recent major Leatherneck assault on an enemy beach, and even though Lawrence Olivier played General MacArthur, the film was so bad that it never had a general release.

The Marines undoubtedly wished that *Full Metal Jacket* (1987) had vanished as quickly as *Inchon*. Stanley Kubrick attempted to mix a portrayal of Marine basic training with a re-creation of the North Vietnamese Tet assault on Hue. The film presents a reasonably accurate look at basic training during the Viet Nam War until a demented recruit blows away his D.I. Without a transition, the audience finds itself in Viet Nam witnessing the battle for Hue. As a result, the film lacked cohesion and failed to make a meaningful statement about the Marine experience in Viet Nam.

In contrast, Oliver Stone's *Born on the Fourth of July* (1989) captured the impact of the war on one Marine despite its many inaccuracies. Ron Kovic clearly loved the Marines and did not direct against the Corps any of his subsequent disenchantment with the war and the government's treatment of him and other paralyzed veterans.

During the 1990s, the Marines found themselves fighting not Vietnamese but Cuban mercenaries in *Heartbreak Ridge*, Martians in

Invaders from Mars, drug dealers in *True Lies*, war with themselves in *A Few Good Men*, and a hired assassin in *The Jackal*.

When the U.S. Army backed away from supporting *Heartbreak Ridge* because of the inaccuracies and use of four-letter words, the Marines agreed to help Clint Eastwood's rendering of the United States intervention in Grenada. In return, the film provided an image of Eastwood's Marine sergeant killing a wounded Cuban and taking a cigar from the body. On the other hand, since the Marines would naturally be expected to fight alien invaders, the Corps provided a few men to battle the Martians in the remake of the 1950s science fiction classic *Invaders from Mars*.

In contrast, *A Few Good Men* offered no benefit to the service; after all, two Marines kill one of their buddies in a hazing incident. They are acting on orders from their commander, played by Jack Nicholson, who lies about his involvement and then after admitting he gave the hazing order, yells that he would do it again. Perhaps even worse, a Navy lawyer deflates the villainous Marine.

During the post–Cold War era, the Marines went on to help Arnold Schwarzenegger destroy a South American drug cartel in *True Lies* and helped save the life of the First Lady in *The Jackal*. Tomorrow's films will undoubtedly show Marines on humanitarian and peacekeeping missions in such diverse places as the Persian Gulf, Somalia, and Bosnia, beating up the bad guys, feeding widows and orphans, and rescuing downed Air Force pilots. At least until the next war.

Clint Eastwood directed and played the part of a Marine sergeant in Heartbreak Ridge *(1986), originally slated to be an Army story. Although the title refers to a Korean War battle, the film was a re-creation of the Grenada intervention of 1983.*

THE Corps Today

THE
Corps Today

By Colonel John Grider Miller, USMC (Ret)

Marines zip upriver ready for action. Modern equipment contrasts with Capt Merritt "Red Mike" Edson's legendary patrol in native dug-out canoes up the Coco River, Nicaragua, in pursuit of Augusto Sandino 70 years ago. (Photo: Greg E. Mathieson)

On any given day, 25,000 Marines—a quarter of the Fleet Marine Force—will be away from their home bases. Since the Persian Gulf War (Operation Desert Storm) in 1991, Marines have answered the alarm bell more than fifty times—an average of once every five weeks—sometimes, in the process, suffering casualties and loss of life.

These deployed units are flexible enough to handle multiple emergencies at the same time. On a single day, the Navy-Marine team known as 22d MEU(SOC) (Marine Expeditionary Unit-Special Operations Capable), afloat on Mamba Station off the Liberian coast, conducted unrelated operations simultaneously in Monrovia, Liberia; Dakar, Senegal; Rota, Spain; Sarajevo, Bosnia-Herzegovina; Sigonella, Italy; Bangui, Central African Republic; Yaounde, Cameroon; Bohinjska Bela, Slovenia; and Volos Bay, Greece. These operations included complex humanitarian assistance (some under hostile conditions)—the protection of U.S. lives and property—and training with allied forces. Although such operations usually fall short of actual warfare, the potential for hot combat is often there.

For example, the dramatic rescue of a downed U.S. Air Force pilot from hostile Bosnian Serb territory came close to crossing the fine line between non-combat and combat. The TRAP (tactical recovery of aircraft and personnel) operation that Marines conducted to bring back Captain Scott O'Grady was a complicated affair, requiring close coordination between land and air forces converging on the rescue scene from several locations. The fact that it worked on an hour's notice was testimony to countless hours of rehearsal—repeating the sequence over and over until each man could execute his part flawlessly on just a single initiating command: "Go!"

Never before has the Marine Corps faced challenges like today's—in the number of operations, their scope, their frequency, and the speed with which they must be conducted.

Top: *A destroyed Iraqi tank is grim evidence of Marine firepower in 100-hour Operation Desert Storm. (Artist: Sgt Charles Grow, USMC. Marine Corps Art Collection)*

Above: *A Marine, training for "TRAP" or "tactical recovery of aircraft and personnel," pops a red smoke canister to signal his location to overhead aircraft. TRAP rescue operations are just one of the special operations capabilities of deployed Marine Expeditionary Units. (Photo: Rick Mullen)*

Previous spread: *CH-53E "Super Stallions," the Marine Corps' long-time "heavy-lifter" helicopters, line up to refuel for another mission during an exercise in the Bahamas. (Photo: Rick Mullen)*

Heliborne vertical assault gives Marines crucial tactical mobility, but aged CH-46 "Sea Knight" helicopters, now more than three decades old, must soon be replaced by new aircraft. (Photo: Greg E. Mathieson)

For more than two centuries, the Marine Corps has stood for a way of life and an approach to living, fighting, and dying. But over the past half-century, dizzying technological advances have brought major changes to the Corps, and, paradoxically, Marines—in the wake of the Cold War—once again find themselves engaged around the world in missions and tasks reminiscent of past eras.

What's the difference between the Marines of the post–Cold War period and those of only a generation earlier? The answer surfaced recently in a conversation between the former commanders of two deployed battalion landing teams.

"I don't get it," said the (relatively) old-timer. "When we deployed to the Mediterranean a dozen years ago, we met every Sixth Fleet training objective. We could do raids and landings, day or night, with or without radio communications, even buttoned up for chemical warfare, if we had to. You name it, we could do it. But people talk like these new MEU(SOC)s can do everything but reproduce themselves. What can a MEU(SOC) do that we couldn't?"

"Well," said the newer commander, mentally scanning a range of possibilities, "on one hostage-rescue drill, with six hours' notice, we took down Charleston airport, with the FBI."

"Oh."

These days, Marines reporting for duty with the Fleet Marine Force keep their seabags handy because they know for certain they will carry their gear on board ship or military aircraft to an overseas destination. The tempo and duration of deployments have increased to the point where a Marine may stay out there for nearly 50 percent of the time. To meet this unique challenge, in the face of resources that are dwindling throughout the Department of Defense, the Corps maintains a tight emphasis on two basic goals: to make Marines and to win battles.

To maintain Marine Corps strength today at 170,000 or higher at least 45,000 recruits must be shipped to boot camp each year. After training attrition and recruits destined for Marine Corps Reserve units are factored out, that leaves about 38,000 for active-duty assignments. Nearly half of today's Corps can be found in the three lowest enlisted pay grades—lance corporals and below. This accent on youth also is reflected in the lowest officer-to-enlisted ratio of all the armed forces— 1:9 (as opposed to 1:5 for the Army and Navy and 1:4 for the Air Force). As a result, every three years, discounting career officers and noncommissioned officers, the turnover is complete. We get a brand-new Marine Corps. The key to the continuity and combat readiness of this new Corps is the transforming power of boot camp.

The pool of Americans providing raw material for new Marines has changed over the past half-century. The World War II generation, hardened by the Depression of the 1930s, was not necessarily well-schooled, but rather was field- and street-wise and took well to military life. By the 1950s, the influx of recruits had changed to the point where platoon sergeants could growl, "We used to get hardened criminals; now all we get is juvenile delinquents."

Right: *The helmet and weapon may be unfamiliar to this Marine's forebears, but his credo "Every Marine a rifleman" is not. (Photo: Greg E. Mathieson)*

Below: *Recruiting posters emphasize Marine readiness and mastery of personal weapons.*

Somehow, the Corps survived this sea change, but by the early 1970s a combination of public disaffection with the Viet Nam War and the end of the draft threw all the armed services into a personnel crisis which took most of that decade to resolve.

Even after substandard Marines from the declining days of Viet Nam were purged, recruiters had to struggle to bring in recruits, 50 percent of whom were high school graduates. Today, as the All Volunteer Force has matured, the percentage of high school graduates has climbed to the high 90s. And the quality of today's recruits is generally strong enough to permit transformation into Marines.

Let there be no mistake—Marine recruit training is much more a process of transformation than one of training. The four-step process begins with the recruiter. In war and peace, recruiting duty remains in the front lines; and when the attractiveness of the All Volunteer Force wilts—whenever war clouds gather or civilian opportunities for upward mobility present themselves to young men and women—the recruiters really wear out their shoe leather.

Unable to match the financial benefits or preferred-assignment guarantees of the larger services, Marine recruiters have an ace in the hole: the prospect of personal transformation and a new grip on life. But to be convincing to prospective Marines and their families, these squared-away sergeants—some of the best in the Corps—must present walking proof of that transformation, and the strength of the core values of Honor, Courage, and Commitment that are instilled in every Marine. Beyond that, they must provide an accurate picture of what lies ahead in boot camp and prepare their charges for its rigors. A disgruntled washout who returns to his neighborhood with tales of having been deceived and misled can poison the well there for years.

With a smooth handoff from recruiter to recruit depot, the transformation can begin. Although a number of reforms have increased the presence and visibility of officers in boot camp, the task of turning civilians into Marines still belongs primarily to the "hats," the noncommissioned drill instructors who wear the distinctive World War I campaign covers commonly bastardized in the vernacular as "Smokey Bear hats."

Carefully selected and trained, these drill instructors (DIs) quickly strip away all signs of each recruit's individuality (the pronoun "I" and its derivatives are forbidden) and begin to show their charges that success lies in teamwork and dedication to a larger cause, in this case, becoming Marines. The training lasts nearly three months, and the hardness and sense of individual responsibility and team purpose that builds each day is capped in the final week during a final event called "The Crucible."

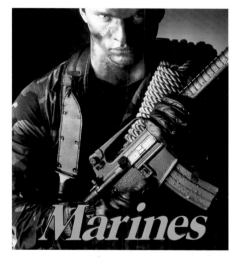

A far cry from the old "Walking John" in dress blue uniform, today's poster shows the Marine with an array of warfighting equipment.

Stretching far beyond a graduation exercise, this three-day ordeal becomes a defining moment in the life of each new Marine—there is no going back. Rousted from their bunks at two hours past midnight, the recruits will be awake and moving forty-six of the next fifty-four hours, through a series of exhausting marches, live-firing and close-combat exercises, and tactical and logistical problems that can be solved only through teamwork. After a nine-mile hike back to the parade deck, the exhausted recruits receive the Eagle, Globe, and Anchor emblem from their drill instructors, who have been with them every step of the way during The Crucible. At last, they are Marines—and they are treated that way during the final days of boot camp building up to their graduation parade for families and friends.

For too many years in the past, the intense atmosphere of boot camp left the brand-new Marines on a temporary high, which would be demolished at first contact with advanced schooling or initial contact with the "real" Marine Corps. In too many cases, the disillusionment would become severe enough to derail a new Marine's sense of purpose, and he would fail to complete his first enlistment.

Today, once boot camp is finished, the recruits are grouped so they can report to advanced training and their initial assignments with two or three friends, instead of going it alone. And when possible, officers and noncommissioned officers from the receiving units visit boot camp to begin working with "their" new Marines. This provides a great

Marine recruits of both sexes now go through a pre-graduation ordeal called "The Crucible" before receiving their Marine Corps emblems. The three-day exercise requires teamwork; it cannot be accomplished alone. (Photo: Sandy Schaeffer)

All Marines in a Marine Expeditionary Unit undergo twenty-six weeks of rigorous specialty training before embarking on a six-month tour afloat in amphibious ships. Here, members of 24th MEU(SOC) prepare for scout-swimmer training at Camp Lejeune, North Carolina. (Photo: Greg E. Mathieson)

boost to unit cohesion and ultimately to combat effectiveness, and it sets the stage for the final phase of a Marine's transformation—"sustainment," which requires strong leadership and positive reinforcement of each Marine's core values throughout his association with the Corps.

More skill, maturity, and judgment are demanded of today's Marine rifleman than any of his predecessors. As always, the central fact of life in the Corps is still that the Marine rifleman is the key to winning battles. The fight is not over until he stands triumphant on top of the final battlefield objective and sets about organizing its defense or prepares to move on.

With the end of the Cold War, many smaller nations and entities (e.g., terrorist organizations) have been released from political and military restraints imposed during that rigid superpower standoff, and an unruly atmosphere reminiscent of the American Wild West days prevails in many unstable areas. Consequently, any deploying Marine unit must be prepared to face conditions that not only are subject to change without warning but also can exist in multiple forms simultaneously. For example, a Marine in one part of a city may be handing out food and clothing in a disaster-relief operation; a block away, his buddies might be standing guard against looters or holding apart two warring local factions; and on yet another block other Marines may be engaged in the difficult and dangerous combat assignment of assaulting and clearing a building under urban-warfare conditions.

As the complexity of the rifleman's task has grown, so have the intricacies of Marine Corps organization for combat. Basic infantry units—fire team, rifle squad, platoon, company, battalion, and regiment—still would be generally recognizable to veterans of World War II and Korea, but beyond that everything is structured as though for an entirely new ball game in a series of new ball parks. Earlier deployments usually consisted of an infantry battalion with support units—formed into a battalion landing team—and a helicopter detachment capable of providing a variety of aviation-support tasks but lacking enough lift for aerial assault of any appreciable size. The battalion landing team still exists today, but as only one of four essential components of today's Marine Expeditionary Unit—and of all Marine Air-Ground Task Forces:

• *Ground Combat Element*, the infantry battalion and its combat support units, including artillery, armor, engineers, amphibious assault vehicles and reconnaissance.

• *Aviation Combat Element*, a composite squadron with attack and transport helicopters, and vertical/short take-off and landing aircraft—the venerable Harrier, serving the Marines for more than a quarter-century.

Below: *F/A-18 "Hornets" find themselves at what is now Marine Corps Air Station, Miramar, California, in the wake of the congressionally mandated closing of the Corps' long-time air station at El Toro, California. (Photo: Carl "Tank" Shireman)*

Right: *The AV-8B "Harrier," a vertical/short take-off and landing aircraft, intended primarily for close air support of ground troops, can operate from helicopter flight decks at sea and minimal facilities ashore. (Photo: Carl "Tank" Shireman)*

• *Combat Service Support Element*, with fifteen days of supplies and equipment embarked, capable of providing a full range of logistical support from the sea or ashore.

• *Command Element*, capable of providing local command and control, communications with adjacent units in the region, and linkage upward through the chain of command to the regional commander-in-chief and the national command authorities.

To earn the extra designation of "Special Operations Capable," each Marine Expeditionary Unit undergoes a twenty-six-week, standardized predeployment training program, culminating in a rigorous evaluation of its capabilities. These include, but are not limited to: humanitarian assistance/disaster-relief operations (as carried out in real time in Somalia, Rwanda, and Bangladesh); noncombatant evacuation operations (real-world applications in Liberia and Albania); amphibious withdrawal (Somalia), raids, assaults, and demonstrations; military operations in urban terrain; peacekeeping and peace-enforcement operations; and signals intelligence/electronic warfare operations, to name but a sampling. Further evidence of the rigor of this six-month work-up

Marines provide Kurdish refugees with care and protection as tent city starts to go up in northern Iraq after Desert Storm. Today's Marine Corps responds frequently to such humanitarian missions. (Photo: JO1 Greg Suaza, USN)

period is that the MEU(SOC) must be able to plan and execute any mission within six hours of notification, and must be able to conduct several unrelated missions simultaneously, as demonstrated in the real world by that single unit on Mamba Station off the Liberian coast, performing missions in nine locations on a single day.

These MEU(SOC)s, with an average strength of 2,200 Marines and sailors, commonly deploy for six-month "floats" in the Mediterranean, the Persian Gulf, and the Pacific and Indian oceans. Embarked in amphibious-ready groups of from three to five amphibious assault ships, they can move freely across the high seas without clearances or other diplomatic restraints. They constitute our nation's most flexible and combat-ready means of exerting U.S. influence abroad. In itself, a three-to-five-ship amphibious task force does not represent a stunning deterrent to a determined adversary. But ever since the days of the Barbary pirates, the appearance of even a single U.S. warship on the horizon has generally had a deterrent effect because of the certainty that others would follow, and would continue to follow until the threat to U.S. interests had collapsed.

Indeed, these amphibious-ready groups with embarked Marines are merely the tip of a massive iceberg of military capabilities. Today, they often operate with aircraft carrier battle groups, guaranteeing significant naval aviation strike support within minutes. And among the MEU(SOC)'s specialties is the quick seizure of lightly defended ports and airfields—to prepare for heavier follow-on forces as needed. These reinforcements can arrive in several ways:

• *The Air Contingency Marine Air-Ground Task Force* may well be the first to arrive if a secure airfield is available near the troubled area. This force can range from a reinforced rifle company to a regimental-sized unit, with its own air combat, support, and command elements.

A stalled jeep is Marine-handled to the edge of a landing zone. These Marines are glad this vehicle is not the much heavier "hum-vee" multi-purpose vehicle that has replaced most jeeps. (Photo: Greg E. Mathieson)

Facing page: *Marines dangle from below a helicopter on a trapeze-like device called a SPIE ("Special Purpose Insertion/ Extraction") rig. Getting to the scene of the action by whatever means possible is the hallmark of special operations capable units. (Photo: USMC)*

Its leading edge is ready to deploy by strategic airlift within eighteen hours of notification—sooner, if a degree of warning exists.

• *The Amphibious Marine Expeditionary Force (MEF)* may appear if the situation calls for more combat power or sustainment to kick open the door in a forcible-entry operation. At full strength, a MEF contains more than 46,000 men and women, organized around a Marine division, aircraft wing, and force service support group.

The three existing Marine Expeditionary Forces (two in the Pacific; one in the Atlantic) are the only standing Marine Air-Ground Task Forces (MAGTFs), both in peace and wartime. They provide the pool from which smaller, task-organized MAGTFs are formed. The amphibious configuration could embark up to two-thirds of a MEF's full combat power. When it arrives in theater, it either can absorb any on-scene MEU(SOC)s, or employ them independently in support of its forcible-entry operation, or use them in support of other operations as designated by the theater commander-in-chief. Today, the amphibious MEF has the only self-sustainable forcible-entry capability in our nation's arsenal.

• *The Maritime Prepositioning Force* truly gives the Corps a sustainable global reach. It consists of three-, four-, or five-ship squadrons stationed in strategic locations near the Mediterranean, Persian Gulf, and Indian and Pacific Ocean operating areas, plus two U.S.-based Aviation Logistics Support Ships, which carry a complete intermediate maintenance capability for Marine aviation units.

Each prepositioned squadron contains the equipment for a mechanized regimental-sized MAGTF, with enough supplies for thirty days of operations ashore. These ships do not need port facilities to carry out their mission. They can offload in the stream, with their on-board cranes, lighterage, and causeways if necessary. They also can pipe water and bulk fuel ashore, wherever adequate facilities are not already in place.

Because of their strategic locations, they can arrive at crisis scenes within seven to fourteen days and commence a buildup of combat power unmatched by any other logistical means. Air movement of the equipment stored by a single Maritime Prepositioning Force squadron, for example, would require more than 3,000 sorties of strategic airlift—or roughly a flight every three minutes around the clock for seven days, if enough aircraft remained up and running and the traffic-congestion problems at both the loading and unloading ends could be solved! In contrast, airlifting the fly-in echelon of more than 18,000 Marines and sailors, to marry up with the prepositioned equipment, only requires 250 sorties of strategic airlift—a 92 percent savings.

Marines on a "NEO" (non-combatant evacuation operation) protectively evacuate U. S. citizens and third-country nationals from strife-torn Tirana, Albania, in 1997. (Photo: PH2 Bret Siegel, USN)

Bottom left: *Marine parachutists begin HALO (high-altitude/low-opening) jump from a heavy-lift helicopter. Free-fall parachuting is a time-honored skill for Marine force reconnaissance units. (Photo: Rick Mullen)*

Bottom right: *Ready to go for a wide variety of missions—from humanitarian assistance to an amphibious assault against a hostile beach—today's Marine Expeditionary Units (Special Operations Capable) or MEU(SOC)s stay afloat for six months in Amphibious Ready Group ships. (Photo: Greg E. Mathieson)*

The revolutionary air-cushion landing craft (LCAC) speeds up the rate of advance from ship to shore from 8 to 50 knots and makes 70 percent—rather than 17 percent—of world's beaches vulnerable to Marine amphibious assault. (Photos: Carl "Tank" Shireman)

With the end of the Cold War and its strategic vision of massive air/land battles over the plains of Europe, war planners' attention has shifted to the littorals as the most likely scenes of future instability. Roughly 70 percent of the world's people live within two hundred miles of a coastline, and 80 percent of the world's capitals lie within three hundred miles of the sea. Therefore, forces that travel by sea and can be launched from the sea maintain an unmatched global, strategic reach for our maritime nation.

For the Marines, getting there may be only half the fun—or half the battle, as the case may be. Long accustomed to operating jointly with the Navy in a seagoing and amphibious environment, the Marines have adapted readily to the newest situation, in which operations of virtually any magnitude or significance quickly turn "purple" and come under the joint task force commander. Indeed, the predeployment training of a MEU(SOC) includes a joint task force "enabler" exercise, in which the Marines open the door for the follow-on joint force. They blend in with the new operating procedures and establish satellite communications to enable the arriving commander to "uplink" with the regional warfighting commanders-in-chief (CinCs).

The Marines have developed command groups and arrangements that can serve as the nuclei for a joint task force headquarters, should a Marine commander be designated. In fact, the nation has had Marine generals as warfighting CinCs of the U.S. Atlantic, Central, and Southern Commands almost simultaneously.

In moving from ship to shore, the Marines unshackled themselves from an eight-to-ten-knot speed in the early 1980s, when they began to acquire the Landing Craft Air Cushion (LCAC). With a sprint speed of greater than 50 knots and a payload of more than 60 tons, these extraordinary craft fly on a five-foot bubble of air and can traverse more than 70 percent of the earth's coastlines (as opposed to the 17 percent accessible to surface-bound landing craft). Arriving aboard a 20-knot amphibious task force, the LCAC provides unprecedented flexibility to amphibious planners and creates new headaches for defenders. For example, a task force approaching Norfolk, Virginia, at dusk could change direction and by the following morning at daybreak send LCACs ashore anywhere between Montauk Point, Long Island, and Myrtle Beach, South Carolina. Faced with such a stretch of coastline to cover, the defender has little choice but to counterattack *after* the landing, thus conceding to the attacker the strategic offense and (initially) the tactical defense—the best of both worlds.

On balance, the Marines are able to shoot, move, and communicate better than ever. Of all the services, the Corps may be the most comfortable amid the post–Cold War uncertainties. In part, this relative comfort zone originated a few years ago when, in anticipation of the future, the Corps examined and restructured itself from the ground up. And in part, it may be that today's Wild West times bear more than a passing resemblance to a period years ago when Marines were fighting small wars in our own hemisphere.

It's a good thing that Marines generally like what they do, because they probably will be doing more and more of it. As the tough old gunnery sergeant told some of the defenders of Wake Island: "I've got some bad news and some good news. The bad news is that we will be filling sandbags until the Japanese attack comes. The good news is that we have plenty of sand."

Today's recruit training, conducted at both San Diego, California, and Parris Island, South Carolina, combines both physical and mental challenges. Emphasis is on mutual trust and confidence, an echo of the World War II Marine Raider war cry: "Gung ho!" or "Work together!" (Photo: Rick Mullen)

A Corps

FOR THE 21st Century

A Corps for the 21st Century

General Charles C. Krulak, USMC

The relationship between the American people and its Corps of Marines is a very special one. The people's high, almost spiritual, expectations for the Corps grew from the darkest days of our nation's history, in times of war, specifically in the early days of any conflict when the situation was in doubt. This was never more evident than in June of 1950 when the North Korean army invaded South Korea. This invasion caught the United States militarily unprepared, and our forces in Korea came very close to being defeated. The Marine Corps quickly put together a combined-arms, air-ground team, and, in just days, sailed to the sound of the guns. Landing at Pusan, they stopped the North Korean advance, then reembarked aboard amphibious shipping to conduct the Inchon landing. The Marine Corps helped save the day.

Two years later, determined never again to be caught unprepared, the 2nd session of the 82nd Congress wrote into law the role and the responsibilities of the United States Marine Corps to the American people. Accompanying that law they wrote the following:

> . . . [history] has fully demonstrated the vital need for the existence of a strong force in readiness. Such a force [must be] versatile, fast-moving, and hard hitting. . . . the nation's shock troops must be the most ready when the nation is least ready . . . to provide a balanced force in readiness for a naval campaign and, at the same time, a ground and air striking force ready to suppress or contain international disturbances short of large scale war.

For the past half century, the Marine Corps has provided that force in readiness—in peace and in war. As our national security interests evolve, it is essential that we, as that "force in readiness," anticipate and adapt to changes looming on the horizon. To do this, the Corps will embrace the forces of change and will, as we have in the past, be aggressive in experimenting and innovating for the future. Yet, in this sea of change, one thing will remain constant—the primacy of the individual Marine. Ultimately, it is the individual Marine—not machines or technology—that defines our success in war. With that as a foundation, let me describe the strategic environment that we see for the Marine Corps in the future, explore a new operational concept that we will use to meet the range of challenges we envision to our national interests, and discuss the programs necessary to make that concept a reality.

The twenty-first century, by all indications, will be a century of change. Changing global political alliances, demographics, and economic power—when combined with the rapid infusion of readily accessible high-technology weapons and information systems—will change both the way our nation projects military power, and the way our adversaries will counter that power projection.

All of our potential foes watched CNN during Desert Storm. They witnessed the futility of attempting to take on the United States in conventional warfare. These same adversaries watched our forces in Somalia and the Russians in Chechnya, and saw a potential Achilles heel. The lesson was not lost on them. Our future opponents will try to fight us

In future warfare—as in the past—success will ultimately be determined by the individual Marine. This Marine trains as a scout-swimmer at Camp Lejeune, North Carolina. (Photo: Greg E. Mathieson)

Previous spread: The hardware of modern warfare is coldly efficient and seldom pretty. This "wet well" of the USS Essex (LHD 2) has in it air-cushioned landing craft or "LCACs." They are preloaded with vehicles of the 11th Marine Expeditionary Unit (Special Operations Capable) for an amphibious landing exercise at Barking Sands, Hawaii, in the spring of 1996. (Photo: Rick Mullen)

Facing page: Marine planners of future battles foresee more and more fighting and unrest in cities and built-up areas. Marines must have the option to use both deadly and non-lethal weapons. Here Marines train in "Urban Warrior" exercises at Quantico, Virginia, in 1997. (Photo: Greg E. Mathieson)

Training bases on both coasts have "combat towns" to facilitate training in "MOUT," the acronym for "Military Operations in Urban Terrain." The grandfathers of today's Marines called it "Combat in Towns" in World War II and Korea and fought it in such places as Naha, Okinawa, and Seoul, Korea. The next generation fought in the battle for Hue in South Viet Nam. Most recently, Marines have contended in operations short of war, but sometimes deadly, in the towns and cities of Somalia. (Photos: Greg E. Mathieson)

where they believe we are weakest—in the cities and in close terrain. By taking the fight to the cities and close terrain, our opponents will attempt to deny us our advantage in command and control, intelligence, firepower, mobility, and logistics systems, all of which were designed to fight another conventional conflict.

Our adversaries will be flexible, adaptive, and highly lethal. They will design asymmetric strategies that counter our strengths and exploit our weaknesses. Among other things, they will target fixed air and port facilities and supply depots in an attempt to deny us access. These changes mandate that the United States field an agile and adaptable Marine Corps and Navy. The nation needs a sea-based force that can quickly react to global conflict, handle missions ranging from humanitarian relief to high-intensity conflict, and function in terrain ranging from open ocean to third world urban slums. This force must blend high-technology and maneuver warfare with the advantages of sea-basing. These requirements gave rise to the Marine Corps' new operational concept: Operational Maneuver From the Sea (OMFTS).

The heart of OMFTS is the maneuver of naval expeditionary forces at the operational level of warfare. Mere movement, however, does not qualify as operational maneuver. In order for it to be considered

Future enemies are likely to use the clutter of built-up areas to negate or diminish the technical advantages of U.S. weaponry and communications. Marines, therefore, must be trained and ready to fight, not on the enemy's terms, but on terms of their own making. Missions in urban warfare can range from humanitarian assistance or peace-keeping to high-intensity combat. (Photos: Greg E. Mathieson)

operational maneuver, our efforts must be directed against an enemy's center of gravity. The extensive use of the sea, as a means of gaining advantage, is what distinguishes OMFTS from all other forms of operational maneuver. The sea is both an avenue of friendly movement, and, simultaneously, a barrier to the enemy and disadvantageous engagements. OMFTS makes use of, but is not limited to, such techniques as sea-based logistics, sea-based fire-support, and the use of the sea as a medium for tactical and operational movement.

To build a Marine Corps capable of conducting OMFTS on the twenty-first century battlefield, we are improving our capabilities in *command and control*, *intelligence*, *mobility*, *logistics*, *fires*, and *force protection*.

To enable the execution of OMFTS we will have a fully integrated Command, Control, Computers, and Intelligence Systems (C4I) capability. This C4I system will be able to "connect" widely separated units (units separated in both function and distance) so that each member of the team has situational awareness of what the others are doing, and the ability to share what they are observing. Our communications nets will insure that all parties from general to private first class will have access to the information *they need*. This will include a "reach-back" capability to a virtual staff of experts to assist in decision making. We will have new

Marines have pioneered in fielding response teams to meet the threat of the terrorist use of chemical and biological weapons. The Marine Corps Chemical/Biological Incident Response Force or "CBIRF," activated in April 1996, has been deployed for such high-risk occasions as the Olympic games in Atlanta, Georgia, and the 1997 presidential inauguration in Washington, D.C. (Top and above photos: Greg E. Mathieson. Above right photo: Sandy Schaeffer)

ways to provide information to those who need it, including "tethered" satellites over the Marine Air-Ground Task Force (MAGTF) area of operations. Hand-held information systems, as simple to use as a pocket calculator, will be distributed all the way down to the fire-team level. One of our goals is to insure that this information network does not possess any seams generated by service-specific architecture. Our Corps will be fully integrated into the joint force, sharing with and providing information for all the players.

We must also protect ourselves from the threat of information warfare. Our C4I, intelligence, and fires systems will be increasingly information-dependent, as will our opponents'. Our opponents will attempt to deny or degrade our information systems—as we will attempt to do the same to them through active and passive deception on air, land, sea, and space, and by direct and indirect attacks upon their data lines of communications.

In the future operating environment, we must be able, quickly and efficiently, to integrate the intelligence, operations, and support assets of the entire spectrum of national power including: industry, academia, government, and non-government agencies and assets. We will coordinate and employ these capabilities just as we do combined arms.

To shape the intelligence effort, we will utilize intelligence systems that provide the joint force with tactical, operational, and strategic level intelligence, accessible to, and tailored for, all participants, allowing them to "see" the conflict's structure and support mechanisms. In this manner we can make educated judgments as to what the enemy's center of gravity is, how best to address it, and whether it is changing as the operation unfolds. This intelligence effort will seek to provide information ranging from sniper locations, to enemy operational maneuver, to cultural information. Most crucial of all, it will focus on identifying the opposition's *intent*. Even with these goals in mind, the Marine Corps recognizes that there is no such thing as "perfect battlespace awareness," nor will we allow ourselves to believe that such perfection is possible. Without a doubt, in the twenty-first century there will still be, as Clausewitz proffered, plenty of "fog of war" and "friction" of battle to go around.

Marines, in even the smallest level of units, will employ a variety of new technologies such as Unmanned Aerial Vehicles (UAVs), unmanned sensors, and "strap-on" sensors for all of our aviation and ground assets. These new technologies, when used in conjunction with other joint systems, and a robust human intelligence (HUMINT) collection program, will help build a much more accurate picture of the operating environment—and help us to see the structural underpinnings of the conflict. In the collection of HUMINT, the Corps will go back to the lessons learned from our

The Marine Corps does not have the luxury of choosing where and when it will fight. It must be prepared to meet a wide range of eventualities and to operate under climatic conditions from arctic cold to jungle or desert heat. (Photo: USMC)

Top: *Marines in combat gear emerge from a just-landed test-model Bell-Boeing MV-22 "Osprey." This tilt-rotor, vertical takeoff and landing, medium-lift aircraft, as revolutionary in its way as the jet engine or helicopter, will carry assault Marines and cargo from the sea to objectives far beyond the targeted beachhead. (Photo: Bell Helicopter Textron Inc.)*

Above: *The revolutionary "Osprey" will replace the Marine Corps' aging "Sea Knight" medium helicopter. The high-speed Osprey has a three-person crew and can transport either twenty-four combat troops or more than five tons of cargo. (Photo: USMC)*

past experiences and employ a comprehensive foreign language and cultural training program designed to insure that our small unit leaders, both officer and enlisted, can operate effectively on the chaotic twenty-first century battlefield.

The Marine Air-Ground Task Force of tomorrow will be highly mobile—at sea, in the air, and on the ground. It will sortie from widely separated sea-bases, and move to objectives deep inside the battlespace. It will have the ability to mass or disperse forces quickly, in all weather and threat conditions. The distinction between assault echelon and follow on forces will blend and merge as we use new methods of establishing forces ashore and sustaining them. These capabilities will allow us to control the tempo of operations, which in turn, will enable us to overwhelm our opponents.

Some of the keystone capabilities needed to execute OMFTS are:

V-22 Osprey. The V-22 allows the OMFTS force to range throughout the entire operational depth of our opponent. Marines must be able to strike from over the horizon and to project land forces deep into the enemy's interior. For the first time, our opponents will know that wherever they try to maneuver, our forces will be within range, embarked upon V-22s flying from naval platforms.

Landing Craft Air Cushioned (LCAC). The LCAC is the workhorse that moves everything, from supplies to vehicles, from ship to landing zones inland. Riding on a cushion of air, it can pick up today's combat loaded main battle tank with crew and "fly" them to shore at several

times the speed of any traditional landing craft. The LCAC has opened almost all of the world's coastlines to us. In times past, an enemy could build heavy defenses covering the few beaches accessible to our landing craft. Now, because there are only occasional limits to where we may choose to come ashore, such defenses are easily negated.

Advanced Amphibious Assault Vehicle (AAAV). The Advanced Amphibious Assault Vehicle (AAAV) will provide the Corps with a unique combination of firepower, armor protection, and high speed mobility. In the water, it will be three times faster than the current Amphibious Assault Vehicle. Once ashore it will have equal to, or greater than, the cross-country mobility of a modern tank. It will be equipped with an overpressure system capable of ensuring the safety of the Marines inside from chemical and biological attacks. The AAAV, in conjunction with the LCAC and the V-22 Osprey, is critical to the successful execution

Already with the fleet, the LCAC (air-cushioned landing craft) forms—along with the MV-22 "Osprey" and the AAAV (advanced amphibious assault vehicle)—the triad of ship-to-shore vehicles that will make possible the Over The Horizon (OTH) assaults envisioned in the Marine Corps new operational concept of Operational Maneuver from the Sea (OMFTS). (Photo: USMC)

The Advanced Amphibious Assault Vehicle (AAAV), now under development, will replace the sixty-year-old "amphibian tractor" technology of the present AAV (Amphibious Assault Vehicle). The AAAV will be able to launch from an amphibious ship twenty-five or more miles from the objective area, move there at three times the speed of its predecessor, and then climb ashore with a high-speed cross-country capability. (Photo: USMC)

The USS Wasp (LHD 1) was the first of a new class of multi-mission amphibious assault ship. Its flight deck can accommodate a variety of helicopters as well as the AV-8B "Harrier" and the MV-22 "Osprey." Its "wet well" deck can launch air-cushioned landing craft (LCACs) and assault amphibian vehicles, including the new AAAV (advanced amphibious assault vehicle).

of the types of Over The Horizon (OTH) assaults that will avoid enemy strengths, exploit his weaknesses, and serve to protect naval forces from increased land-based missile and sea-based mine threats.

New Amphibious Shipping. Sea-basing allows the Navy-Marine team to establish a "presence" that can serve either to deter a brewing conflict or, if conflict is unavoidable, to create a condition of operational shock upon our opponent. Additionally, unlike land-based air power-projection, a sea-based force can move into and remain in an area, without regards to issues of sovereignty or access. This ability to stand offshore allows us to "control the clock" indefinitely. With adequate

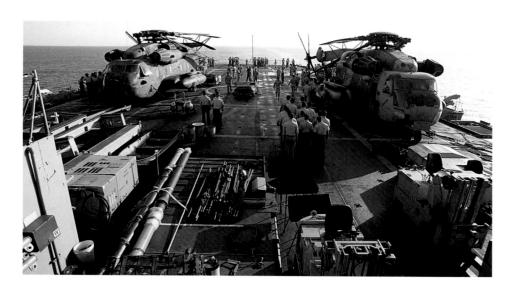

Marine CH-53E "Super Stallion" helicopters, the Corps' "heavy lifters," squat on the deck of an LPD (amphibious transport dock). Upgraded several times over the years, they will come to the end of their service life early in the twenty-first century. (Photo: Rick Mullen)

amphibious shipping, the Marine Air-Ground Task Force can conduct a simultaneous engagement through the use of fixed-wing air support from short take off and vertical landing (STOVL) Joint Strike Fighters (JSFs), and amphibious assault via LCACs, V-22s, and AAAVs. The procurement of the *Wasp* class LHD (amphibious assault ship), the *San Antonio* class LPD (amphibious transport dock), and enhanced Maritime Prepositioning Shipping is a key enabler of the OMFTS concept.

If we are to project forces deep within the battlespace, and shift them effortlessly, they must have the logistics support they require. This will be no simple feat when the forces are dispersed. The OMFTS logistics support apparatus will be the enabler which allows us to achieve our objectives and generate the tempo advantage that will be key to overcoming our adversaries. We will have the flexibility to support operations ranging from humanitarian assistance to high-intensity conflict. The logistics infrastructure must, and will, operate seamlessly with joint and non-government organizations (NGOs). For large-scale humanitarian operations, the OMFTS force will often be the first on the scene, providing initial crisis response before transitioning the effort to joint civil affairs units or to appropriate NGOs.

To support the twenty-first century's OMFTS mission profiles, we will employ new and more efficient combat service support methodologies and technologies. Some of these include: precision logistics, remote equipment status monitoring and diagnosis, on-site manufacturing and repair of equipment with robots, and, taking a lead from industry, near real-time delivery.

Marines of the twenty-first century will have greater choices in

Marine Corps reservists from heavy helicopter squadron HMH-769, working inside an operations tent at Twenty-nine Palms, California, contribute their efforts to the Marine Air Ground Task Force in a CAX (combined arms exercise). (Photo: Rick Mullen)

weaponry and will be able to employ both lethal and non-lethal fires. These fires will be delivered from a mix of manned and unmanned air, ground, and sea-based platforms, and they will be fully integrated with other elements of the joint force. Some of the new fire support technologies we will employ include: weaponized UAVs, low-yield precision-guided munitions for our manned attack aircraft, unattended ground-based fire support systems, a whole range of non-lethal and less-than-lethal weapon systems, information warfare systems, and improved psychological operation tools.

Key to providing necessary fire support to the Marine on the ground will be the Joint Strike Fighter (JSF). Stealth technology, combined with short takeoff and vertical landing (STOVL) flexibility, allows the Marines to employ this aircraft from a variety of platforms, strike critical deep targets, provide close-air-support, escort V-22s, suppress enemy air defenses, and conduct counter-air missions. Like the V-22, the JSF gives the Navy-Marine Corps power-projection force tremendous capabilities in operational depth, shock, and interoperability, all of which create operational dilemmas for our opponent.

The twenty-first century operating environment will be much more deadly than anything we have encountered in recent times. Land bases can present lucrative targets as we have seen with the bombings in Beirut and Saudi Arabia. The inherent mobility associated with sea-based forces offers significant protection over those assigned to fixed bases.

There is, however, a danger in viewing twenty-first century weapons and tactics from too much of a technological standpoint—thereby underrating the human dimension. The Marine Corps will not do this! Our focus rests, as it always has, upon the enhancement of the individual Marine, and his ability to win in combat. Therefore our most important

The always tough Marine "boot camp" has been made even tougher by the addition of the "Crucible," conducted at Quantico, Virginia, for officer candidates and at Parris Island, South Carolina, and Camp Pendleton, California, for enlisted recruits, male and female. (Photos: Sandy Schaeffer)

OMFTS enhancement will be in the training of the individual Marine.

On the battlefields of the twenty-first century, the junior enlisted Marine will have access to more information and firepower than a battalion commander might today. This Marine will be comfortable with high-technology weapons and information systems, and will be trained to know what to do with them. Above all else, the individual Marine

will be a warrior without peer. We will leverage technology to provide demanding and realistic training for our Marines—allowing them continually to expand their warfighting edge.

In the twenty-first century our Marines will fight something we call the "three block war." In the morning they may be feeding and clothing displaced refugees—providing humanitarian assistance. A few hours later, they may be holding two warring factions apart—conducting peacekeeping operations. Later that night, they could be engaged in a lethal, high-intensity urban battle. Junior enlisted Marines must have the tools to prevail in combat operations that span the entire spectrum of conflict, in the same day, all within three city blocks. To do this they must be as physically tough and as mentally agile as any who have borne the title U.S. Marine. And they will be. These Marines will be forged in the same furnace of shared hardship and tough training that has produced the world's finest warriors for generations.

To meet the challenges of the twenty-first century battlefield, we have enhanced our recruit and combat training. We increased the length of our already arduous recruit training program, and added an event called the "Crucible." The Crucible is the defining moment in recruit training. It is a fifty-four-hour ordeal that stresses teamwork, toughness, and the values required to prevail on the twenty-first century battlefield.

Refined organizations, derived from our Advanced Warfighting

The "Crucible" is a fifty-four-hour ordeal each recruit must go through before earning the coveted Eagle, Globe, and Anchor emblem and the right to be called by the title, United States Marine. Building the Corps' values and requiring physical and mental endurance, the Crucible demands teamwork. The individual alone cannot survive it. (Photos: Sandy Schaeffer)

The Marine aircrew members in the cabin of a UH-1N light helicopter can engage the target with either a GAU-2B minigun or a .50-caliber machine gun. The UH-1N is the latest of a long line of "Hueys" used by the Marine Corps, going back to the Viet Nam War. (Photo: Rick Mullen)

An LAV (light armored-vehicle) belonging to the 11th Marine Expeditionary Unit (Special Operations Capable) drives off the ramp of an LCAC (landing craft, air-cushioned) during Operation RIMPAC '96, an amphibious training exercise conducted in the Pacific. Thought by some to be "too light to fight," the LAV proved itself in screening and reconnaissance missions in desert fighting in the Persian Gulf War and in urban conflict on the streets and roads of Somalia. (Photo: Rick Mullen)

Experiments (AWEs), filled with these tested and proven men and women of character, will fight and win our nation's battles in the next century. The cohesion between the Marines in these units will be more important than ever as they face the challenges of the more lethal and more chaotic battlefields of the future. As such, we have implemented new manpower assignment policies aimed at keeping Marines together—as a team—throughout their first enlistment. On the future battlefield, as it was in our battles past, teamwork will be paramount. As it always has been, our core values of Honor, Courage, and Commitment will continue to steel the backbone of the individual Marine—and his or her team.

Preparing the Marine Corps for the twenty-first century requires more than tough training or procurement of new equipment. It requires an institutional commitment to change. "Laminating" future technology on current doctrine and organizations is not the answer.

The Marine Corps has begun the process of combining new technology with innovative new organizations, doctrine, and training. One of the Corps' most important initiatives is the Marine Corps Warfighting Laboratory. Just as we used the Marine Corps Schools at Quantico, Virginia, to redefine the science and art of amphibious assault during the 1920s and 1930s, so will the Warfighting Laboratory help us chart a course to master the challenges we see ahead. At the forefront of this effort is the testbed we call "Sea Dragon." Sea Dragon is not one particular innovation or idea, but rather a commitment to innovation. It is not a predetermined force structure or a predetermined operational technique, but a method of evaluating potential structures and techniques as well as training, education, and doctrinal ideas. It is through this commitment to innovation that the Marine Corps will develop the doctrine, tactics, equipment, and training techniques that will bring victory in the future.

To prepare the Corps for the twenty-first century we are aggressively making the changes necessary to build an OMFTS force, we are innovating for the future, and, as always, we are focusing on enhancing the warfighting abilities of the individual Marine. We are changing, but our purpose does not change. We will continue to make Marines and win battles for our nation. We will continue to be the force that is the most ready, when the nation is least ready. This is the legacy of the Corps. This purpose, incommutable by time, is our raison d'être.

Gen Charles C. Krulak, the Corps' thirty-first commandant, made the central mission of his tenure the preparation of the Marine Corps for the challenges of the twenty-first century. His description of the two fundamental things the Corps does for America is captured on this poster "Since 1775: Making Marines, Winning Battles."

Editors and Authors

EDITOR-IN-CHIEF:

BRIGADIER GENERAL EDWIN HOWARD SIMMONS
("Since 1775" and "The Commandants")
was commissioned in the Marine Corps in June 1942 after graduating from Lehigh University. He retired in January 1996 after thirty-six years in uniform—including combat in World War II, Korea, and Viet Nam, where he commanded the 9th Marines and was assistant division commander of the 1st Marine Division—and eighteen years as a civil servant. For the last twenty-four years he served as the Director of Marine Corps History and Museums and is currently the Director Emeritus. He is a founder of the Marine Corps Historical Foundation, now the Marine Corps Heritage Foundation, and a recipient of its Distinguished Service Award. He has written or contributed to numerous books; has published more than three hundred articles, essays, and reviews, and has lectured around the world.

EDITOR:

J. ROBERT MOSKIN
("Chronology")
graduated from Harvard and during World War II served as a sergeant in the Army in the Southwest Pacific. After the war he earned a master's degree in American history at Columbia University, covered the news as a magazine correspondent in Berlin, the Middle East, Korea, and Viet Nam, and spent five years as the foreign editor of *Look* magazine. He has written six books, including *The U.S. Marine Corps Story*—for which he received Distinguished Service Awards from both the Marine Corps Combat Correspondents Association and the Marine Corps Historical Foundation—and, most recently, *Mr. Truman's War*, the story of the final five months of World War II.

THE AUTHORS:

GENERAL CARL E. MUNDY, JR.
("The Marine Corps Experience")
as a small boy during World War II was determined that he would be a Marine. He enlisted at age eighteen in the Marine Corps Reserve and was commissioned in 1957 upon graduation from Auburn. He retired at age sixty from active service in July 1995 after completing four years as the thirtieth commandant of the Marine Corps. He is now president of World USO. See also page 290.

LIEUTENANT COLONEL JON T. HOFFMAN
("The Iwo Jima Flag-Raising and the Monument")
has served on active duty as an infantry officer and an instructor at the Naval Academy, and now, a Reserve officer,

as a military historian. His writing has won him numerous awards including the prestigious Wallace M. Greene, Jr. Award, named in honor of the twenty-third commandant, from the Marine Corps Historical Foundation for his biography of Major General Merritt A. "Red Mike" Edson, *Once a Legend* (1994).

LIEUTENANT COLONEL CHARLES H. CURETON
("Parade Blue, Battle Green")
was commissioned in the Marine Corps in 1972 following graduation from Sonoma State College, California, and served on active duty as an amphibious vehicle platoon commander. Leaving active service in 1975 for graduate school, he joined the Marine Corps Reserve and has been assigned to the Marine Corps Historical Center since 1983, including service as a combat historian in the Persian Gulf War, Somalia, and Haiti. He received his master's in history in 1978 from East Tennessee State University and his doctorate in 1985 from Miami University of Ohio. His special interest, for many years, has been the evolution of Marine uniforms.

COLONEL BROOKE NIHART
("Muskets to Missiles")
holder of the Navy Cross, was commissioned in 1940 and, on active service, commanded machine-gun and anti-tank platoons, a ship's Marine detachment, infantry battalions, and a regiment. He saw combat in World War II and Korea. In retirement he headed the Marine Corps museums program for many years. He is a founder of the Marine Corps Historical Foundation and has received its Distinguished Service Award. Internationally known as a weapons expert, he himself was a match pistol and rifle shot.

COLONEL JOSEPH H. ALEXANDER
("The Vital Link: From Ship to Shore")
spent twenty-eight years on active service in the Marine Corps, most of them as an assault amphibian vehicle officer, including two tours in Viet Nam and five years at sea on board amphibious ships. He is a graduate in history from the University of North Carolina, has advanced degrees from Georgetown and Jacksonville, and is a distinguished graduate of the Naval War College. A prolific and prize-winning writer, he is also extremely active in military history television documentaries.

LIEUTENANT COLONEL RONALD J. BROWN
("Corsairs, Cobras, and Phantoms")
was on active duty as an infantry officer from 1968 to 1971, with a combat tour in Viet Nam. Subsequently, as a Reserve officer from 1975 to 1996, he served as a Marine Corps historian. This included deployment to the Persian Gulf and

northern Iraq, and the writing of numerous official histories. In civilian life he taught American history in Michigan high schools and continues to coach championship football teams.

COLONEL JOHN R. BOURGEOIS
("The President's Own")
became the twenty-fifth director of the United States Marine Band in 1979. He retired in 1996 having served nine presidential administrations—from Eisenhower to Clinton. In retirement he continues to teach, conduct, and contribute to both band research and the preparation of musical editions.

CAPTAIN JOHN C. CHAPIN
("The Sergeants Major of the Marine Corps")
entered the Marine Corps in 1942 as an officer candidate on graduation in history from Yale. Receiving his commission, he served with the 4th Marine Division, was wounded in the Marshall Islands and again, more seriously, on Saipan. Physically retired, he earned a master's degree at George Washington, had a career largely in public service, and continues to study and write Marine Corps history, including his *Uncommon Men: The Sergeants Major of the Marine Corps* (1992).

LAWRENCE H. SUID, PH.D.
("Marines in the Movies")
is a military historian with interests ranging from motion pictures to nuclear munitions. He is a graduate of Case-Western Reserve, has master's degrees from Duke and Brandeis, and returned to Case-Western Reserve for his Ph.D. The first of his several books, *Guts and Glory: Great American War Movies* (1978), is based on his doctoral dissertation. He has taught at Winona (MN) State University, the University of Vermont, and the Marine Corps University.

COLONEL JOHN GRIDER MILLER
("The Corps Today")
was commissioned after graduation from Yale in 1957. His service included two combat tours in Viet Nam and a deployment to the Mediterranean. He wrote speeches for three commandants (Generals Chapman, Cushman, and Wilson) and finished up with a tour as Deputy Director, Marine Corps History. Since retirement in 1985 he has been managing editor of the U.S. Naval Institute *Proceedings* with time left over to write three books.

GENERAL CHARLES C. KRULAK
("A Corps for the 21st Century")
began his four-year term as commandant of the Marine Corps on 1 July 1995. His overriding concern has been preparing the Corps for the challenges of the next century. Born in Quantico, Virginia, the son of the distinguished Victor H. Krulak who rose to lieutenant general, he is a Naval Academy graduate, served in Viet Nam, and during the Persian Gulf War directed the Marines' forward logistics effort. His whole life has been steeped in the Marine Corps. See also pages 290–291.

Acknowledgments

Many individuals and agencies, within and outside the government, have assisted in the development of this book. Absolutely essential has been access to the resources of the Marine Corps Historical Center at the Washington Navy Yard and the Marine Air-Ground Museum at Quantico. Of particular help at Headquarters, Marine Corps, have been the Commandant's Staff Group and the Division of Public Affairs. Farther afield, the Marine Corps Research Center at Quantico and the San Diego Command Museum have lent their aid. Navy friends of the book include the Navy Historical Center, the U. S. Naval Institute, and the U.S. Naval Academy Museum. The vast holdings of the National Archives and Records Administration, the Library of Congress, and the Smithsonian Institution have been tapped.

Among the many individuals who have been especially helpful are Ronnie D. Alexander, Robert V. Aquilina, Annette D. Ammerman, LtCol T. Brant Bailey, Capt Frank Byrne, LtCol Scott R. Campbell, Fred A. Carr, Jr., Dr William Cogar, Col Edward M. Condra III, LtCol Leon Craig, Jr., Danny J. Crawford, David B. Crist, Dr William S. Dudley, Maj John T. Dyer, Sara Elder, Evelyn A. Englander, MSgt James A. Fairfax, Jane Farnol, Ann A. Ferrante, LtCol Timothy Foley, Benis M. Frank, Marylou Frank, Lynn C. Goldberg, Frederick G. Graboske, Sgt Anthony U. Greene, Dolores Haverstick, Gordon H. Heim, Jr., Col Dennis J. Hejlik, W. Stephen Hill, Charles O. Hyman, Gail I. Job, Lena M. Kaljot, Catherine A. Kerns, MGySgt Andrew Linden, Richard A. Long, Donald S. Lopez, Col Michael F. Monigan, Gale Munro, Patricia Mullen, Cpl Pauline L. Render, Col Charles J. Quilter, MGySgt Michael Ressler, Jack Shulimson, Charles R. "Rich" Smith, Kenneth L. Smith-Christmas, Col Jay Sollis, BGen Clifford L. Stanley, Michael E. Starn, Sgt Dieter Stenger, Robin Stewart, A. Kerry Strong, Robert E. Struder, LtCol Robert J. Sullivan, SSgt Eric C. Tausch, Larry "Staples" Walsh, Charles A. "Tim" Wood, Deborah T. Zindell.

Suggested Reading

GENERAL MARINE CORPS HISTORIES

Col Joseph H. Alexander, *A Fellowship of Valor: The Battle History of the United States Marines* (1997)

Col Robert D. Heinl, *Soldiers of the Sea* (1962)

Jeter A. Isely and Philip A. Crowl, *The U. S. Marines and Amphibious War* (1951)

LtGen Victor H. Krulak, *First to Fight* (1984)

Col Allan R. Millett, *Semper Fidelis* (1980, 1991)

J. Robert Moskin, *The U.S. Marine Corps Story* (1977, 1982, 1987, 1992)

BGen Edwin H. Simmons, *The United States Marines* (1974, 1975, 1998)

PRE–WORLD WAR II CAMPAIGNS

Theodore Roosevelt, *The Naval War of 1812* (1882)

K. Jack Bauer, *Surf Boats and Horse Marines* [Mexican War] (1969)

Ralph W. Donnelly, *Rebel Leathernecks* [Civil War] (1989)

Jack Shulimson, *The Marine Corps' Search for a Mission* [post–Civil War] (1993)

Ivan Musicant, *The Banana Wars* (1990)

Col John W. Thomason, Jr., *Fix Bayonets!* [Semi-fiction: World War I] (1926)

Col John W. Thomason, Jr., *. . . and a Few Marines* [Semi-fiction: World War I and China duty] (1945)

WORLD WAR II

Frank O. Hough, *The Island War* (1947)

Fletcher Pratt, *The Marines' War* (1948)

Robert Leckie, *Strong Men Armed* (1962)

Col Joseph H. Alexander, *Storm Landings: Epic Amphibious Battles in the Central Pacific* (1997)

Richard B. Frank, *Guadalcanal* (1990)

John Hersey, *Into the Valley* (1943)

Robert Sherrod, *Tarawa* (1944)

Col Joseph H. Alexander, *Utmost Savagery: The Three Days of Tarawa* (1995)

Robert Sherrod, *On to Westward* (1945)

Richard Wheeler, *Iwo* (1980)

Col Victor J. Croizat, *Across the Reef: The Amphibious Tracked Vehicle at War* (1989)

James D. Ladd, *Assault from the Sea, 1939–45: The Craft, the Landings, the Men* (1989)

Leon Uris, *Battle Cry* [Semi-fiction] (1953)

KOREAN WAR

Col Robert D. Heinl, *Victory at High Tide* [Inchon] (1968)

Eric Hammel, *Chosin: Heroic Ordeal of the Korean War* (1981)

Robert Leckie, *Conflict: The History of the Korean War* (1944)

T. E. Fehrenbach, *This Kind of War* (1963)

VIET NAM

LtCol Ronald H. Spector, *After Tet: The Bloodiest Year in Vietnam* (1993)

Robert Pisor, *The End of the Line: The Siege of Khe Sanh* (1982)

Col Gerald H. Turley, *The Easter Offensive, Vietnam, 1972* (1985)

Col John Grider Miller, *The Bridge at Dong Ha* (1989)

LtCol Gary D. Solis, *Son Thang: An American War Crime* (1997)

Frank Snepp, *Decent Interval: An Insider's Account of Saigon's Indecent End* (1977)

COLD WAR

Col Joseph H. Alexander and LtCol Merrill L. Bartlett, *Sea Soldiers in the Cold War* (1995)

Eric Hammel, *The Root: The Marines in Beirut* (1985)

PERSIAN GULF WAR

Michael R. Gordon and LtGen Bernard E. Trainor, *The Generals' War* (1994)

Molly Moore, *A Woman at War: Storming Kuwait with the U.S. Marines* (1995)

MARINE CORPS AVIATION

Robert Sherrod, *History of Marine Corps Aviation in World War II* (1952)

Cdr Peter B. Mersky, *U.S. Marine Corps Aviation, 1912–Present* (1983)

MARINE CORPS WEAPONS

Col Robert H. Rankin, *Small Arms of the Sea Services* (1972)

Edward Clinton Ezell, *Small Arms of the World* (updated periodically)

MARINE BAND

Paul Bierley, *John Philip Sousa: An American Phenomenon* (1973)

Elise Kirk, *Music at the White House* (1986)

MEMOIRS AND BIOGRAPHIES

Karl Schuon, *U. S. Marine Corps Biographical Dictionary* (1963)

Jane Blakeney, *Heroes, U. S. Marine Corps, 1861–1955* (1957)

Charles L. Lewis, *Famous American Marines* (1950)

Marine Corps Association, *Home of the Commandants* (1956, 1966, 1974, and 1995)

Werner H. Marti, *Messenger of Destiny* [Archibald Gillespie] (1955)

Lowell Thomas, *Old Gimlet Eye: The Adventures of Smedley D. Butler* (1933)

Col Frederic W. Wise, *A Marine Tells It to You* (1929)

MajGen John A. Lejeune, *The Reminiscences of a Marine* (1930)

Gen David M. Shoup, *The Marines in China, 1927–1928: A Contemporaneous Journal* (1987)

BGen Robert Hugh Williams, *The Old Corps: A Portrait of the U.S. Marine Corps Between the Wars* (1982)

Gen Holland M. Smith, *Coral and Brass* (1949)

Burke Davis, *Marine! The Life of Lt. Gen. Lewis B. (Chesty) Puller* (1962)

Gen Alexander A. Vandegrift, *Once a Marine* (1964)

Col Allan R. Millett, *In Many a Strife: General Gerald C. Thomas and the U.S. Marine Corps, 1917–1956* (1993)

Jerry E. Strahan, *Andrew Jackson Higgins and the Boats that Won World War II* (1994)

LtCol Jon T. Hoffman, *Once a Legend: "Red Mike" Edson of the Marine Raiders* (1994)

Capt John C. Chapin, *Uncommon Men: The Sergeants Major of the Marine Corps* (1992)

OFFICIAL HISTORIES

Purposely omitted from this reading list are the hundreds of official operational histories, reference pamphlets, monographs, unit histories, bibliographies, and chronologies published by the Marine Corps History and Museums Division over the last three-quarters of a century. A complete listing of these official histories and how to obtain those still in print can be obtained by writing the Director, History and Museums Division; Headquarters, U. S. Marine Corps; Washington, D.C. 20374-5040.

Index

358

Photography and Art Sources

All other images are courtesy of the U.S. Marine Corps or the authors. All sources are cited within image caption.

Associated Press: 113

Bell Helicopter Textron Inc.: 224, 226, 344

President Jimmy Carter Library: 251

Gary Delscamp: 136

David Douglas Duncan: 74, 75, 76, 77, 79, 88, 89, 94, 95, 218

Grumman Corporation: 229

Harpers Illustrated Weekly: 155

Hohner Company: 245

President Lyndon B. Johnson Library: 248

Library of Congress: 60, 241

Litton/Ingalls Industries: 201

Lockheed Aircraft Corporation: 226

Eric Long: 110–111, 115, 138, 140, 143, 146, 153, 154, 156, 157, 158, 159, 160, 161, 162, 163, 165, 170, 171, 174, 185, 188, 210, 211, 216, 238, 258–259, 263, 291

Marine Band Library: 234, 235, 240, 244, 246, 247

Marine Corps Air-Ground Museum, Quantico: 141

Marine Corps Art Collection: 15, 28, 34, 36, 37, 39, 40, 41, 42, 43, 45, 49, 52, 53, 55, 56, 62, 66, 78, 80, 82, 83, 92, 106, 109, 116, 117, 130, 131, 132, 134, 135, 136, 137, 145, 147, 148, 149, 152, 153, 154, 155, 156, 158, 159, 164, 166, 169, 170, 178, 211, 212, 215, 217, 224, 225, 233, 235, 265, 284, 292, 321

Marine Corps Historical Library: 138, 139, 140, 234

Marine Corps Museum: 260

Marine Corps Recruit Depot, San Diego: 81

Mariners Museum: 38

Greg E. Mathieson/MAI: 27, 98, 100, 101, 102, 103, 128–129, 133, 141, 147, 150-151, 205, 230–231, 320, 322, 323, 324, 326, 327, 331, 332, 333, 338, 339, 340, 341, 342, 349

McDonnell Douglas Corporation: 227, 228

Rick Mullen: 12–13, 18, 19, 23, 24–25, 29, 30, 31, 96, 97, 98, 99, 100, 228, 321, 333, 335, 336–337, 346, 347, 348, 352

Museum of Modern Art, Film Stills Archives: 300

National Archives: 50, 234, 236

The New York Times: 250

President Ronald Reagan Library: 252, 253

Sandy Schaeffer/MAI: 323, 326, 350, 351

Carl "Tank" Shireman: 204, 205, 206–207, 228, 229, 327, 328, 334

Mark Stewart, Stewart Studios: 215, 216, 218

Texas Instruments: 168

U.S. Army Art Collection: 191

U.S. Coast Guard: 64, 69, 190

U.S. Naval Academy Museum: 35, 37, 38, 85

U.S. Naval Institute: 85

U.S. Navy: 47, 100, 107, 108, 180, 182, 194, 200, 201, 202, 329, 333

U.S. Navy Art Collection: 28, 162, 189, 217

Col Charles Waterhouse, USMCR (Ret): 32–33